Home of the Braves

❖

Home
of the Braves

❖ ❖

*The Battle for Baseball
in Milwaukee*

❖

Patrick W. Steele

The University of Wisconsin Press

The University of Wisconsin Press
728 State Street, Suite 443
Madison, Wisconsin 53706
uwpress.wisc.edu

Gray's Inn House, 127 Clerkenwell Road
London EC1R 5DB, United Kingdom
eurospanbookstore.com

Printed in the United States of America

This book may be available in a digital edition.

Library of Congress Cataloging-in-Publication Data

Names: Steele, Patrick W. (Patrick William), author.
Title: Home of the Braves: the battle for baseball in Milwaukee / Patrick W. Steele.
Description: Madison, Wisconsin: The University of Wisconsin Press, [2018]
| Includes bibliographical references and index.
Identifiers: LCCN 2017043651 | ISBN 9780299318109 (cloth: alk. paper)
Subjects: LCSH: Milwaukee Braves (Baseball team)—History.
| Baseball teams—Wisconsin—Milwaukee—History.
Classification: LCC GV875.5 S74 2018 | DDC 796.357/640977595—dc23
LC record available at https://lccn.loc.gov/2017043651

ISBN 9780299318147 (pbk.: alk. paper)

This work is dedicated to the most important fan of the Milwaukee Braves that I ever knew, my mom, **Kathye Steele**, and my favorite fan of the Atlanta Braves, my granddaughter, **Macy Hoot**.

Contents

Foreword

Bob Buege

Milwaukee has had a long and sometimes glorious baseball history. Since 1900 it is the only city in America that can lay claim to two different teams in both the National League (1953–65 and 1998–present) and the American League (1901 and 1970–97). In addition, for more than half of the twentieth century, Wisconsin's version of Metropolis was home to a ball club in the highest minor league, the American Association, playing their home games for appreciative crowds in splintery old Borchert Field.

The four major league franchises that called Milwaukee their home enjoyed varying degrees of success. The 1901 American League Brewers, who helped inaugurate baseball's "junior circuit," lasted just one year before pulling up stakes and moving to St. Louis and becoming the Browns. Fifty-two years later they became the Baltimore Orioles, which they remain today. I wonder how many modern Milwaukee fans think of the Orioles as "our" team.

By every measure except longevity, Milwaukee's Braves were the brightest star in the Wisconsin baseball constellation. The passage of time and the otherworldly idolatry toward the Green Bay Packers have obscured how amazing the Miracle of Milwaukee truly was. What happened inside Milwaukee County Stadium and throughout Wisconsin from, say, 1953 to 1957 was without precedent or parallel in the history of professional sports.

On April 8, 1953, the day the Milwaukee Braves arrived in their new home city for the first time, they were greeted by an army of enthusiasts at the North Western depot and loaded into open convertibles for a motorcade down Wisconsin Avenue. At the Schroeder Hotel they were ushered into a ballroom festooned with holiday decorations, featuring a gigantic Christmas tree surrounded by gift-wrapped presents for every man on the roster: shaving kits, theater passes, cuff links, wallets, fishing lures, underwear, pen and pencil sets, you name it. The players thought they had died and gone to heaven.

That night the new Milwaukee Braves met the public at a lively rally inside a packed Milwaukee Arena. Of course, Governor Vernon Thompson and Mayor Frank Zeidler took their places among the speakers, but the crowd reserved its loudest applause for three men—manager Charlie Grimm, Miller Brewing Company president Fred Miller, and Braves owner Lou Perini.

Grimm had been the manager of the American Association Brewers in Borchert Field during the 1940s and along with charismatic owner Bill Veeck had won the hearts of the city with a mixture of high jinx and solid, pennant-winning baseball. Miller was a selfless civic leader who generally received credit for persuading Perini to uproot his Boston Braves losers and move them to the unknown hinterlands of Wisconsin. And then there was Perini.

Lou Perini was a Boston-area native and a self-made millionaire. While the Braves were building a World Series contender and ultimately a champion, Perini's construction company was busy excavating a large portion of the St. Lawrence Seaway. He was familiar to Milwaukee baseball fans, having purchased the minor league Brewers effective October 1, 1946. Perini needed a viable farm club at the AAA level, so he bought one. Simple as that. He used his wealth to leverage his needs, not necessarily by flaunting it but certainly never by concealing or underplaying it.

There was a story told about Perini trying to sign teenaged Johnny Antonelli, a can't-miss left-handed pitcher in the days before there was a free agent draft. Antonelli's father, who owned a construction company, was playing hard-to-get with Perini, boasting about his own business and telling Perini, "I own two steam shovels. How many do you have?" Perini paused before answering, "I'm not sure. I think about fifty." Antonelli signed with the Braves for a reputed $65,000, the largest bonus up to that time.

Perini was also a visionary. In January 1948 he delivered a talk to the Milwaukee Athletic Club in which he expounded on his view of big league baseball in the not-too-distant future. He cited pressure from the Pacific Coast League to expand the major leagues by adding four West Coast cities—San Francisco, Los Angeles, Oakland, and Hollywood (maybe he meant Anaheim). "But adding four cities would give us ten teams in each league," he said, "and we can't run with ten teams." Instead, two more would need to be added, to have twelve in each league. Perini stated boldly, "Milwaukee will be in a major league within five years." Five years later, in 1953, he was right on the money.

Speaking of money, local citizens and county officials made certain that neither the Braves ownership nor their ballplayers suffered for lack of it. Even with just a few weeks for presale of tickets, overwhelming demand all but guaranteed profitability at the gate. What's more, the Milwaukee County Board did its part by crafting a lease on County Stadium that charged the Braves a nominal amount: one thousand dollars. That's for the season, not per game. Even the woebegone Boston Braves could have made that payment.

And the players? Commercial establishments and fans could not do enough for them. Automobiles were provided free of charge for their use by Dodge dealer Wally Rank. Free gasoline, free dry-cleaning service, free wrist watches, all were theirs for the asking. Eddie Mathews recalled that he and about a dozen of the Braves rented rooms at the Wisconsin Hotel in downtown Milwaukee. "For every game a pitcher won," Mathews explained, "he got a case of Miller High Life. If you hit a home run, you got a case of Miller High Life. They'd deliver it right to your room at the hotel. Well, I had twenty-seven home runs at the All-Star break, and that was just me. We had to rent another room just for the beer because besides Miller there were other breweries—Blatz, Schlitz, Pabst . . ."

Mathews and his teammates reciprocated in a couple ways. First and foremost, they played top-notch baseball starting on day one and lasting many years into the future. They never did experience a losing season. Second, the ballplayers made themselves available to the fans. They lived among the fans in normal neighborhoods like real, ordinary people. Everyone in town, it seemed, had some connection to a genuine Milwaukee Brave. Your cousin used to baby-sit for Lew Burdette's kids, or your uncle went to the same barber as Andy Pafko.

In addition, every school and church had a social event, a smoker, a sports night, a testimonial banquet, and every one of those get-togethers featured celebrity athletes, which in the 1950s meant Milwaukee Braves. At age eight I felt privileged to attend, with my dad, the Lettermen's Club Spring Banquet at the high school from which I would later graduate. I still have the dinner program from that evening, autographed (legibly) by each of the featured guests: Eddie Mathews, Danny O'Connell, Joe Adcock, George Metkovich, and Bob Forte of the Green Bay Packers. Bear in mind, this was simply a semi-annual event at an ordinary high school in a working-class suburb of Milwaukee, to which no admission was charged, for which the ballplayers were not compensated, at which autographs were free. Those were the days.

From Opening Day 1953, Braves attendance became a subject of more than academic interest or fiscal importance. It was a matter of civic pride. Every day a "thermometer" graph in the newspaper compared Milwaukee's daily and cumulative attendance with the analogous figures from 1952 in Boston. It was strictly no contest, of course. The Boston home opener had drawn a pitiful 4,694 to watch Warren Spahn face the Dodgers. After thirteen games Milwaukee's total surpassed Boston's entire season, so the newspaper began comparing with 1948, the year that Boston won the pennant. When that number was exceeded, the comparison was switched to Brooklyn's record year.

The team that all those 1,826,397 Milwaukee Braves loyalists paid to watch was well worth the price of a ticket. Mathews led the majors in home runs in 1953. Spahn led in earned run average and games won. Billy Bruton led in stolen bases. The Braves finished second behind the Dodgers, but Milwaukee won ninety-two games, more than any Boston Braves club since 1914.

In 1954 Henry Aaron joined the Braves. He and Mathews proceeded to hit more home runs in their careers as teammates (863) than any other pair of sluggers, surpassing Babe Ruth and Lou Gehrig. The mound duo of Spahn and Lew Burdette won more games as teammates (412) than any other pair of hurlers since World War I. Six ballplayers who wore the Milwaukee Braves uniform are today enshrined in the Hall of Fame in Cooperstown. Three of them nearly everyone can name; the others are Red Schoendienst, Phil Niekro, and Enos Slaughter.

In the Milwaukee Braves' fifth season, they reached the top of the mountain. After a narrow miss on the final weekend of the 1956 campaign, Fred Haney's club captured the 1957 National League flag and subdued the Yankees in the World Series. Derided by New York as "bush," Milwaukee sat proudly atop the baseball world.

In 1962, though, once-revered Braves owner Lou Perini wanted out. What followed was relatively swift and not pleasant to watch. By mid-season 1963, the rumors had reached avalanche proportions: the Braves were bound for Atlanta. How could such a profound love affair between a city and its baseball team turn so toxic?

Patrick Steele has studied that question in scrupulous detail. This book, *Home of the Braves*, grapples with that issue, and its conclusions may surprise you. They surprised me.

Bob Buege is the author of *The Milwaukee Braves: A Baseball Eulogy*.

Acknowledgments

In the course of this work, countless individuals have helped along the way and a simple thanks does not seem quite adequate, but I will try. Joel Willems and the staff at the Chudnow Museum of Yesteryear, in Milwaukee, are the first of a very long list. A chance to present a paper there on Milwaukee baseball lit a fire in me to complete this book. Rick Schabowski and the other members of the Milwaukee Braves Historical Association and the Ken Keltner Badger State Chapter of the Society for American Baseball Research provided answers, encouragement, and support when I needed inspiration and help. Dave Klug helped me with some photographs that I simply could not find anywhere else. Kevin Abing and Steve Schaffer, of the research staff at the Milwaukee County Historical Society, were true professionals and helped me find relevant materials and photographs that complemented the text.

A special word of gratitude for Bob Buege is in order. His work inspired my interest in the Milwaukee Braves, and he was a tremendous resource. He answered questions and pointed me in the right direction as I worked through the research materials. He also provided several of the photographs that appear in the book. I am especially thankful that he agreed to write the foreword to the book.

My editors along the way were extremely essential from the beginning to the final draft of this book. Gwen Walker of the University of Wisconsin Press was phenomenal to work with, and she gave great guidance and direction during the final draft process. The help provided by Kristin Schultz and Meghan Steffens reading the drafts and providing insightful comments was indispensable. They also helped me focus on the narrative. During this process they were always available to support me with ideas as well as words of encouragement and prayers as I worked through various problems within the book. Words alone cannot express how thankful I am for them. Susan Willems, Claudia Beck, Mike Tews, Katelyn Shields, and my father, Oscar Steele, also participated along the way, and their respective suggestions were greatly appreciated. Without all of their unselfish work, this process would still be ongoing.

I am extremely thankful to my parents, Oscar and Kathye Steele, who helped and supported me during the hours of research and writing. My undying gratitude also goes to my best friend, Robert Klug, for all he has done for me over the years. My colleagues at Concordia University Wisconsin supported my work and helped ensure my completing the research and writing. In particular, Steve Crook helped me work through some of the complicated issues that surround the story of the Milwaukee Braves.

My children, Jessica and Scott, have been inspirational. Jessica was always there with words of encouragement and jokes when I needed them the most. Scott asked about the progress and created the attendance chart that appears in the book. My granddaughter, Macy, helped by sitting on my lap as I wrote, and she listened to me work though some of the chapters. She also attended a Braves-Brewers game in Atlanta and kept us all entertained for nine innings.

Finally and most important, I am most grateful to the person who has put as much into this as I have: my wife, Lynet. She has always been there for me, encouraged me, and sacrificed so this book could be completed.

All conclusions and any errors that might appear in the text are my own.

Home of the Braves

Prologue

The Board of Directors of the Milwaukee Braves, Inc.,
voted today to request permission of the National League
to transfer their franchise to Atlanta, Ga., for 1965.
Milwaukee Braves publicity director Ernie Johnson,
October 21, 1964

It was a warm summer night and the Braves were preparing once again for a series opener under the lights at Milwaukee County Stadium. Over the last seven years the team had established itself as one of the best not only in the National League but in all of baseball. More than twenty-one thousand fans filtered into the ballpark to catch a game that, on paper, was not especially significant because the Braves were playing a team they were supposed to beat. Taking the mound for the Braves was one of the preeminent pitchers in their storied history and perhaps even the best of his generation. Years later, when he walked away from the game, he would be elected to the Baseball Hall of Fame. Tonight, from the first inning through the ninth, the wily veteran did not disappoint.

Unfortunately for many in the stands, it was not Hall of Famer Warren Spahn, the pitcher who had so often carried the Braves to victory during their twelve years in Milwaukee. Instead, it was Greg Maddux and this game, played on June 1, 1998, marked the first regular season game the Braves played at County Stadium since they pulled up stakes at the end of the 1965 season to become the Atlanta Braves.

Tom Flaherty of the *Milwaukee Journal Sentinel* noted that for the hometown Brewers, the game was a "historical moment lost on players." By this point, the Braves had been in Atlanta for thirty-three seasons and the Brewers had been Milwaukee's major league representatives for twenty-eight years. Now, because the Brewers had been transferred to the National League, the two teams would meet on a regular basis. Braves third baseman Chipper Jones said his teammates were aware of the acrimonious history between the club and Milwaukee, but "we're in Atlanta now and Milwaukee is in the National League so we have to play these guys and beat them as much as possible." Braves pitcher Denny Neagle added, "That's just where we came from. . . . The Atlanta Braves had to start somewhere."[1]

The commissioner of baseball and former owner of the Brewers, Allan H. "Bud" Selig, said after the game that the Braves' return was indeed "a great night, a wonderful night . . . I guess there's a lot of fulfillment. I remember the last game here thirty-three years ago. Now, the Braves are back, and all's well that ends well."[2]

For some in Milwaukee, however, all did not end well. To be sure, the passage of more than three decades had diminished the residual anger that many Milwaukeeans had about the franchise that was arguably, at one point, more beloved than the Green Bay Packers. That night of the first Braves game back in Wisconsin, the Brewers even passed out a photo commemorating the Braves' return to County Stadium. But a small percentage of fans still believed that they would never get over the heartbreak of the Braves' departure and the years of seeing an empty stadium sitting rejected in the Menomonee Valley. One fan noted that some people in Milwaukee still "hate the Braves. They hate 'em. . . . People who've been around since the '50s, some of 'em have never been to a game since. Some old men I know, they'll never come back." Lou Chapman, an iconic sportswriter in Milwaukee who originally covered the Braves, later said that there was "still a lot of bitterness over what the Braves did, and that's because people here don't forget easily."[3]

Over the years, many fans have blamed the move on sheer greed—absentee owners determined to improve their profit margin. The owners, for their part, have pointed to the declining attendance of the early sixties. "The fans left us," declared Lou Perini, who had owned the team until 1961. "They were spoiled by our early success."[4] Even today, the Braves maintain that rationale for the move to Atlanta.

As for me, my passion for the team began nearly a decade after they had already left Milwaukee. My journey to understand the reasons for their move began in 1974, when I received a book on baseball greats for my birthday. As a seven-year-old, I pored through the book again and again, enthralled by the stories of my favorite player, Henry Aaron. Over time, I noticed that in several photos he was wearing an *M* on his cap rather than the familiar *A* of the early 1970s. When I asked about it, my mom explained that the Braves had once played for Milwaukee. She then told me about how much she loved going to Braves games, especially to the Ladies Day promotions at County Stadium. In her eyes I could see the love she had for the team and how much it hurt when they left. Perhaps even worse for her was that the Braves organization blamed the fans for a lack of support as their reason to leave.

I felt, even then, that there had to be more to the story. The more I spoke with my parents and grandparents about the Braves, the more my fascination grew. Whenever I went to County Stadium I would talk to ushers who had worked the ballpark since back in the fifties. Most were more than happy to answer a young boy's questions about the glory days of the Braves that became known as the Milwaukee Miracle. I could not help but wonder why the team left, if it was so good and the ballpark was full. My great-grandfather took me to a game in Aaron's last year and pointed out the places in the ballpark where history had been made: the spot where Aaron's pennant-winning home run cleared the fence in 1957, where the row of evergreens known as Perini's Woods used to be, and where Eddie Mathews became a Hall of Fame third baseman. For Christmas in 1988 I was fortunate to get Bob Buege's classic, *The Milwaukee Braves: A Baseball Eulogy*. I read the book many times and still pick it up from time to time to reread some of the great stories that Buege lived through and wrote about.

While Wisconsin now roots for the Brewers, the defunct Milwaukee Braves continue to capture the public imagination. Miller Park still honors that history with a Milwaukee Braves Walk of Fame and a memorial to all who played for the team. Milwaukee Braves jerseys and caps still dot the bleachers and vending stands. A historical association has formed to preserve the team's memory. There are several sites on social media where fans share stories of love and heartbreak of the Braves, as well as many books that recount the team's success. What has been missing is a detailed examination of how the team eventually failed in Wisconsin and why they left.

Unlike other baseball books, *Home of the Braves* does not deal with batting averages, managerial decisions, or players. There is minimal focus on what Atlanta did to draw baseball to Georgia because the subject has been covered elsewhere. Instead, the focus is primarily on the operations of a professional baseball team in Wisconsin in the postwar era and the relationship of the club to the public. While this is predominantly a Milwaukee narrative, the incredible draw of the team across the state and the region has made it a larger story for all Braves fans. More broadly, the history of the Braves sheds light on the potential rewards and pitfalls of relocating a major sports franchise, a now common practice.

Over the years since the Braves left Milwaukee, mutual finger-pointing has led to overly simplified versions of what went wrong. In delving into this history, I draw on newspaper reports, archival research, and interviews of club officials and locals who worked to move or retain the team. Taken together, these sources tell a more dynamic, more complex, and ultimately more interesting story.

To diehard fans like my mother, the Braves were stolen—but not by Atlanta. Multiple parties' competing interests converged with rapidly changing circumstances in Wisconsin and throughout the country. It was these disparate forces, coming together, that "stole" the Milwaukee Braves, leaving an empty spot in the heart of the city and memories of past glories: a sold-out stadium, passionate fans, and the team that delivered the Milwaukee Miracle.

1

"You Keep the Brewers, We'll Keep the Braves"

1945–1953

Judas Priest, no wonder Lou Perini wanted to get out of Boston.

Branch Rickey, Pittsburgh Pirates general manager,
March 19, 1953

Milwaukee's Baseball Heritage

Fans of Milwaukee baseball have always believed that their city has a special relationship with America's pastime. In addition to a strong minor league tradition that dates back to the late nineteenth century, the Milwaukee Brewers were a charter member of the American League, which was founded at the Republican House hotel in downtown Milwaukee in 1901. While those major league Brewers lasted only a single season before they relocated to St. Louis to become the Browns, better days were ahead. For the next fifty years, Milwaukee's baseball heart was predominantly with the new American Association (AA) Milwaukee Brewers. Games were played at the oddly shaped Borchert Field, where the Brewers won eight league titles, two of them in their last years in Milwaukee, 1951 and 1952.[1] The success of the minor league Brewers in their dilapidated old wooden ballpark ultimately paved the way for major league baseball to return to Milwaukee in 1953.

The AA Brewers went through several owners during their existence, but none was more important to the future of Milwaukee baseball than William Veeck Jr. His father had been the president of the Chicago Cubs, and the

7

younger Veeck grew up around the game. In 1941 Veeck put together a group to purchase the minor league Brewers, who at the time were on the verge of financial collapse. There were even rumors that the American Association was going to exercise legal action to take over the team. Through clever promotions, stadium improvements at Borchert Field, and shrewd management of the club's finances, Veeck turned the club around.[2] With a collection of good players, the Brewers won three pennants during the World War II years. When the war ended, Veeck returned from service in the Marines and was ready for another challenge. He had always wanted to own a major league team, but because that did not appear possible in Milwaukee he sold the Brewers in 1945 and put together a group that bought the Cleveland Indians, the first of three teams he would own in his lifetime. Milwaukee fans had always treated him well, and Veeck hoped that one day he could return to Wisconsin with a major league club.

Without Veeck's creativity, the Brewers most likely would have failed and left Milwaukee. Without the Brewers, there would have been no pressure to build a municipal stadium in the early 1950s, which was a primary reason the Boston Braves originally looked at Milwaukee in the spring of 1953.

After Veeck sold the Brewers to a Chicago lawyer, the team was sold again, in 1946, to Louis R. Perini and the ownership group of the National League's Boston Braves.[3] The acquisition gave the Braves a farm club in the largest city in the American Association, a city with a well-earned baseball reputation. Moreover, the postwar political and civic leadership in Milwaukee County was planning a program of infrastructure improvement and urban renewal that many believed would make Milwaukee a greater place to live: new highways, a zoo, libraries, an expanded airport, a multiuse arena, and a war memorial. The centerpiece of the municipal investment was a publicly funded baseball stadium, ostensibly for the minor league Brewers. Mayor Frank Zeidler proudly said, "Milwaukee had its chance at greatness and it grasped and made splendid use of the opportunity."[4] The stadium was projected to be big enough to host a major league baseball franchise and games for the National Football League's Green Bay Packers. With expansive parking and amenities that were arguably greater than those of contemporary major league ballparks, Milwaukee County Stadium was one of the key selling points of Milwaukee to Perini and the Braves.

While ground would not be broken for the stadium until 1950, the slow-moving cogs of bureaucracy were already grinding behind the scenes. In fact, the idea of building a new stadium to replace Borchert Field dated further back in the twentieth century. Several proposals were discussed over the decades, but none were ever acted upon. In the 1930s, a city alderman, hoping to attract federal dollars under the Public Works Administration, resurrected the stadium project. The concept, however, languished during World War II, although a new stadium push was revived shortly after Veeck sold the Brewers to the Braves. Leading the charge to get the project done were many local officials and journalists who championed this attempt to replace Borchert Field. This pattern would be replicated in other cities where boosters would help get stadium projects built in existing major league towns or in places that desperately wanted to attract a franchise. It was especially important in an era when several owners of second-tier teams were looking for a brighter future and a new ballpark.

Several locations were proposed but eventually the Milwaukee County Board settled on a site around the Story Quarry in the Menomonee River Valley.[5] A segment of it was federal land under the Veterans Administration. In 1949, after some local political battles, President Harry S. Truman signed legislation that leased the twenty-two acres to Milwaukee County for the paltry sum of one dollar a year. The county also purchased almost a hundred acres of land around the parcel for parking.[6] Without realizing it at the time, one of the greatest traditions of Milwaukee sports was secured. Unlike other teams that were landlocked in decaying urban centers with ballparks that had limited space for cars, a large parking lot was part of the new stadium. The proposed stadium was to seat twenty-five thousand with possible expansion to sixty thousand.[7] Ground was broken for Milwaukee County Municipal Stadium in October 1950, but construction was delayed because materials were scarce during the Korean War. Slowly a stadium began to emerge from land that had been used as the garbage dump.[8] Its location was expected to attract fans in the suburbs who could easily attend sporting and other events at the crown jewel of Milwaukee County.

What really made County Stadium unique compared with other facilities at the time was not its design or dimensions but its financing. Unlike most ballparks that were primarily built by team owners, Milwaukee County taxes paid for the new stadium. While this was not the first time that tax dollars were used for a stadium project in the United States, it was the first to be promoted as a major source of revenue for the community that built it. Other municipalities recognized this, along with sports owners who saw the benefits of new publicly funded stadiums to their bottom lines. Rather than just waiting for expansion or an owner to want to come and build a stadium, cities without major league sports understood that they had a greater chance of attracting a team with an existing facility, or the promise of a new one. Several other cities, including Atlanta, used the Milwaukee method to become major league.

The Boston Braves Look West

It might be hard to believe now, but for five decades before the Braves' relocation to Milwaukee in 1953, no major league baseball franchise moved; the sport was fairly static. From 1903 to 1953 the highest level of professional baseball was primarily a Northeast phenomenon. While there were hundreds of minor league teams spread out across the nation, the St. Louis Browns and Cardinals shared the distinction of being both the farthest west and south that big league baseball had ventured. Many of the cities that had major league baseball split their fan base between two franchises, or in New York's case, three. Often, one of the teams, such as the Cardinals or the Boston Red Sox, seemed to capture the majority of the fans, and the other teams, like the Browns or the Braves, were second class in the minds of the fans. This was the business model, however, that brought baseball through the dark days following the Chicago Black Sox scandal of 1919 and the years of the Great Depression and World War II.[9] The prosperity of the postwar years, as well as population shifts to the west, ultimately challenged that model and brought baseball into a modern age of new stadiums and cities.

The Boston Braves were one of several unlucky clubs that played a secondary role to another team in their market. Because the Braves played in a stadium without the charm of Fenway Park or the iconic players of their crosstown rivals, like George "Babe" Ruth or Ted Williams, they struggled for attention from fans and paying customers.[10] The team had been in Boston since 1871 and was a charter member of the National League in 1876. They had won their only World Series in the distant past, 1914, when they swept the Philadelphia Athletics. A year later they christened the new Braves Field, which was nicknamed the Wigwam and remained their home until September 21, 1952. At the time it was built it was the largest ballpark in the United States and could seat forty thousand fans.[11]

Regrettably, attendance at Braves Field underperformed the National League average more often than not, as the team was usually not very good. In fact, between its championship in 1914 and its last year in Boston, 1952, the team had only eleven winning seasons and one pennant. The team was so desperate for fans it even changed its name in an effort to alter its fortunes. The "new" Boston Bees had five losing seasons, from 1936 to 1940, before it reverted back to the Braves name. As overall baseball attendance grew after World War II, the Braves finally broke the million mark in 1947. It peaked at fewer than 1.5 million a year later when the Braves went back to the World Series but dropped again in 1949 to just over 1 million before the bottom fell out the last two years at the Wigwam. By the end of 1952, attendance was the lowest in all of baseball with just over 281,000,[12] compared with over 1.1 million for the crosstown Red Sox, and the Braves consistently lost money.[13] This hurt not only the owners of the Braves but also those of the visiting teams that received a percentage of the ticket sales for games in Boston.

Lou Perini, a minority owner of the Braves since 1941, spearheaded a trio of Boston contractors nicknamed "Three Little Steam Shovels" who purchased the team in 1944. Perini, along with Guido Rugo and Joseph Maney, created a syndicate that bought out the rest of the Braves' stockholders in 1943. The financial resources of Perini's construction company, along with the support of his younger brothers Joseph and Charlie, contributed to his shares, and they eventually attained half of the stock of the Braves.[14] In 1945, upon the retirement of team president Bob Quinn, Perini took over those responsibilities and would remain the Braves' president until 1957. Quinn's son John remained with the team as general manager and is remembered for leading the club during the tumultuous move to Milwaukee. During his time with the Braves, the younger Quinn built three pennant winners and one World Series champion.[15]

The new Perini ownership group seemed to infuse a bit of excitement into the moribund franchise, and the team got better on the field. In an effort to improve on one of the smallest farm systems in the major leagues, the Braves purchased the American Association Milwaukee Brewers in 1946 for $270,000. A year later the group was operating fifteen minor league teams, including the Brewers. This new direction helped the franchise on the field as the Braves went to the World Series in 1948. They took on Bill Veeck's Cleveland Indians in the Fall Classic, but the success of the season was diminished a bit when Boston lost in six games. The 1948 National League pennant was the apex of the Perini ownership in Massachusetts. The team floundered in 1949 and 1950. It would take time for many of the better young players in the minor leagues to matriculate up to the majors. Even the addition of Sam Jethroe, the 1950 National League Rookie of the Year and the first minority player in all of Boston, could not return the Boston Braves to the World Series or profitability. As performance on the field struggled, abysmal attendance at the Wigwam and increased payroll created financial losses that were not sustainable. This situation, combined with its second-class status in Boston, meant the Braves were in deep trouble. Perhaps in an effort to get out before the situation got worse, Rugo sold his shares of the team to Perini and Maney in 1951 and was removed as the club's vice president.

Improvements were made at Braves Field to increase fan interest in the team, but the product on the field did not match Perini's expectations. In 1952 rumors began to swirl that the team might relocate to solve its financial problems. Fueling that speculation was a move in November 1952 by Perini and his brothers to buy out the 45 percent of the stock held by eight other owners, including the last of the original trio, Joseph Maney. Boston papers conjectured that Perini might be leaning toward moving the Braves to another city, most likely Milwaukee.[16] Whatever Perini's decision was, he kept it to himself, telling no one, including his own family.[17] The world would not get wind of this until news broke on March 13, 1953, that the Braves were looking to relocate to Wisconsin.

Milwaukee seemed to be perfectly located and ready for major league baseball, whether with an expansion club or transfer of an existing team. Located on the shores of Lake Michigan, it was a hub of industrialism that thrived during and after World War II. The population of the state had gone up more than 9 percent since 1940, with Milwaukee County alone at 871,000 out of a total of 3.4 million. That number increased to more than 1.1 million if you included Ozaukee, Racine, Washington, and Waukesha Counties in southeastern Wisconsin, which represent the greatest draw for Milwaukee baseball. There were also more than 1.2 million vehicles in Wisconsin alone that could travel along more than twenty-nine thousand miles of state and county highways to potentially funnel into the expansive parking lots at Milwaukee County Stadium.[18] At the same time, Boston was struggling to support two teams, despite a city population of 801,000 and a metropolitan area that brought the prospective fan base up to more than 2.3 million.[19] While Braves Field did not have much parking space, public transportation was the norm in Boston. There were plenty of ways to get to the ballpark, but not many people seemed interested in going to the games.

Here Come the Milwaukee Browns?

With the opening of Milwaukee County Stadium looming for the spring of 1953, Milwaukee civic leaders began to look for a team to call it home. The Brewers, coming off of back-to-back American Association titles, were the logical choice, but the Greater Milwaukee Committee and the Milwaukee Association of Commerce believed that they could attract an existing major league team to transfer and play in their new stadium. The most logical one to pursue was the team that had left Milwaukee five decades earlier. The American League's St. Louis Browns had never met with much success in either city and had won only a single pennant in its existence. That was in 1944, when most able-bodied men were fighting for their nation, not playing baseball. Like the Braves in Boston, the Browns were a clear second-class team compared with the Cardinals. Even worse, both clubs had played in the same ballpark since 1920. Although Sportsman's Park was originally built for and still owned by the Browns, the Cardinals continually outperformed the Browns in attendance and wins. Ironically, both clubs were rumored to be considering a move to Milwaukee when County Stadium was still under construction.

Speculation was rampant as early as 1951 that the Browns were under consideration to be replaced in the American League by a new Milwaukee franchise. Frederick C. Miller, the energetic president of Miller Brewing, was reported to be in line to purchase the floundering club to operate in Milwaukee's new stadium.[20] It has been said that whatever was good for the region received Miller's economic support and his leadership. He was not only active within the brewing industry, he also maintained control of the family lumberyard and was the first president of the Air Force League. More importantly, through his role in the Greater Milwaukee Committee he was instrumental in the development of the Milwaukee Arena, County Stadium, the new public library, airport enhancements, and other civic improvements. He had also been an All-American football player and team captain at Notre Dame, where he played for renowned coach Knute Rockne. He served as a vice president of Miller Brewing for eleven years and was promoted to the top spot in 1947. Miller also served on the board of directors of the Green Bay Packers. He was truly Milwaukee's sportsman.[21]

Unfortunately for Miller, the restless Bill Veeck put together a syndicate and purchased the Browns from owners Bill and Charlie DeWitt at the eleventh hour. The irrepressible Veeck did everything in his power to turn the fortunes of the Browns around, but he soon came to realize staying in St. Louis would be difficult. It was also believed at the time that the St. Louis Cardinals might be moving to a new city and Milwaukee might be a good fit. Cardinals owner Frederick Saigh was being pressured to sell his club because he faced federal charges for tax evasion. There were several cities mentioned as a possible landing spot for the Red Birds, including Milwaukee. Lloyd Larson of the *Milwaukee Sentinel* claimed that an unnamed team official told him that "Milwaukee and the State of Wisconsin are entitled to more than a big league franchise. They should have the best baseball can work out. The transfer must come from a western city. That means the Cardinals are it. So we are ready to move when the stadium is completed." Fred Miller was again linked to the Milwaukee attempt to buy the Cardinals, especially after the Browns were sold to Veeck. Regrettably for the Milwaukee fans, Saigh declined their offer of $4 million. Instead, August Busch Jr., president of Anheuser-Busch Brewery, stepped up and purchased the Cardinals in February of 1953 for $3.75 million.[22] The strong financial backing of Anheuser-Busch clearly and immediately ended all hopes of the Cardinals coming to Milwaukee. Even more, it exacerbated the competitive imbalance in Missouri. Veeck now needed to find a new home for the Browns, and Milwaukee was appealing. After all, it had a new ballpark, and he had maintained a good rapport with baseball fans in southeastern Wisconsin. In fact, after the sale of the Cardinals, it now appeared to be a given that the Browns were coming to County Stadium.

Before this could happen, two major obstacles had to be overcome. The first was approval by the American League owners, who were not likely to grant it to Veeck. He had created many enemies among his fellow owners, and some even hoped to force him to sell his franchise and be removed from baseball once and for all. The second was the Boston Braves. They would have to sell the rights to the territory in Wisconsin they had maintained since purchasing the Brewers in 1946, and it appeared to Veeck that Perini was not in a selling mood. The Browns owner truly believed that Perini would have been "willing to sell" the territorial rights to Milwaukee if he had made this proposal a year earlier, in 1952, or a year later, after the Braves had improved in 1954.[23] But it did not work out that way for Veeck, and despite heavy lobbying on his behalf by some Milwaukee journalists, the Browns would not be leaving Missouri for Wisconsin any time soon.

It was now apparent that Perini had seriously been considering moving the Braves, most likely to Milwaukee, since at least 1950. Charlie Grimm, the last manager of the minor league Brewers, was promoted to manage the Braves in late spring 1952. He later wrote that he was selected because of his rapport with Milwaukee city officials and Wisconsin baseball fans.[24] If Perini wanted to be in Milwaukee, with its new stadium and a potentially enthusiastic fan base, he had to find a way out of Massachusetts. However, it would be difficult for him to abandon Boston in the same manner that Braves fans had deserted the Wigwam. He was not completely convinced that Milwaukee would be able to support a major league franchise, even if it was good. They had a plethora of young prospects filtering through the Braves' farm system, and the future on the field was brighter than it had been in recent years.[25] Moreover, Perini loved Boston, had many business contacts there, and did not want to leave unless there were no better options for his team. But soon he would have to make a difficult decision.

On March 3, 1953, it was reported that Veeck had offered the Braves $500,000 to transfer the Brewers from Milwaukee to Toledo and make room for the Browns in the new ballpark. Veeck later wrote that he actually offered Perini $750,000 for the Milwaukee territory, which was almost three times the amount that Perini originally spent on the Brewers. If the Braves accepted the offer, Veeck claimed that Perini would still get to keep the minor league team as well as the rights to Toledo. The transfer of the Brewers would clear the Milwaukee market for the Browns, and the move would take place before the 1953 regular season began. The Braves, however, declined the offer, citing the need for a franchise similar to the Brewers and what they had in Milwaukee. Braves vice president Joseph Cairnes told the *New York Times* that the team was not interested in the cash, but instead wanted another minor league team that could perform the way the Brewers had, and he did not see how this could "be worked out in a few days or a few weeks." Clifford Randall, chair of the Greater Milwaukee Committee, added that he had made the offer to the Braves on behalf of the Browns, but the Boston club just "wasn't interested."[26]

"A matter of form if the Braves agreed to the move"

Perini made it clear to the Milwaukee boosters that were pressuring him to allow the Browns in that he would not stand in the way of the city getting into the majors. In a published telegram exchange with R. G. Lynch, sports editor of the *Milwaukee Journal*, Perini encouraged Milwaukee's civic leaders to pursue a major league club by going through the proper application channels. He did not see the decline of the sale of the Brewers as anything significant, because they had refused offers to sell for the last three years. Perini further added that if Milwaukee did pursue it through the appropriate channels, the Braves would make clear "any preference we might have to make Milwaukee available" for major league baseball. The Braves would also "abide by whatever decision baseball might make" regarding the major-minor league rules of baseball. Veeck himself said that Perini was not "at all unreasonable and was acting within his rights by rejecting an offer at a time when clubs are preparing to open their season." He added that he knew "Milwaukee is a sound baseball city" and he was positive that "it would support a big league team," including the Browns. Veeck also believed that the Browns would be a pennant contender in 1953. But Veeck did not "foresee any change of franchises in the near future."[27]

Lynch appeared to be losing his patience with the obfuscation of the Braves front office in regard to the Browns situation. He pointed out that Milwaukee had spent $5 million to build County Stadium and the net result would be an increased cost to buy the city out of its "bondage to Louis Perini and the Boston Braves." It was clear to all that without the Braves' opposition, the Browns would be in Milwaukee on Opening Day. Even more frustrating to the Milwaukee fans was Perini's assurances of support to help, or at least not hinder, the city to succeed in their attempts to enter the major leagues. Now it appeared that not only were the Braves obstructing, but talking to them was like running "into a stone wall." Time was also becoming an issue because of a thirty-day cancelation clause in the stadium agreement between the county and the Brewers. This clause was added because the Braves wanted options in the unlikely event that the major leagues granted Milwaukee a franchise. The only thing that could help at this point, Lynch argued, was for the public to show their support for a major league team. Perhaps that would persuade Perini to allow Veeck's team to become the Milwaukee Browns or, most likely, return to the Brewers name. If the Browns could not wait, the Philadelphia Athletics were rumored to be looking for a new home, and Milwaukee might still be available in 1954.[28]

Mayor Zeidler attempted to get the Braves to explain why they opposed relocating the Browns and was told that it was too late to get the approval of baseball commissioner Ford Frick. Furthermore, a move would disrupt the American League schedule as well as the American Association and even break up the latter. This was a dubious claim coming from a National League club that would not be affected by these changes at all. The Braves reiterated that they were not interested in cash but rather a place to develop their players. Lynch challenged these claims in the March 5 edition of the *Milwaukee Journal*. He argued that Frick's permission was necessary "only as a matter of form if the Braves agreed to the move." Moreover, there was no deadline for major league clubs to announce they were moving into a minor league territory. It was assumed that the deadline was December 1 of the year previous to the move, but that applied only to minor league teams moving to another city. The most doubtful argument from the Braves was the disruption of the schedule. Milwaukee was closer to the rest of the league than St. Louis, so how could that really impact their scheduling? It would save the league an estimated $70,000 in travel expenses over the course of the season. The fear of the disintegration of the American Association was groundless because the city the Brewers would move to under any agreement was Toledo, a city that had a forty-year history with the AA. Lynch closed his comments by suggesting that Zeidler would be "justified in feeling that these statements were an insult to his intelligence."[29]

Wisconsin governor Walter Kohler joined the calls for a resolution to the impasse between the Browns and the Braves. The citizens of his state were growing impatient with the process, and he decided to step in to expedite a solution. The state senate concurred and unanimously adopted a joint resolution that suggested the "time is ripe to make good" on Perini's promise "not to stand in the way of the plans to bring baseball to Wisconsin." Kohler communicated personally to Frick and Perini that the transfer of Veeck's club was a "matter of tremendous importance" to Milwaukee and Wisconsin. He added that he hoped that "the interests of the public will not be overlooked in the consideration of the matter."[30] Meanwhile, on March 6, 1953, Veeck told reporters that it had become increasingly clear that the Browns would have to remain in St. Louis for the upcoming season. He said he was approached the previous September by a group spearheaded by Clifford Randall of the Greater Milwaukee Committee to buy his club and bring it to Milwaukee. Veeck was not interested in selling, but Randall offered the next best thing, a move of the Browns to Milwaukee under the existing ownership.[31]

The dreams of Randall and his Milwaukee boosters appeared to be dying because the Braves were being neither honest nor supportive of Milwaukee's efforts to bring major league baseball to County Stadium. On March 11, rumors persisted that the Browns would not return to St. Louis for the pending season. Frick stated that a team did not need his approval to relocate, and he would settle only "controversial matters between clubs." This would bring the Braves and Browns dispute into Frick's domain, and he clearly left "the door open for a shift of baseball franchises and some move appears to be under serious consideration." However, overruling the Braves in this matter seemed "unlikely if not impossible."[32] Frustration with Perini and the Braves seemed to reach a boiling point on March 12 when banner headlines in the *Milwaukee Journal* sports pages announced that Perini formally asked for a new rule at the owners' meeting in Vero Beach, Florida. Perini's proposal would prevent the "transfer of a major league franchise to a minor league city" with the exception of a window between October 1 and the December 1953 baseball meetings. If approved, this plan was believed to kill any last hopes for a major league team in Milwaukee for the 1953 season. Despite all previous assurances to Milwaukee, it was clear that Perini was making this move to prevent the Browns from relocating and to protect their investment in Milwaukee.[33]

To local sportswriters it was abundantly clear that the Browns wanted to come to Milwaukee right away and Perini had made every effort to prevent it from happening. Veeck's plan appeared to be stalled long enough that the Browns might abandon any plans to relocate in Wisconsin. Particularly galling to the fan base was the substantiation that Milwaukee could have had the Browns if only Perini had agreed to move the Brewers.[34] The news became more devastating the following morning when Lloyd Larson reported that Veeck was now finalizing a deal to take the Browns to Baltimore instead. The situation in St. Louis was now toxic for Veeck and his club, and if Milwaukee was not going to work out, then he needed to find another city that was fully prepared to accept a major league team. Negotiations between Veeck and Baltimore officials continued in the background, despite the public efforts to take the Browns to Milwaukee. Although Veeck hoped that when the 1953 season opened the Browns would be in a new city, either Milwaukee or Baltimore, it did not happen. The relocation of the Browns would have to wait until 1954. For Milwaukee fans, Veeck's collaboration with Baltimore had to be devastating news. Even worse, it involved moving the minor league team in Baltimore to Toledo, where the Brewers were supposed to go if a major league team came to Milwaukee. The prospects of a big league team inaugurating a brand new County Stadium in 1953 were now very remote.[35] Despite the plethora of bad news about the Browns, no one outside of Lou Perini and a few of his close insiders knew the world of baseball was about to change forever.

Behind the scenes, the Milwaukee County Board proceeded to act to terminate the contract between itself and the Milwaukee Brewers. Five members of the board introduced a resolution that invoked a thirty-day termination clause in the contract to make room for whichever major league team came first. This left the Brewers without a place to play because Borchert Field, the home of Milwaukee baseball since the 1880s, had already been demolished. It was a risky move for Milwaukee, but the political and civic leaders wanted a big league club in their new stadium.[36]

"Milwaukee May Get the Braves"

Despite this imminent development, it is clear that this would not be the last time Milwaukee baseball fans would feel they had been deceived by the Braves organization. From Perini's perspective, he had to keep his decision very close because his primary business interests were headquartered in Massachusetts and he could not afford to antagonize the public or politicians in Boston. In addition, the Braves and their few remaining Boston fans had an extremely close relationship. Perini's heart was in Beantown, and he had been committed to win a World Series for the Boston faithful, but fans and the Braves family were shrinking. Receipts had dropped so much that in one game in 1952, the visiting Pirates' share of the gate totaled exactly twenty-four dollars.[37] Horace Stoneham, owner of the New York Giants, added that his team "never took a nickel out of Boston."[38]

Perini still hoped to salvage the team's future in New England by either moving to a new ballpark in the Boston suburbs or even sharing Fenway Park with Tom Yawkey's Red Sox. The Perini group had already attempted to make Braves Field a better experience for the fans. They had invested in expanding the seating capacity to closer to fifty thousand, improved the concessions, and added more bathrooms. In January 1953, mere months before the move was announced, Perini had asked the National League's permission to reconfigure Braves Field to give fans a better view of the game. He looked into moving home plate closer to the stands, as well as elevating the infield or the seats in the stands. A new outfield fence would be built to accommodate the changes and keep the ballpark's measurements the same. Warren Giles, the National League president, denied Perini's petition, and no major changes were slated at Braves Field for the upcoming season.[39]

If Perini had to move the team, he clearly preferred to wait until 1954. The fiasco with Veeck, however, had forced his hand and now a decision had to be made. Just weeks before the 1953 opening day, Perini could merely wonder why only 420 season tickets to Braves Field had been sold.[40] The Wigwam was primed and freshly painted for the upcoming season, but major league baseball would not be returning. The magic of the 1948 pennant season was long gone, and with no other option readily available, the move to a new city became inevitable.

Working behind the scenes with Perini as the Browns debacle unfolded, Fred Miller tried to convince Perini that now was the time to move the Braves to Milwaukee. The two had known each other for several years through the beer sponsorship of the Brewers, and Miller was the former president of the Brewers. Miller had even attempted to purchase the Braves from Perini after his deal to buy the Browns fell apart. While Perini did not want to sell the Braves, he was intrigued enough by Milwaukee to promise Miller that he would not stay in or leave Boston without first conferring with Miller. Perini had concerns that had to be overcome before any decision was made about where the Braves would play in 1953: to leave Boston would mean losing money up front from cancelation of tickets already sold for games at Braves Field, as well as $320,000 in advertising for radio and television broadcasts for games in Boston. Miller promised Perini that his brewery would pay a million dollars for sponsorship for the first five years the Braves were in Milwaukee; in return, Miller Brewing would have preferential treatment, including exclusive rights to sell beer at County Stadium. Miller later backed down, and all of Milwaukee's beer companies had their brands inside the ballpark. Miller also committed his company to purchase $25,000 in tickets annually for five years for Miller Brewing promotions.[41]

The news of Veeck's decision to focus on Baltimore instead of Milwaukee was devastating to the local boosters who still believed that their city was major league even if it did not yet have a team. Perini's obstruction on the Browns' relocation had exasperated many in Milwaukee and indeed across much of

Wisconsin. Angry letters, telegrams, and cards arrived at Braves headquarters, decrying the ongoing impediment to major league baseball in Milwaukee. Then, when the future seemed darkest, *Sporting News* broke a story that Frick had called for a meeting of National League executives the following Monday to discuss and ratify a request by Perini to relocate the Braves from Boston to Milwaukee.[42]

The headlines in the Friday edition of the *Milwaukee Journal* announced that "Milwaukee May Get the Braves." According to a story reported earlier that day and confirmed in Florida, Milwaukee, and even St. Louis, an emergency meeting would address the Browns and Braves moves. Perini was to meet with Frick and Giles to discuss the possibility of relocating the Braves to Milwaukee— and, in turn, the Brewers to Toledo. Approval by Perini's fellow National League owners was not guaranteed. When asked directly about the veracity of the report, Perini replied, "I can't say yes and I can't say no." He added that there were issues that made his situation different from Veeck's in St. Louis. To move from St. Louis, said Perini, Veeck only had to sell his ballpark to the Cardinals and the Anheuser-Busch Brewing Company. Perini did not have another owner waiting in the wings to purchase Braves Field because the Red Sox were ensconced at Fenway Park (and remain there today). Estimated to be worth more than $8 million in 1952, Braves Field was sold to Boston University for a reported $340,000 in 1953.[43] At the time of the sale, it seated forty-one thousand and, according to BU president Harold Case, would be used for athletics and "commencements, baccalaureate services and other academic programs."[44] Rechristened Nickerson Field, it was the home of BU football, soccer, and lacrosse, as well as the American Football League's Boston Patriots in 1961–62. In 2017, only the right field pavilion area remains as part of Nickerson Field, more than a decade after Milwaukee County Stadium and Atlanta Fulton County Stadium have been demolished and even after the Braves left Turner Field in Atlanta.[45]

"You won't be sorry"

As the story of the potential move was unfolding in Florida, Miller realized that his big league dreams for Milwaukee were coming true. He had used all the economic leverage he could to lure the Braves from Boston. When he "heard of the Baltimore move . . . I called Perini in Florida and asked him if the Braves could be moved here this year," he told reporters. One of the issues holding up Perini's decision, he said, was cost: "about $500,000 in lost revenues" if the move happened now. More encouraging for Milwaukee fans was what Miller said next. He noted that there could be potential changes in the ownership if the Braves came to Milwaukee, but he did not go into detail. He added, "I can't really answer that now . . . but there would be some Milwaukee ownership."[46] Miller also said that the mission to get the Braves to Milwaukee had already been going on behind the scenes for two years. It was always his goal to land a professional baseball team for the new County Stadium and now the hard work was paying off. Milwaukee had "finally won them over two days ago" when the Braves made the decision to relocate. Perini himself would later say Miller made the most compelling argument He told Perini if the Braves came to Milwaukee, "You won't be sorry."[47]

On the day the story broke in *Sporting News*, Miller met with members of the Milwaukee County Park Commission as part of an overall effort to secure a stadium deal for Perini. Miller told reporters that he would remain connected to the Braves ownership and that negotiations had been conducted through Joseph Cairnes. The deal was reported to be worth $1,000 a year for the first two years and 5 percent of receipts for the following eight years. This agreement would later be reworked as the Milwaukee Miracle unfolded.[48] In addition to use of the ballpark, the Braves wanted improved lighting, more seating capacity, and office space at County Stadium. Miller told the press that it was not clear what the ball club would be called when it finally played in Milwaukee. It might be the Braves, the Brewers, or maybe "a contest might be held to pick a name."[49]

"Long Live Yawkey and the Red Sox"

Meanwhile, Perini faced a hostile Boston sports media, bitter about the likely loss of the Braves, who had been there since the 1870s, long before the American League's Red Sox.[50] An apologetic Perini told the press and the few Braves fans that he was truly sorry for the decision. He knew that uprooting his team from its home and family-oriented fans would impact not only fans but sportswriters and businesses across Boston. He also stated the obvious: Boston could no longer support two teams, and the Red Sox were there to stay. Someday, he added, Tom Yawkey might sell Boston's favorite baseball team and Perini might be in a position to buy it.[51] Giles told reporters that Perini was highly respected and had dealt quite nobly with the decline of interest in Boston Braves baseball. Perini said money was not the only issue that forced his decision; the pronounced negative attitude and general apathy of Boston fans caused him the most concern.[52]

Fans of the Boston Braves did not have enough time to maximize any efforts to save the team. A decade later, during the Braves' last three years in

Milwaukee, amid rumors of a move to Atlanta, civic leaders organized to try to preserve major league baseball in Wisconsin. But in 1953, although the Braves had not drawn well for several years, fans were shocked by Perini's decision. Eventually, however, the city would get over the loss of the Braves and the financial blow to the hotel and restaurant industry, the transit system, and taxis.[53]

Massachusetts governor Christian Herter, Boston mayor John Hynes, the state legislature, and the Boston Chamber of Commerce met on March 16 to plot a strategy to keep the Braves in Boston. There was still hope among some that the league owners might not approve the move, as had the American League owners with Veeck, but that was not likely. Herter told reporters that he was "shocked to learn of the plan to move the Braves' franchise" and that he did not "know too much about what led up to this situation, but it would be a blow to the pride of Boston and Massachusetts to lose the Braves and become a one-team city." Fans of the departing club began to gather in opposition to the move, but their options were fairly limited. Hynes personally appealed to Perini to reconsider, but Perini said that he had already lost $700,000 in 1952 and that support for the team, even before the announcement, "had just about evaporated." A follow-up telegram from the governor and mayor begged Perini to reconsider the move. They added that alternative "arrangements may be worked out" so that other interests could "purchase and retain the franchise in Boston."[54]

Between the announcement of the pending move and Perini's final decision, the few remaining fans of Boston's National League club called the team's front offices in a futile attempt to get him to change his mind. The estimated financial loss to the Boston area was over $1.25 million per year, and Hynes told reporters that the National League would regret this move. He believed that "Milwaukee cannot or will not be able to support the Braves as well as Boston did." He believed that that Boston "was deserving of better treatment." Even after the formal approval of the transfer was announced, members of the Boston Chamber of Commerce who had traveled to Florida in an unsuccessful last-ditch attempt to keep the team sent a telegram to Boston. It simply read, "Long Live Yawkey and the Red Sox."[55] Red Sox general manager Joe Cronin added that he was "sorry to see the Braves leave Boston, but that Perini did what he believed was best for baseball."[56] Once the owners voted, Boston became a one-team city.

It should be noted here that, unlike the Milwaukee Braves relocation to Atlanta in 1966, a stadium lease did not hamper the Boston Braves move to Wisconsin. Because Perini owned Braves Field, he was not contractually obligated to remain in a city whose residents did not seem to want them. Owners, besides Veeck, who owned their ballparks or had short-term leases were the most likely to be ready to move when attendance fluctuated or new and growing television and radio markets offered greener pastures. Immediately after approval, it was evident that the Braves' move was most likely the first of many sweeping changes to the baseball map of the future. There remained only one question for Giles: "how big a handicap two teams in one city will be under in this day of television." Walter O'Malley, the Brooklyn Dodgers owner, added that there was only one "thing I'm sure of. . . . This transfer is going to set off a chain reaction and there are bound to be some more transfers."[57] The relocation of the Braves did not modify the structural framework of the National League or fundamentally change travel schedules, as was the case with some of the later franchise moves, but it was a step in that direction. Two more franchise changes took place before 1954, and the Dodgers themselves would play their last game in Brooklyn in September 1957. Unlike the second-rate status of the former Boston Braves, the Dodgers enjoyed a rabid fan base and phenomenal attendance. Their move was for greater profitability rather than simple survival.[58]

The Game of Baseball

Unfortunately for those few remaining fans of the Boston Braves, very little, outside of taking the team over by eminent domain, could have been done to keep the team in New England.[59] The reality of professional baseball is that it really represented two games, one played on the field and the other in the owners' boxes. From the earliest days of legal challenges to baseball, over players' contracts and other issues, the courts had continually ruled that because baseball was a sport, it was not subject to antitrust legislation regarding interstate commerce. The owners had absolute control over the game, the players, the revenues, and the cities where it would be played. They also worked hard to keep their ranks more exclusive than even the United States Senate. After all, by the end of the 1950s there were one hundred senators but only sixteen major league principal owners.

American League owners exercised their power over the game by refusing the transfer of Veeck's St. Louis Browns to Baltimore in 1953, regardless of what would happen to the team. The next day Veeck said he had been a "victim of duplicity by a lot of lying so-and-sos. The only reason they can give for voting against me is they are silly or malicious. I prefer to think they are malicious." He added that this decision was merely "postponing the inevitable" because he had lost $400,000 in 1952 and "I just don't have that kind of dough to lose."[60]

Clearly the animosity aimed at Veeck influenced the decision. The March 24 vote on the Browns' relocation was 5–3 against the move. Veeck tried again on September 27, and the vote was tied 4–4 so nothing was done. A mere two days later, following Veeck's agreement to sell the Browns to a new ownership group, the owners unanimously agreed to transfer the club to Baltimore.[61] The team was renamed the Orioles and brought more than one million fans through the turnstiles, which was more than three and a half times as many as the Browns had drawn to Sportsman's Park in St. Louis in the 1953 season.[62] Even more interesting, the final lame duck season of the Browns in 1953 drew 297,238 fans.[63] This was almost sixteen thousand more than the Boston Braves in 1952, when no one knew it would be their last.

Revenues for the Braves, and frankly the Browns, were hurt by more than just low attendance at their ballparks. By the early 1950s major league clubs made money selling "novelties, clothing, radio and television rights" and they appeared to be willing to rent out "everything but the kitchen sink." Teams also understood that they needed to branch out into other areas as "the money made in these extra enterprises enables baseball to keep its admission prices" at prewar levels and cover the cost of developing new players. Without fans in the stands, the teams lose money not only from the gate receipts but concession sales. These had long been considered part of the ballpark experience, and the teams collected approximately 25 percent of the gross concession sales. In lean years, concession sales alone helped to finance spring training trips by some teams. The Chicago Cubs and St. Louis Cardinals benefited by owning their concessions and reportedly earned fortunes. In 1950, Cardinals owner Fred Saigh stated that two decades earlier, the team received about $20,000 in concessions while now it grossed "$600,000—and that's exclusive of our farm system." The Cincinnati Reds front office acknowledged the most important advancement in concessions at ballparks was "the trend toward sound merchandising." Even more, good "concessionaires have learned that merchandising just like a store will pay dividends. No longer can a ball club expect its patrons to just accept any old item." Sales of sponsorships and broadcast rights could help teams cover the cost of annual ballpark maintenance that was estimated to run between $250,000 and $400,000.[64]

Owners also generated revenue by selling players' contracts to other teams, and the Braves had not been above this in the past. By the end of the 1952 season, however, the lack of success on the field, few fans in the stands, few great players, and reduced concession sales all contributed to the mounting yearly losses that the Braves had suffered since 1948. Fortunately for the Braves' plans to relocate, the National League owners actually liked Perini. Enthusiasm for the team in

Milwaukee meant fans in the stands who would buy food, shirts, pennants, and baseball caps. It also meant that the visiting teams would get larger checks for their trips to County Stadium than to Braves Field.

The Braves Quit Hub

On March 18, 1953, the National League formally approved the transfer of the Braves to Milwaukee after a three-and-a-half-hour owners' meeting. It was a testament to Perini's character and esteem among the owners that the move was approved so quickly and seamlessly. Giles announced there had been no substantive opposition to the first franchise shift in fifty years, and Perini agreed to compensate the American Association $50,000 for its loss of Milwaukee. Despite Fred Miller's previous comments on the team name, the Braves name would continue in Milwaukee and the only change for the uniforms was the replacement of the white *B* on the caps with an *M*.[65] Because the Braves were now in the Midwest rather than on the East Coast, Giles also told reporters that most of the discussion revolved around swapping the Braves and Pirates 1953 schedules to ease traveling, as well as their respective divisions. After the meeting Perini commented that it was more than low attendance and financial losses that brought him to this point. It was apparent that "since the advent of television Boston has become a one-team city . . . and the enthusiasm of the fans for the Boston National League club has waned." Moreover, the "interests of baseball can best be served elsewhere and Milwaukee has shown tremendous enthusiasm." Perini forewarned that this could be the start of a trend of baseball relocation and that other communities "can take a page from the Milwaukee book by providing for major-league facilities." He added that he regretted the loss and disappointment to Braves fans and for the impact upon so many members of the Boston media.[66]

Tickets already printed for the 1953 season at Braves Field were destroyed, and Perini wrote a personal letter of apology to the 420 fans who had applied for season tickets, an all-time low for the franchise. "In spite of all our efforts," he wrote, "the large majority of Boston and New England fans" were not going to support the ball club, and the only way the Braves could stay financially viable was to move the team "to where more people would give them the whole-hearted support which they deserve."[67] Raynhild Stenberg, the secretary for the Boston Braves for twenty-five years, declined an offer to follow the club to Milwaukee. She had witnessed profound shifts in the organization during her time at Braves Field, including three changes of ownership and a single pennant. She would "never find a job as interesting," but she was not "as near suicide as some of the old fans" of the Braves.[68] Devotees' last opportunity to see their club play in Boston was a pair of exhibition games at Fenway Park against the Red Sox. Fans booed Perini and Miller, seated together to watch the end of a rivalry that had begun in 1901 when the Red Sox entered the American League as a charter member. The National League players were introduced for the first time as the Milwaukee Braves and received a mixture of boos and cheers from the Boston faithful.[69] The old crosstown rivalry was now over, and the Braves, unloved in their last years in New England, were "besieged" by their nostalgic remaining fans.[70]

And with that, the Braves were gone. Outside of exhibition games, they were not to return to Boston again until 1997 with the introduction of interleague play. But they were not far from the minds and hearts of the fans remaining behind, and there were signs of bitterness. Ten days after the move was announced, a vandalized shipment of women's handbags from New Bedford, Massachusetts, arrived at a Milwaukee department store. The inside flaps of the handbags had been scribed with the following messages: "You can't support the Brewers. How can you support the Braves?" and "You keep the Brewers. We'll keep the Braves." It was also said that not "since the Redcoats tried to slap a tax on their tea have this city's residents been so unanimously united." Some believed that Boston was still a two-team town, and all they had left were "those crummy Red Sox."[71]

Richard J. Cushing, the archbishop of Boston, defended the decision and Perini in particular. He said to a grieving public that the shift to Milwaukee might be a blessing if it reminded those with civic pride not to take too much for granted. The loss of the Braves could "arouse the citizens of this community to undertake several courageous projects," including beautification of the city, and perhaps even have a greater concern "in the helping of the poor, the needy, the handicapped and the helpless." He added that Perini was a great contributor to charitable causes in the city. A few months later, as the Braves got off to a hot start in Wisconsin, some said that if they won the pennant, half of the city of Boston would move to Milwaukee. It still pained longtime fans to pass the empty Braves Field or read that the Milwaukee Braves were now in a pennant race. Even worse, the team that had not drawn enough fans to the Wigwam to keep each other warm was regularly selling out County Stadium.[72]

On March 20, 1953, award-winning sports columnist Harold Kaese of the *Boston Globe* published an open letter to the new fans in Milwaukee. "Dear Sudsy," he began, and proceeded to vent as a fan of a club that had abandoned him. Yet he tried to remain optimistic about the Braves franchise, if not their new hometown. He asked if the Milwaukee fans were prepared for a team that had more history with failure than success and would charge more to see them than a minor league team. He was defensive about the low attendance at Braves Field the last couple of years. He encouraged Milwaukee to treat "our team well. Treat it better than we did" but be careful. Do not think of the new major league team as a "sacred trust" because the Braves were not sacred in their old hometown. Kaese argued that the Braves "won't be sacred in Milwaukee. Only as sacred as the money in your pants pocket, Sudsy old boy."[73] No one would truly understand the veracity of this warning, nor was Sudsy really prepared when their wallets were empty and Atlanta's were flush with cash.

2

Home of the Braves
1953–1954

Unless baseball becomes part of TV, it will find itself in
direct competition with the most powerful entertainment
medium in America.

Warren Giles, president of the National League,
1953

Joy in Sudsville

Many baseball experts originally believed that Braves owner Lou Perini did not
have much of a chance to relocate the team to Wisconsin. But when the news
arrived that the National League had approved, Milwaukee almost immediately
gave "a transfusion to the sport . . . [and] that is why folks are exceedingly wary"
to make more predictions about the Braves.[1] Sending congratulations to Perini,
Bill Veeck said he was "very happy over the decision to move the Braves to
Milwaukee." He assumed that it would be good for baseball, and the baseball
fans of southeastern Wisconsin were "certainly deserving of major league
baseball."[2]

The people of Milwaukee were in a mood to celebrate the biggest news
to hit their city since the end of Prohibition. Neighboring communities also
planned celebrations. On April 8, 1953, ten thousand people greeted the Braves
at the railroad station, and eighty thousand lined the parade route, including
many children, some on spring break. Fireworks went off as the Braves moved
west in convertibles along Wisconsin Avenue—temporarily renamed Braves
Drive—toward County Stadium, forty blocks away from downtown Milwaukee.
During the festivities it was announced that Wisconsin governor Walter Kohler

28

would throw out the ceremonial first pitch on Opening Day.[3] Gushing about the scene unfolding before him, Perini said there was "never anything like this in Boston. . . . Even in 1948, when we won the pennant and went to the world series for the first time since 1914, there wasn't a demonstration like this. This is just out of this world." Fred Miller could not have been happier with the turnout as the motorcade wound its way to County Stadium. He told those around him that this could indeed be the "beginning of a championship. . . . It's how they start." Perini added that it "could lead to anything" and the Braves would certainly embrace this. He wished that "all of the other ball club owners in the major leagues could be here today and see this. It would show them better than anything else the hold that baseball has on the public's heart." After a short reception where gifts were presented to the team, the Braves went out on the field for their first official workout at County Stadium.[4]

While parties, parades, and the tapping of countless kegs of Milwaukee's finest signaled the beginning of a new era in the city's history, there was work to do before the first games could be held: converting the headquarters of the former minor league Brewers to offices for the major league Braves and assembling a staff to sell tickets, answer phones, and prepare the stadium for exhibition games as well as Opening Day. One of the first issues to be hammered out was the scheduling of games brought about by the swapping of divisions between the Braves and the Pittsburgh Pirates. Another issue to be addressed was the schedule of Green Bay Packers games booked at County Stadium that might conflict with the baseball schedule, especially if the Braves went to the World Series.[5] The Braves also planned on playing thirty-two night games in Milwaukee, four more than scheduled had the team remained in Boston.[6] Albert Oliver, the grounds superintendent at Braves Field who inspected the Milwaukee field in mid-March, told the local press that County Stadium was in "near-perfect" shape for major league baseball. His list of things to be accomplished before Opening Day included working over the infield with a different field mix and painting some of the fencing in the outfield green to give the hitters a better view of the ball.[7] Two moving vans were sent to Milwaukee to carry the team's maintenance and office equipment, including typewriters and anything else needed at County Stadium. Oliver said this was "stuff we think they'll need immediately in Milwaukee." Included among the material rescued from Braves Field was the organ, which was placed along the first base side of the ballpark.[8]

Substantial changes to the ballpark had been agreed upon before the team moved, some of which created dissatisfaction among local leaders.[9] According to the lease, the county was obligated to spend an estimated $500,000 immediately and an additional $1.5 million over the next two years to bring the new ballpark up to major league standards. The costs involved increasing the number of permanent seats to a minimum of forty thousand, expanding concession space, replacing wooden planks in the upper deck with seats, and changing the offices.[10] The lighting at County Stadium was improved with permanent light stanchions that could illuminate the field 2,500 times brighter than a full moon.[11]

In addition to these extra costs, it was projected that Milwaukee County would most likely lose approximately $30,000 per year in rental fees because it was not getting the full value of its stadium lease. These financial concessions were, in the minds of the Milwaukee County Board, essential in the deal to secure the Braves, and certainly the fans did not complain.[12] It was further recommended that the City of Milwaukee budget $100,000 to break up traffic bottlenecks around the stadium anticipated to be worse than those of minor league days.[13] Unfortunately, the reduced lease rates would create a problem in the future when the terms of the original deal were met and a new lease was negotiated. Only then did the county insist upon a rental agreement that benefited Milwaukee County at the expense of the Braves and the rest of the baseball fans in the region.

"We all have a chore to do"

Anticipation of the Braves' arrival impacted many different institutions, including schools, colleges, and universities. Concordia College in downtown Milwaukee welcomed the Braves with a spoof in the student newspaper, the *Concordia Courier*. Under banner headlines, the reporter, simply named "Dickins," claimed that a game had been arranged between the college faculty and the Braves. All proceeds from the game, scheduled for "April 32," were to go to the "Retired Professors" fund. The Concordia uniforms specified "dark navy blue suits with black bow ties."[14] Humor in advance of the home opener, however, did not match the excitement at the box office.

On March 24, 1953, the first tickets emblazoned with *Milwaukee Braves* arrived at the stadium, but these would only partially fill the demand for the first eleven home dates scheduled. The Milwaukee ticket offices needed help organizing for a major league team. Cincinnati Reds ticket manager Charles Morris arrived to help, as the Braves' ticket manager, Blaze Romeo, had remained behind in Boston.[15] Despite every effort to streamline the process amid the timing of the Braves' move to Milwaukee and the exodus of the minor league Brewers to Toledo, the ticket office was simply overwhelmed. More than twelve thousand tickets for the Brewers needed to be exchanged, and the Braves required even more reserved seats. Brewers fans who had purchased box or reserved seats for the American Association opener could exchange them for their Braves counterparts if they paid the price difference. Some Braves supporters even came out to County Stadium to see where their seats would be before ordering them. Charles Sands, the Braves' public relations director, told the local media that it "was a terrible mess and we don't blame a lot of people for being angry. . . . There just were a lot more complications than we thought there would be in making a last-minute switch of cities." As late as April 3, the club officials were concerned that up to two thousand Brewers tickets still needed to be exchanged, and it was evident that some of the minor league fans would be disappointed with their seats in the new stadium.[16] The home opener scheduled for April 14 was sold out eight days before first pitch. The last tickets sold for the game were in the bleachers, which required the Braves to get a National League waiver because of a preexisting ban on the sale of bleacher seats. It was estimated that more than two thousand fans were in line at 9:30 a.m. on April 6 when the last of these tickets were released. By the end of the day, the tickets were gone, including a sale to a pair of men from Kenosha who had ridden a tandem bike to the stadium lot to get in line before sunrise.[17]

Ticket requests via mail orders were so overwhelming that new requests often arrived before the last ones had been processed. Window sales were limited to accommodate mail customers who did not have the luxury of driving to the stadium and standing in line. Fans in line were allowed to buy tickets for only one home stand at a time. The next series would be offered for sale only when the Braves went back on the road. By the end of the 1953 season more than 80 percent of the total capacity of County Stadium had been sold.[18] The rush of activities impacted the local media, as both the *Milwaukee Journal* and the *Milwaukee Sentinel* were obligated to add more switchboard operators and reporters to cover the team. Mayor Frank Zeidler told the *New York Times* that Milwaukee was "highly pleased" to be included in the "select circle of major league baseball cities." He spoke of the virtues of the city and added that Milwaukee thanked the owners for their expression of confidence in Wisconsin and he hoped the Braves would win a pennant at the earliest date.[19] The Braves would accomplish this feat a mere four years after moving to Milwaukee.

Lou Perini and his brothers had to be optimistic about Milwaukee's future when more than ten thousand fans showed up at County Stadium in the rain to see an exhibition game with the Red Sox. Attendance at County Stadium, in a cold, rainy exhibition game that lasted only two innings, almost doubled that of the 1952 Boston club's matchup with the Red Sox at Braves Field—and it could be presumed that the previous year's matchup in Boston included fans of both teams. When the season started, local businesses immediately felt the positive financial impact. On nights when the Braves played, restaurants and bars across southeastern Wisconsin were forced to change the hours they served dinner so fans could get to the games. Many taverns also chartered buses to take their fans to and from County Stadium to ensure there would be some business before and after the games on an otherwise quiet night. Restaurants around the stadium were overwhelmed, even on Sunday nights, as people came from all over the state and beyond to see the new home of the Braves.[20]

Perini was enthused by what he saw at County Stadium, but remained cautious about the Braves future. He told a crowd at a baseball banquet in Milwaukee that the city and state would be competing with much larger metropolitan areas and therefore attendance was imperative for the survival of the team. Perini believed that the Braves would have won more games in Boston "if the fans there had displayed this wonderful enthusiasm you have shown us here." He was also grateful that the local press had been friendly because the Boston sportswriters "didn't realize that their critical writing would kill the enthusiasm of the three and a half million fans who had backed the Braves for seventy-five years." Therefore, for the team to thrive in Milwaukee, Perini noted that "We all have a chore to do."[21]

Robert Creamer, senior editor for *Sports Illustrated*, editorialized two years later that Milwaukee was indeed a great baseball city, "by far the best in the major leagues." Baseball was truly part of the city's persona, as much "a part of the town as beer," and the Braves and the local brewing industry were "part of Milwaukee's civic pride." Milwaukee had a reputation of having "Ladies Day crowds" that cheered "wildly and indiscriminately at anything, even foul balls," he said, but fans "yelled at the right places and for the right things." In 1998, Johnny Logan, who had played for the old minor league Brewers and later the Braves, said there was always "a full-capacity crowd, but not the crowd you see today. Not the tailgating crowd or the Summerfest crowd. A sports-minded crowd. An adult crowd."[22]

On March 31, 1953, the team sold the radio broadcast rights to Braves games for the next five years. Miller Brewing was the title sponsor and had won the rights over six other bidders at a cost estimated to be in excess of $1 million. Fred Miller had been instrumental in the negotiations with the ball club, and his family's brewery had sponsored radio broadcasts in Milwaukee for the previous thirteen years. Braves games were ultimately simulcast on two Milwaukee stations. Earl Gillespie, the play-by-play announcer for the minor league Brewers, became WEMP's voice for the Braves. WTMJ's Blaine Walsh joined Gillespie in the booth for home and away games. This new Braves radio network extended across Wisconsin, Upper Michigan, portions of Minnesota, northern Illinois, and even into Iowa.[23] The agreement to simulcast the games was unusual for traditional broadcasting, but both stations were willing because of the civic interest in the Braves.[24] Many restaurants across the region played the Braves games in their establishments to keep their customers from bringing portable radios. WTMJ's station manager reported that listening increased up to 28 percent during day games and 38 percent for night games. If weather interrupted a broadcast, it only took a few moments for listeners to call WTMJ's switchboard to find out what was happening in the game.[25]

There were a few ominous notes, however, in the euphoria that surrounded the team, particularly in regard to the new medium of television. The broadcast agreement included a Miller Beer–sponsored weekly program called *Back Your Braves*, which aired on WTMJ-TV, but not television rights for broadcasting live games. Braves executive vice president Joseph Cairnes made it clear that these telecasts were not for sale.[26] Perini later said that no matter what he was offered for television rights, "the sum would not satisfy me if the park were empty."[27] Many felt that televising games would dilute fan interest in coming to the ballpark, and no regular season home games were televised locally until 1962. By the time the Braves came to Milwaukee, more than a third of all American homes had television sets. Many baseball owners believed that telecasts were responsible for the 30 percent decline in attendance at major league games since 1948.[28] They were already giving away games for free through radio; why should they do the same through TV? Arguably, neglecting this new medium would contribute to the failure of the Braves in Milwaukee, and if Perini understood its value, perhaps the Braves could have sustained the tidal wave of fan support far longer than it did.

Another issue that would become problematic for the Braves was concessions, in particular, beer sales. The Dairy State led the nation in per capita beer consumption in 1952, with an estimated 26.6 gallons annually per Wisconsinite.[29] In Milwaukee, the many breweries that made up a good percentage of its manufacturing gave their employees free or low cost beer on a regular basis. Beer was always available to Braves spectators. They could bring their own or purchase it at the ballpark. The average customer spent as much as $1.10 in the stands (almost $10 in 2016) for an estimated total of $450,000 (more than $4 million in 2016).[30] In 1961, the team and the Milwaukee County Board, wanting to get a larger cut of the stadium concession sales, banned beer carry-ins (see chapter 4). This rule would have a dramatic impact on attendance at the ballpark, even after it was rescinded.[31]

Fans in the Stands

The first major league game in Milwaukee since the American League Brewers left for St. Louis at the end of the 1901 season was played before a sellout crowd of more than thirty-five thousand. It was a different experience for the veterans of the club who came of age playing before thousands of empty seats at Braves Field in Boston. With temperatures in the mid-fifties and an enthusiastic populace, the game had been expected to set an attendance record in Milwaukee for any given sport. The previous mark was just over thirty-three thousand for a stock car race at the Milwaukee Mile at State Fair Park in 1950.[32] By July 5, 1953, the team had already drawn almost seven hundred thousand fans in only twenty-seven home dates, which at this point was more than any other big league team could claim. Even more telling, the Braves brought in twenty-five thousand more fans in Milwaukee than the 667,130 they had both home and away from Boston in 1952. They averaged almost twenty thousand more fans per game at the same time major league baseball lost about 8 percent in attendance. By October 1953 the Braves parking lots, with a capacity of 9,400 vehicles, had accommodated more than 470,000 cars. This was almost 200,000 more cars than the Boston Braves had fans in 1952. There were also spaces for forty buses, but demand required double that number. Rivalry games, like those with the Chicago Cubs, upped the bus spots to 150.[33]

With enthusiasm for the team spreading throughout the region, railroads ran special trains to Milwaukee, and one airline sent planes from Minneapolis and St. Paul. Local hotels offered special weekend packages for out-of-town fans. Official mail from the city was stamped with "Milwaukee . . . the home of the Braves," and local cabbies relayed the scores of the games until it was discovered that Federal Communications Commission regulations forbade "the use of their short-wave stations for purposes other than routing" cabs to clients. The Milwaukee Association of Commerce projected that interest in the team would bring around $8 million per year in additional, subsidiary businesses. Mayor Zeidler relished the newfound prosperity that the Braves phenomenon had unleashed.[34] A survey by the Milwaukee Association of Commerce indicated that 97.6 percent of all fans from outside Milwaukee County spent money in some manner during their trip to the games. Up to 30 percent of all fans were from outside the county, and many "tickets were bought in blocks by bus companies, railroad companies, tourist courts, hotels, restaurants and bars and no one knows how those tickets were redistributed." Almost 40 percent of the fans from outside Milwaukee County spent at least one night in an area hotel.

Combined, this brought between $4.9 and $5.9 million ($43–52 million in 2016) into the county through baseball alone.[35]

"The doggondest thing I ever saw in my life"

So many fans were coming out to the ballpark by late June that the team agreed to restructure the existing stadium lease. The new terms were negotiated because the Braves felt that the "response, enthusiasm, and support" had already surpassed their expectations. The original $1,000-a-year contract was replaced with a $25,000-a-year agreement. The new arrangement also allowed the Braves to retain the concession rights at County Stadium, pending oversight by the Milwaukee County Board.[36] The new team in town clearly transcended Milwaukee's other professional team, the National Basketball Association's Milwaukee Hawks, and Ben Kerner, owner of the Hawks, was a bit upset that the Braves got "every break in the book" in regard to their stadium deal. Kerner, who was actively looking to move his moribund team to a new city, said that it was "high time major league basketball got a little consideration, too."[37] Ironically, he got his wish—basketball got little consideration from the county and the community, and the Hawks were soon gone, first to St. Louis and, by 1968, to Atlanta.

The Braves began to win so soon that excitement for the team on the field matched the newness of being in the major leagues. Donald Davidson, the Braves' acting publicity chief, told reporters that it was "not enough that the fans are clamoring for tickets faster than we can sell them"; some fans were angry that it was too early to make reservations for the World Series. Increased attendance at the gate generated more revenue and the Braves were able to invest in better players. Other owners were paying attention to the Braves' success and began to look for options to increase their own revenue streams. In some cases, owners considered new cities with new stadiums.[38] After all, if a perennial cellar dweller like the Braves could make the move in March and be contending immediately, surely other teams could do the same. In particular, Brooklyn Dodgers' owner Walter O'Malley saw the Milwaukee Braves' experience as a model for the future of baseball. Either in Brooklyn or elsewhere, O'Malley believed, a new stadium would create fan interest and increase attendance at the park. More fans obviously equaled more money.[39]

Players and coaches enjoyed some unexpected bonuses, including free beer, gasoline, clothes, food, dry cleaning, car rentals, and many other gifts. Home runs, shutouts, and double plays paid extra cash. Some employees at restaurants and hotels wouldn't accept tips from players. The Braves had truly found a home.[40] When asked about having surpassed the previous year's attendance total in only eighteen home dates in Milwaukee, manager Charlie Grimm said it was "the doggondest thing I ever saw in my life." Amazed at their reception in Milwaukee, Grimm said, "The one thing I have to guard against is that they don't smother us with kindness, sauerbraten, beer and invitations."[41]

In August the team ran a full-page ad in the local papers to thank the Braves fans from Milwaukee and all across Wisconsin. It stated simply, "The Milwaukee Braves' Baseball Team; all personnel, and Management, wish to express our sincere gratitude to the loyal fans of Milwaukee and Wisconsin for their enthusiastic and spirited support." It noted that County Stadium was the first ballpark to surpass the million-fans mark in 1953.[42] Attendance was surpassing the highest mark at this point of the season for the 1948 Boston Braves, was almost double that of the 1953 Red Sox at this juncture, and would remain that way through the end of the season.[43] What was particularly impressive about the 1953 season was not that the Braves won ninety-two games, but that they put 1,826,297 fans into the seats at County Stadium. This feat set the all-time National League attendance record and was done without the benefit of any preseason sales promotions. It broke the record set in Boston during the World Series year of 1948.[44]

In October the Braves announced that after a single season in Milwaukee, they had eliminated the $1 million deficit that the team had generated over the last three seasons at Braves Field. Speaking on behalf of his brothers and the rest of the ownership, Perini said, "I want you to know you have completely wiped out that loss in our one year of operation here." He was vague about how much the team actually made, but one could presume the Braves ownership was confident that they had made the right decision moving to Milwaukee.[45] Humbled by the response that the team received in Milwaukee, he said, "We should be honoring you, instead of you honoring us, not only for what you have done for the Braves, but for all of baseball."[46] But it was not without a cost. Many business owners across southeastern Wisconsin believed that fans without tickets to the games stayed close to home or wherever they could listen to radio broadcasts of games rather than spend their time and money as they had in the past. There was also the negative financial impact on businesses close to the Detroit Tigers and the Chicago Cubs, which both recorded significant losses in attendance, most likely because of the Milwaukee Braves in 1953.[47]

National League president Warren Giles noted that the success of the Braves "pointed to further shifts in big league cities."[48] It was evident that Milwaukee had unintentionally created its own gold mine and a new model for success, as teams "with poor attendance could reinvent themselves by moving to one of the many communities desperate for major league baseball." The Milwaukee Miracle had "awakened baseball owners to the possibilities of regional franchises" in cities that aspired to be big league by drawing in an existing franchise with "the lure of a publicly funded stadium," which translated to "profits, prestige, financial rewards and spiritual benefits."[49] Milwaukee had indeed proven that it was not the size of the population that should determine whether a city is big league in stature. However, in the context of baseball's new era of franchise mobility, one Boston reporter predicted that the Braves would "be gone from Milwaukee within ten years."[50] It would simply take another city with greater prospects and a stadium even newer than the brand new County Stadium that looked so promising in 1953.

Requests for Braves tickets continued to flood the ticket office well into the off season. The Braves' new ticket manager, William Eberly, reported that since the end of the season he had received around five thousand letters requesting individual tickets for 1954. During the season he had about twenty full-time staffers responsible for sales in Milwaukee and sixteen other ticket agencies across Wisconsin and northern Illinois. After studying the season, they estimated that more than 70 percent of attendance came from within fifty miles of County Stadium.[51] Opening Day tickets were in greatest demand. Eberly said the response was going to be the same for all requests, that he was sorry "but you will have to wait until our schedule is approved by the National League. The general ticket sale is tentatively set for Feb. 15." In addition, many of the 1953 season ticket holders wanted better seats. During the off season, the Braves ticket office staff consisted of Eberly and eight others located at County Stadium and a downtown office. Lou Chapman, the *Milwaukee Sentinel*'s sports editor, joked that Eberly was now the "most popular Brave." More than seven thousand of the twelve thousand season tickets were already sold by early December. Braves Christmas gift certificates sold at the rate of around twenty-five a day for box or reserved seats.[52]

"You better get busy and build those parks"

In late 1953 Lou Perini visited San Francisco at a time when the city was trying to secure a major league franchise. While there, he answered questions about baseball's future and discounted discussion on the expansion of baseball. He thought a proposal to expand to twelve teams in each league was just "plain silly" because if you were the "eleventh or twelfth place team, you couldn't give your baseball away." Ominously, he added, if "you want major league baseball out here, you better get busy and build those parks. Montreal and Toronto are hot after franchises, and so is a fine Midwestern area (the twin cities of Minneapolis–St. Paul). If they beat you to the punch, you may have to wait a long, long time." He also said that he did not believe that the relationship between Milwaukee and the Braves was temporary and the skeptics who argued "wait until the honeymoon is over" were not from Wisconsin. He added that their recent second-place finish would have drawn only about 400,000 people in Boston compared with the 1.8 million in Milwaukee. Perini was optimistic that the attendance record would go up in 1954 because County Stadium was already expanding by eight thousand seats. There was not much "in the way of entertainment to divert the citizens from baseball." The Braves front office believed that Wisconsinites love crowds and "enjoy being in a jammed ball park." When asked about the possibility of selling the Braves to Fred Miller, one of the men most instrumental in the club coming to Wisconsin, Perini stated that he wanted to keep the team. The only way that he could see himself parting with his franchise was if he "could buy the Red Sox from Tom Yawkey," which was not likely. Therefore, Perini publicly claimed that he would "own the Braves for a long time."[53]

An interesting side note to 1953 was a column by nationally syndicated columnist E. V. Durling, who wrote in November that Seattle, Washington, could be a "second Milwaukee in baseball." Milwaukee had been a great city for the big leagues and he believed that Seattle would be as well. It was a fantastic town for all sports, and a major league team in Seattle would "draw fans from all over the great Northwest."[54] Unfortunately for the fans in Milwaukee and the first attempt at major league baseball in Washington State, the 1969 Seattle Pilots, both teams would fail. More importantly, both franchises would dramatically change Wisconsin's sports landscape in the decades to come.

"The best we can do is none too good"

The years 1953 and 1954 were exciting for Milwaukee and the Braves. Every season seemed to bring the team closer to the World Series and the city to a championship. Lou Perini made it clear when his team arrived in Bradenton, Florida, for spring training in 1954 that the World Series was the goal for the franchise. He believed that off-season moves to improve the team could make the upcoming campaign special for the city, and Milwaukee deserved it. It was "a fabulous city and Wisconsin is an amazing state. I wouldn't be much of a guy if I didn't go out and get them the best there is in baseball." But Perini did not want to build up false hopes for the Wisconsin fans. However, "no matter what happens, I want those loyal fans to know we are trying our best without promising anything for 1954." The team wanted to keep the fans happy, and "we are going to do it with a championship ball club. The best we can do is none too good."[55]

Milwaukee fans even followed the Braves to Florida to watch spring training, between 500 and 750 people every day. The dedication of Braves fans surprised many, especially their emotional investment in the team.[56] The Braves broke camp in late March 1954 and were scheduled to play a three-game series in Atlanta against their Double A farm club, the Atlanta Crackers of the Southern League. This would not be the last time the Milwaukee Braves played in Atlanta.[57] In April another parade greeted them in Milwaukee, this time, however, numbering only around thirty thousand fans, but with plenty of Welcome Home signs. The ticker tape parade again went from the downtown train station to County Stadium, where the Braves opened a three-game exhibition series with the Red Sox.

In contrast to 1953, however, only 6,074 fans braved the weather for the first game, the smallest turnout at County Stadium since it opened in 1953.[58] It did not appear to reflect a decline in interest, and it was far different from the reduced attendance to be noted in the early 1960s. In early May, the Braves played before a crowd of 12,383 that was showered with snow and a high temperature of 37 degrees. For eleven minutes during the game, the crowd sang "Jingle Bells" in weather that made the stadium look like a snow globe. In August, County Stadium hosted more than forty-eight thousand fans for a game against the St. Louis Cardinals, the largest crowd in the young ballpark's history to date. Braves attendance continued to grow, while declining attendance for many other teams made the Milwaukee experience somewhat abnormal in 1954. The question remained, how long would this continue?[59]

Until changes made at County Stadium interfered, patients at the Wood Veterans Hospital had been able to enjoy the games from a small grandstand that overlooked the ballpark. To accommodate them, the Braves donated eight hundred dollars to build a new set of stands, for about three hundred patients, about a tenth of a mile from the park.[60] Eventually, those stands would also be eliminated through further expansion of the stadium.

The Braves appeared to be in the pennant race that summer, but the ticket office did not get excited about their postseason prospects. Even though the "whole town's talking about the Braves' pennant chances," assistant ticket sales director Charlie Blossfield said it would be no problem to meet the demand. The Braves had turnout similar to an All-Star Game or World Series every day, and even when the prospects of the pennant were not particularly high, the team still had around fifteen hundred customers seeking tickets that morning and demand remained high. The Braves had no plans for additional season tickets for the remainder of the year, "but of course we'll add some for the series" if that happens.[61]

The Braves finished eight games back of the eventual world champion New York Giants, but they were far more successful than 1953 in attendance. Lou Chapman claimed that the recent season had been "the most fabulous year in the city's history, as more than two million fans filed through the turnstiles to make the 1953 debut look like a second-run show."[62] When the regular season ended in September, major league baseball reported that paid attendance increased more than 10 percent that year. The American League paced the increase with an almost 14 percent increase in their gates, mostly because of the Yankees and the success of the Baltimore Orioles' transfer from St. Louis. Interestingly, the Red Sox were low for the second year in a row compared with where they were in 1952. Apparently only a small number of Boston Braves fans migrated over to Fenway Park. The National League saw a rise of slightly more than 7 percent, once again because of the phenomenal attendance in Milwaukee, but this year was also assisted by the Giants doing particularly well at the turnstiles in the decaying Polo Grounds.[63] These gains were enough to counter flat or declining attendance in several cities, particularly among noncompetitive teams. Milwaukee's civic enthusiasm, however, was credited with being "forerunner in the modern trend toward territorial realignment in the majors."[64]

Perini was so confident, and frankly grateful, about the Braves' future that for the second year in a row he voluntarily increased the Braves rent. The original cost was negotiated at $25,000 for 1953 and 1954, but the Braves presented Milwaukee County with a check for $225,000 in September. The owner told the County Park Commission that he "appreciated the reception given to him by the Milwaukee fans and officials" and wanted to make this change to the rental agreement. The commission agreed to accept the money and park commission president Walter Bender said that the county appreciated "very much the marvelous expression" of generosity by Perini and the Braves.[65] The county board was surprised by this move by the club because three more years remained on the stadium agreement. Because rental fees were based on a percentage of gross receipts, projections were that the year ahead would bring in $95,000 for rent, but the Braves left open the possibility of another gift in the season ahead. It seemed that the investment the taxpayers made in the municipal ballpark was paying tremendous dividends throughout the region. Based on this success, some in county government as well as many fans hoped for a further expansion of County Stadium.

A proposal was forwarded to add 10,500 seats at the ballpark, which would bring its capacity up to fifty-three thousand. The upper and lower grandstands would be extended farther down both lines and some of the bleacher seating would be eliminated. At a cost of approximately of $1.6 million, the expansion might help the Braves when they hosted the All-Star game in July 1955.[66] Opponents convinced the county board to reject the proposal by a vote of 14–10. Milwaukee County had already spent enough money on the ballpark, they argued, and, perhaps ominously, despite the attendance record, there had been only sixteen sellouts of County Stadium in 1954 compared with thirty-nine in 1953. Because the Braves themselves did not request the addition and parking was limited, county supervisor John L. Doyne argued that there was no "use buying the seats if you haven't the parking space for an additional 2,500 autos."[67] This 1954 proposal was not the last time that the interests of the county, the stadium, the public, and the Braves would conflict.

Major league baseball was to impact the geography of southeastern Wisconsin as engineering plans were already under consideration in 1954 to facilitate access to the stadium. Los Angeles roadways were studied for layout, and costs were believed to be in the range of $8 to $10 million per mile. It was felt that cities had no choice but to accommodate cars and commercial haulers or they would all slowly go out of business. The newly designed roadways and infrastructure were projected to have a capacity of more than one hundred thousand vehicles a day. A downside would be the addition of stop signs and stoplights hindering the flow of traffic in and out of Milwaukee.[68] As the interstate system in southeastern Wisconsin was just getting underway, the I-94 project was moved closer to County Stadium and its extensive parking lots.

Telecast the Braves?

In March 1954 Milwaukee fans petitioned Lou Perini for televised broadcasts of Braves road games. Copies of the petitions were circulated throughout the community, and within two weeks more than thirty thousand signatures had been gathered. The petitioners claimed that it was not an organized drive. Rather, they just "talked it up and started a petition to show the newspapers and the Braves what people are thinking." They were clear that they were not "asking for the home games," but they thought Perini was "wrong about TV of road games doing the club any harm." They were hoping to at least interest the ownership in broadcasting the games.[69] But Perini remained adamant that television would harm the club.

Kal Ross, a director of operations for the local CBS station, made it clear that it was the Braves' right to determine their own telecast policies. He believed, however, that they were wrong about telecasts, for example, Perini's belief that banning telecasts was "a foolproof preventive against poor attendance." Warren Giles had previously said baseball must either embrace telecasts or resign itself to playing all of its games during the day. If it did not become part of the TV landscape, baseball would find itself in "direct competition with the most powerful entertainment medium in America." Ross agreed that telecasting home games was not an option because the home dates "must be protected if the ball club is to be prosperous and successful." Perini would be "performing a public service for the thousands of fans who are unable to buy a ticket to the many home games that are sellouts," despite the real possibility that television could cost the Braves up to $200,000 in lost revenue. Ross also predicted that television would "be rightfully creating new fans for the ball club out of people who heretofore knew little about big league baseball . . . and cared less." Moreover, if the Braves "refuse to use television, at least on a limited basis, other nationally televised sporting events carried by Milwaukee television stations could conceivably keep the baseball fan at home." This would certainly ring true in Wisconsin by the early 1960s, as telecasts of the Green Bay Packers and of space missions added to the diminishing support for the Braves. In fairness, baseball owners did not yet know the real impact of television on sporting events. It was too new of a medium to risk losing fans in the stands if they could watch from the comfort of their own living rooms.[70]

Perini felt he was justified in the fight to keep the Braves off television in Wisconsin. When the Boston Braves went to the World Series in 1948, they drew close to 1.5 million fans. In the years that followed, Perini allowed most home games to be televised, at a cost of $40,000. What followed was an 81 percent drop in attendance at Braves Field by the end of the 1952 season. Because Perini believed that television had killed his team in Boston, he did all he could to prevent *any* Braves telecasts, locally or nationally, in any market that would draw fans to County Stadium. In fact, before relenting in 1962, the only time the Braves games were telecast locally was during the World Series trips in 1957 and 1958. Perini said at the time, "We have come to believe that TV can saturate the minds of the fans with baseball. We would like very much to guard against that."[71]

Television had completely changed the landscape of baseball. Not only did it impact the home markets of the major league clubs, it brought big league baseball into the heart of the minor league cities. As a result, minor league baseball grew less popular, and many teams fell by the wayside. It was said that TV "pushed the minors so far into the periphery of American life that they fell right off to oblivion." Television also came to highlight generational differences.

By the late 1960s, young people tended to prefer to watch football on TV while older Americans preferred baseball. None of this mattered to Perini. His refusal to listen to petitioners, television executives, or the local media caused incredible harm to the Milwaukee Braves by the early 1960s, and Milwaukee's loss would become Atlanta's gain.[72] It is a bit ironic that Perini had previously approved of broadcasts of the American Association Brewers games by WTMJ television in Milwaukee.

Simply Nothing Left for the Athletics

It was evident immediately that the Braves' ownership under the Perini brothers had made the right decision to come to Milwaukee. The first two seasons had seen record ticket sales and revenue for the ownership and the community. Other owners with and without deep pockets were also looking for their own "miracle" in a new city, or revitalized interest in their old one. A franchise shift to a new market could bring instant prosperity to the club from revenues generated by a new ballpark and/or generations of new market fans. The St. Louis Browns shift to Baltimore was first, and the next would be the Philadelphia Athletics of the American League. The Athletics (the A's) had been owned and managed by the Mack family since the early twentieth century. There were a few successful years, with six pennants and five World Series wins, but the last was a quarter of a century ago. Connie Mack, the iconic owner and manager of the club for five decades, had retired in 1950, and the franchise had fallen further into hard times. Like the hapless Browns, the A's now shared their stadium with their National League counterpart, in this case, the Phillies.

The most recent A's campaigns had been extremely damaging to the club and the city. They finished sixty games behind the Yankees in 1953 and attendance plummeted. So did the payroll and the number of minor league teams in the A's farm system. The only things that helped the team come close to breaking even were the Phillies' rent payments on their stadium and cash advances from the company that ran the concessions. They needed to draw more than five hundred thousand to break even in 1954 but only three hundred thousand came. Even a "Save the A's" campaign failed to generate local interest, and now the younger members of the Mack family were anxious to sell and get out of baseball. They made it clear that they were not necessarily looking for a new city and hoped a buyer could be found in Philadelphia. A few groups were interested and wanted to see the team stay, but others, with deeper pockets, were looking to follow the Milwaukee formula of success in a fresh city with a new ballpark.[73]

American League president William Harridge called a meeting in September 1954 to resolve the issue with the Athletics. Co-owner Roy Mack was strongly opposed to any sale that would take the team from Philadelphia. There was a substantial offer on the table from Chicagoan Arnold Johnson, who wanted to move the team to Kansas City, currently a minor league city controlled by the New York Yankees. Johnson was the owner of Yankee Stadium, and the Yankees supported his effort to purchase and relocate the Athletics. Harridge said the purpose of the meeting was to determine the fate of the Athletics, either in Philadelphia or a new city, and added that no application for franchise movement could be considered until October 1, 1954. It would take a minimum of six other American League owners to approve any transfer. Clark Griffith, the owner of the Washington Senators, was already opposed to any move that involved Kansas City because it would "unbalance the whole league and add considerably to the burdens of travel." The owners of the Boston Red Sox and Detroit Tigers also appeared to oppose selling the club to Johnson, who had made what he considered to be a very fair offer to the Mack family in early August. Johnson had reportedly offered up to $4.5 million for the team and the ballpark, or $2.5 million for just the team.[74] Many believed that Kansas City was already a "better prospective big league city than Milwaukee" when the team left Boston.[75]

In October the owners met again to discuss the Athletics when it was apparent they had no future in Philadelphia. There remained interested parties in the city to buy the team, and the club apparently accepted a formal offer on October 17. But after Johnson objected that his offer was better than the Philadelphia syndicate's offer, Roy Mack reversed his previous agreement and sold the team to Johnson. On November 9, 1954, the owners, who a year and a half earlier had been so vindictive toward Bill Veeck, met again to unanimously approve the sale of the A's to Johnson. The owners also endorsed the transfer to Kansas City 6–2, with Griffith's Senators and the Cleveland Indians being the only dissenting votes.

This was the third transfer of a professional club since 1953, but unlike the Braves, there was new ownership as well, as had been the case with Baltimore. As with the Braves and the Orioles, the move would pay dividends immediately, for the A's drew more than a million more fans in 1955 and 1956.[76] Unlike the Boston situation in 1952–53, the Philadelphia Athletics fans had a whole summer to prepare for the inevitable, even though many did not think it would happen. In Boston, it was said that until the move was announced, "Boston for many years had turned nothing but its broad 'A' and equally broad back upon the efforts of the hapless Braves." The Athletics were clearly the number two team in the city, and there was basically nothing left for them. Even a change in owner-ship within the city could not keep the team solvent.[77]

Either way, local fans were going to lose. Compared with a local business, such as manufacturing, sports teams and the loyalties of their fans go far deeper into the hearts of the community. While municipalities suffer when businesses close or move to new cities, those companies were not premised on spectators coming to their location to cheer on their workers. Therefore, while owners of teams cannot sustain financial losses any more than manufacturers or other businesses, they are unfairly held to a higher standard of community loyalty. Nevertheless, owners too often considered their franchises as merely a straight-forward business that they could relocate as readily as any other endeavor. Ultimately, neither the owners nor the fans truly understood the position of the other, but those who owned the teams held most of the cards. This was evident with the Athletics situation.

Commenting on the final decision, Arthur Daley of the *New York Times* wrote that "the handling of the transfer of the Athletics' franchise was a stupid, disgraceful bungle all the way. The only thing comforting about it is that the sorry story is ended—for Philadelphia. It begins anew under a veil of disillusion-ment and dampened enthusiasm in Kansas City. The only consolation is that this miserable business is finally settled." Daley was surprised that Johnson did not "pack his three and a half millions in his valise and quit in disgust." If that had happened, the American League would have been stuck with a dying franchise and the feuding Mack brothers to drive the franchise into insolvency. Daley felt that despite the signs of discontent among several other owners, this might be the last franchise move for a while, as the A's were the last of the second-tier teams in cities that could no longer support more than one baseball team. The transfer of the hapless A's to Missouri did not guarantee success like that of the Braves in Milwaukee, and a losing team would not sustain the novelty of big league baseball in Kansas City. Yet arguably, all of the American League owners would benefit from the Athletics move because it was presumed the gate receipts would be at least initially higher in the new city, much as they were in Milwaukee and Baltimore.[78] With minimal consideration to the fans who had supported the team for decades, the Philadelphia A's became a footnote in baseball history as the franchise, like the Braves, ultimately intro-duced major league baseball to two different cities. Perhaps surprisingly the elder Connie Mack wished the Athletics well when they moved to Kansas City. In fact, he said that he planned to meet the team when they reported for spring training in 1955 and hoped they would win a pennant for their new hometown.[79]

As the crowds eventually dwindled in Kansas City and after Johnson died in 1960, the Athletics' new owner, Charles O. Finley, would look to move to Atlanta, Louisville, and even Milwaukee. Finley's flirtation with Atlanta would be the beginning of the end of the Milwaukee Braves, as Finley convinced Georgia officials to pursue building a new stadium to attract a major league team.

Musical Chairs in New Cities and Stadiums

With the approval of the Athletics' transfer to Kansas City, the geography of baseball continued to change. The impact of a baseball team on a community certainly varies from city to city and even from one season to the next. Duplicating the immediate success of the Milwaukee Braves was going to be hard for any city, whether new to baseball or with a well-entrenched team, because too often fans took their teams for granted. Escalating costs of baseball weighed against thinning attendance meant teams were not easily sustained. Writers warned fans to expect more changes to the game as it looked to expand and advance into new markets.[80]

In November 1954, Walter O'Malley, the principal owner of the Brooklyn Dodgers, foreshadowed another relocation when he announced that the team was going to do at least part of its spring training in California starting in 1956. He made it clear that he had "no intention of selling the Dodgers. . . . Nor are there any plans to move it" or to discuss the subject with the other owners. He added, however, that "what the future holds for us I just wouldn't know. We are confronted by two serious problems. One is at the turnstiles. The other, which you might say dovetails with the first, has to do with the parking situation at Ebbets Field." Brooklyn's attendance had dropped to about half of Milwaukee's, and O'Malley saw the revenues that fans generated for the Braves and he believed the financial disparity would create a competitive imbalance. At one time, he said, he had given "serious thought to exploring the possibility of moving the Dodger franchise to Los Angeles."[81] This was not an idle threat and was alarming to the traditional fabric of major league baseball. No one could argue the Dodgers were a second-tier team or did not have strong fan support. The only reason they would move was to find greater riches elsewhere.

At a meeting in December 1954, owners agreed to look at an expansion plan that would lead to two leagues each with ten teams and might include new cities in California. Both the American and National Leagues formed committees to look at the feasibility of this westward expansion by 1956, as well as the necessity of a 162-game schedule rather than the current 154. Cities being considered were Los Angeles, San Francisco, Toronto, Montreal, Houston, Dallas, and the Twin Cities in Minnesota. The committees were to report back to the owners at the All-Star Game in Milwaukee in July 1955.[82] In the end, all of the cities originally listed would get either an expansion team or, in the case of Los Angeles, San Francisco, and Minneapolis–St. Paul, a franchise transplanted from the East. Interestingly enough, Atlanta was not seriously discussed as a major league prospect at this time.

Despite the interest in expansion, only a month later, in January 1955, the National League announced that it had effectively abandoned any immediate plans to expand to ten teams. Giles said there was "no sentiment for a ten-club league at this time," although no formal discussion was held on this topic. He added that there were cities that hosted minor league teams that would eventually be in the majors but when that would be he could not say. Giles also argued that there was considerable interest to move a franchise if a city could offer the National League and the team as much as Milwaukee had for the Braves. But he also cautioned communities that he was "not advocating that a city go out and pass a big bond issue for a new stadium as any guarantee that it will be accepted into the majors." Still, said Giles, "if it were not for Milwaukee [County] Stadium and all it has to offer, they wouldn't have the Braves there for big league baseball today."[83] As we have already seen, and will again note later, if a city was serious about getting major league baseball, it had to have a facility ready to go or far enough along in the process to make it worthwhile for an owner to make the move.

Death of a Salesman

The success that the Braves had achieved since moving to Wisconsin arguably meant that the future of Milwaukee baseball was far brighter than when the Braves first relocated from Boston. By their second season in Milwaukee, the Braves had topped more than two million in attendance for the first time in franchise history, and fan enthusiasm had not dissipated.[84] The baseball experience in Milwaukee seemed to have developed far better than anyone could have anticipated when County Stadium was first proposed and sold to the community. But the future of the Braves in Milwaukee was dealt a great blow by the untimely death of the Braves' most important fan, Frederick C. Miller. His vision of major league baseball in Wisconsin had been realized when the Braves arrived, but the promise of the Milwaukee Miracle ended on a cold winter evening when the forty-eight-year-old Miller was killed in a plane crash on December 17, 1954.

Sports Illustrated reported that the brewery president and community leader had been rumored to be negotiating to purchase the Braves from Lou Perini's organization at the time of his death.[85] Contemporaries of Miller have speculated for years about the veracity of these negotiations, but it is not clear whether there was serious discussion about Miller purchasing the club. He may have merely mentioned to Perini that he would like to invest in or buy the Braves at some point in the future. Perini himself would later testify that he had not agreed to sell to Miller or anyone else in Milwaukee.

Miller understood the economic power of advertising for the benefit of his business and local sports teams. In the recent past his brewery had paid for the radio broadcasts rights of the minor league Milwaukee Brewers, as well as their telecasts in the late 1940s and early 1950s. The company even sponsored special events at Borchert Field and at the new Milwaukee Arena.[86] Through his connection to the Brewers, Miller had developed a personal and professional relationship with Perini that was instrumental in convincing Perini to move the team in 1953 and to "give the Braves a fair chance by moving them to Milwaukee, where they could be appreciated."[87]

On the day of the accident, Miller left the office for General Mitchell Field for a flight to Canada for a weekend of hunting with his twenty-year-old son, Frederick Miller Jr. Approximately one minute after takeoff, the nine-passenger Lockheed Ventura suffered engine failure and struck the ground. Miller, Frederick Jr., and pilots Joseph and Paul Laird were fatally injured. The elder Miller was the only one to initially survive the accident. When found outside the flaming wreckage, he yelled to those who arrived to help, "My God, don't bother about me. There are three others in the plane." He was taken to a local hospital where he succumbed to his injuries in the waning hours of the night.[88]

Memorials to Miller flooded into Milwaukee from throughout the nation. He was far more than a philanthropist and businessman who had made Miller Brewing one of the leading brewers in the nation. Mayor Zeidler said most people knew Miller "for only a few of the many facets of his character." Lloyd Larson of the *Sentinel* editorialized that Milwaukee had indeed "suffered a loss so great as to be almost beyond comprehension," as Miller had been a "big leaguer through and through."[89] His wife and six daughters, ages ten to twenty-two, survived him.

It is evident that the community still feels Miller's loss well into the twenty-first century. He was truly a fan of baseball and the Braves, but more importantly he was a prominent salesman of Milwaukee and southeastern Wisconsin to the national community. It was said that he was indomitable in courage and his destiny was only the small part of the great future of Milwaukee and Wisconsin, as well as the nation. He was considered a "man of great Christian principle, and a man devoted with complete heart to his family."[90] Miller would be sorely missed in the years ahead, particularly after Perini decided to sell the Braves.

A year after plane crash, Perini set up a $200,000 foundation to provide for scholarships in Miller's name for Wisconsin high school students. Perini said that he did not "know of a better way of simply saying thanks" to the fans of his club. In true charitable mindset, the scholarships were for "young persons who cannot otherwise afford to get a college education."[91] Suggestions to rename County Stadium "Frederick C. Miller Stadium" or something of the like did not come to fruition, but his name was evident inside the stadium. In 1955 Miller Brewing Company paid to put its name on the $75,000 scoreboard it had donated with a $5,000 check cut to the Milwaukee County Parks Commission, to be paid annually.[92] Although today the National League Milwaukee Brewers play in Miller Park, it is unfortunate that the name was primarily a commercial deal for the brewery and not a memorial to the local man who was instrumental in bringing major league baseball to Milwaukee.

3

Bush Leaguers

1955–1957

> The Braves have been good for Milwaukee and Milwaukee
> has been good for the Braves. We hope this mutually
> advantageous relationship continues for many years.
>
> Joseph F. Cairnes, president of the Milwaukee Braves,
> November 26, 1957

Keen Observers of Baseball

At the second annual Milwaukee Diamond Club dinner in early January 1955, it was made clear that the Braves would be a pennant contender for the upcoming 1955 season. Anticipation of success on the field translated into another record-setting preseason ticket drive for the Braves. As early as November 1954, the Braves reported more than ten thousand season tickets had already been sold for 1955, up from 9,008 tickets for 1954. Previous season ticket holders had the right of first refusal on their seats and would be given priority in reordering. Because the Braves planned on limiting season ticket sales to twelve thousand, there would be high demand for the remaining tickets.[1] By January 1955, more than 11,100 season tickets had been sold, a number that promised attendance of more than 804,000 at County Stadium for the 1955 season. That advance sales alone represented more than half the total paid attendance of four National League clubs in 1954 was astonishing. Moreover, individual tickets were not scheduled to go on sale until March. The Braves were confident that they would break their previous year's National League attendance record of 2,131,388.[2]

Just before Opening Day the *Sentinel* reported that a total of 1.2 million tickets for the 1955 season had been sold and the Braves were now close to the twelve thousand season ticket mark. Only "28 good singles are left, scattered among boxes, lower grandstand, and upper boxes." The club again promoted special nights, including Lutheran Night, which was expected to draw more than twelve thousand, and Wisconsin State Knights of Columbus Night, fourteen thousand. Games against the Giants and the Dodgers were close to sellouts, and advance sales among the many civic organizations were fantastic. Even sixteen thousand Chicago Cubs fans were expected to migrate to County Stadium for games.[3]

Enthusiasm for baseball in Wisconsin was so strong that the *New York Times* reported that police in Milwaukee were called to break up a January baseball game being played by eleven-year-old boys in near zero-degree temperatures. The *Times* sarcastically blamed the Braves. Officers told the children to wait on playing baseball at least until the weather warmed up. Even the Braves' players themselves appeared to be impatient to start the 1955 season, as commissioner Ford Frick fined several of them for reporting to spring training too early. The Braves officially opened their spring training camp on March 1, amid pennant speculation for the season ahead. It was felt that they had the right mix of pitching, hitting, and defense to leave the other teams in the National League behind in the final standings.[4]

Meanwhile the Milwaukee County Board inspected the ballpark as part of the annual preseason maintenance program. County Stadium manager William Anderson took the supervisors throughout the ballpark and the parking lots to highlight the changes made since 1954. Modifications included three hundred additional parking spaces allotted for season ticket holders and other changes to facilitate the movement of cars and fans going to and from the games. New office spaces for Braves executives were completed, as well as areas available for county usage, including the stadium personnel offices.[5] The symbiotic relationship between Milwaukee County and the Braves was still strong at this juncture. Their irrevocable breakup a mere decade later was unthinkable.

The first games scheduled in 1955 were a series of exhibitions between the Braves and the Cleveland Indians, the first meeting of these two clubs since the 1948 World Series. With the Braves considered to be favorites in the National League, it was presumed to be a World Series preview. A bit alarming were reports that only four hundred fans greeted the team when it arrived in Milwaukee, although it should be noted that the team came in a day earlier than scheduled. Unlike the previous two years, the City of Milwaukee did not schedule a parade, ostensibly because the Braves arrived on Good Friday. Club officials who spoke to the local press said that it was good to be back in Milwaukee and they were optimistic for the year ahead. Perhaps auguring future miscommunications, about seventy-five fans waited for the team at the Milwaukee Road station while the Braves actually arrived at the Chicago & Northwestern facility. It was reported that they "stood around impatiently before being apprised of the Braves' destination."[6]

The first game of the exhibition series opened in front of 19,991 enthusiastic fans, who were reported to be more sophisticated than those from the early days of 1953. More restrained and no longer cheering for long foul balls, the fans were used to good baseball and now applauded only the best.[7] Braves shortstop Johnny Logan noted the maturation of Braves fans while he served as a representative for a local brewery. The fans are now becoming "keen observers of baseball," Logan said, and they understood the game was "far more than eighteen players running around the beautiful stadium we have here in Milwaukee."[8]

Perhaps the primary highlight of the 1955 season in Milwaukee was the major league All-Star Game held at County Stadium in July. The National League won the game 6–5 in dramatic fashion, which certainly pleased the locals.[9] One Braves fan, seventy-five-year-old Calvin Smith from Stevens Point, was so thrilled that after collapsing in the grandstands he declined to go to the hospital because he "did not want to leave." Smith was one of the 45,314 fans at the largest crowd of the year to date at County Stadium. At least five thousand fans arrived via thirty-two special stadium buses while more than 10,200 cars were squeezed into the stadium parking lots.[10] Cars were noted from thirty-eight states and the District of Columbia. The most license plates found in the lots, besides those from Wisconsin, were 617 vehicles from Illinois, followed by forty-four each from Iowa and Minnesota.[11]

Milwaukee area fans embraced their moment in the sun, and local stores and streets fell quiet during the game. Fans stopped and watched the game on TV sets in department store windows, hotel lobbies, and local taverns. A group of television representatives attending a convention in Milwaukee installed about thirty television sets and abandoned their business to watch the game. A fan listening to the game on the radio missed her bus because she became so engrossed in the game. New York sportswriters reported that Milwaukee was perhaps the "most partisan town in baseball."[12]

The Braves finished the regular season in second place, but thirteen and a half games behind the front-running Brooklyn Dodgers. Baseball attendance, buoyed by a franchise move, was up almost seven hundred thousand fans over the course of the year. Most of that was attributed to the excitement of Kansas

City fans for the Athletics now ensconced in Missouri. More than 16.6 million fans were in attendance for all sixteen major league teams combined. Milwaukee again paced the majors with more than two million fans at County Stadium in 1955.[13] The National League's dip by almost 340,000 was blamed on the hot start of the Dodgers and an uncompetitive pennant race. Milwaukee fans apparently enjoyed night baseball more than others because the Braves drew more than one million to thirty-three night games at County Stadium, more than two hundred thousand above the highest American League team, the Kansas City Athletics. Combined attendance for Milwaukee in three seasons was just shy of six million, almost double that of the last six years of the Boston Braves.[14]

"The Braves had it too easy"

After leading the Milwaukee Braves through the formative years of the Milwaukee Miracle, manager Charlie Grimm was unceremoniously fired when it appeared that the Braves were going to miss the pennant again in 1956. The official story from the Braves was that Grimm resigned, but the truth was fairly obvious. Grimm later wrote that it was evident the Braves were up to something when the owner and other front office personnel arrived in Brooklyn to see the Braves play the Dodgers at Ebbets Field. After losing for the twelfth time in seventeen games, Braves traveling secretary Duffy Lewis told Grimm to go see general manager John Quinn at his hotel suite. According to Grimm, "I walked into the execution chamber. Officials of the Braves and the Milwaukee newspapermen were sitting around, saying nothing, looking slightly embarrassed. I don't even remember if Fred Haney, my successor, was there." Furthermore, it "seemed like hours before Joe Cairnes, the executive vice-president, broke the news. I got up and left the room."[15] Grimm went out that night with Lewis and "spun" one before he said good-bye to the team the following morning and went back to Milwaukee. His managerial record in Milwaukee was a stout 290–218, but his talented teams were devoid of pennants.

Later that night, Lou Perini and Cairnes, along with Quinn, announced that Fred Haney had been promoted to the manager's position. Quinn said Haney was not "an interim manager," and Perini added that "his future as our manager will depend on his performance for the rest of this season. He has taken the job on that basis." The owner added that Grimm had been offered another position with the team, and the former manager would make his decision later. Grimm answered reporters' questions and spun the story of his resignation, adding "fan reaction had nothing to do with it. I gave it a good try, like I always have" throughout his baseball career, but it "just didn't work out."[16]

Haney was handed a team that Perini, and many Braves fans, thought would win the pennant. It took just a month from the time Haney took over on June 17, 1956, for the Braves to solidly rise to first place. On Labor Day they were still in front of the Dodgers by three and a half games but, despite going 68–40 down the stretch, fell one game short of going to the World Series. Haney said there were three reasons the team lost: failure to hit at four specific positions, poor bunting, and weak base running. Everybody "has hitting slumps; ours just happened at the worst possible time. When we needed them the most, we weren't getting any runs," he said. Others, including Jackie Robinson, said the Braves choked. The Brooklyn legend said the Braves were too busy drinking when they should have been thinking, and a "couple of key men on the club . . . did not take care of themselves down the stretch." The Braves were also accused of not being hungry enough to win the pennant. Because of the tremendous response the team had in Milwaukee and the massive crowds that regularly filled County Stadium, "the ball club is bulging with money—and it has been more than generous in paying big salaries to young players who, on other clubs, might have had to work a little harder and wait a little longer to attain the same financial gains. The Braves had it too easy."[17] Meanwhile the first-place Dodgers played their final World Series at Ebbets Field before they moved to Los Angeles.

"Dedicated to the people of Milwaukee and Wisconsin"

Perini had maintained operational control over the Boston/Milwaukee Braves since 1943 and served as the club president since 1945. That all changed in January 1957 when he stepped aside from the presidency in favor of Joseph Cairnes. Perini said that part of his decision was the need to have the team's leadership located in Milwaukee, as there "are many advantages to the president of any organization residing in the organization's home community." He was optimistic this move would help the team secure the pennant in 1957 and if this change had been made last year, "the Braves might have won because they would not have had to depend upon a man who was far away and busy with other things for direct supervision." The Braves board of directors quickly elected Perini as chairman, and he continued to serve the new president in an advisory capacity. Cairnes had been with the team since 1947 and was the business manager of the farm system before he was promoted to executive vice president in 1953 and moved to Milwaukee with the team. In this role, Cairnes handled all the transactions for the team on and off the field, including the

Braves' minor league franchises. The new president said that the transition from Perini's to his day-to-day control would "continue to follow along with the ball club dedicated to the people of Milwaukee and Wisconsin."[18]

There were reasons to be optimistic in 1957. With a roster full of all-stars and future hall-of-famers, the team was favored to win the pennant. Quinn had opportunities to make some trades, but he believed that Milwaukee had "a team, which, just like it is, can win the pennant. We went into the winter meetings prepared to trade" and talked to every team in the National League, but they all wanted too much in return. Fred Haney believed that the Braves would "win the pennant if we play the type of ball we're capable of and have the right frame of mind: desire."[19]

Meanwhile, the fan experience was enhanced at an expanded County Stadium. It could now hold forty-five thousand with virtually no bad seats in the house. Among the best seats were those in the lower grandstand, along the baselines, that cost $1.85 per game. *Sports Illustrated* reported that the "interior of the ball park is very neat, rest rooms spacious and heated, concession counters easily available and popular." The best sellers included "delicious bratwurst on large rye buns, plus beer." Ushers were "eager to please" and "surprised when tipped." The Miller Brewing–sponsored scoreboard was enlarged for the season ahead to provide more information about other games in progress. It was noted that the front office was reluctant to cancel games in bad weather. Furthermore, since the Braves averaged "30,093 fans a game, a certain amount of slow-moving traffic is unavoidable" when the game was over. It was recommended that the best "procedure, therefore, is to stay put for a while in stands, enjoy another bratwurst and beer and appreciate a beautiful ball park."[20]

"Buying sandwiches without knowing or caring what was in them"

Record-breaking fans in the stands meant big business in concessions. Earl Yerxa, concessions manager at County Stadium, said that at one Ladies Day promotion in August, almost 7,300 women purchased tickets at a special price of fifty cents. More than five thousand children were in the crowd, some of whom purchased tickets through the Knothole Gang, a fan organization that sold ten-cent tickets to children between the ages of ten and fifteen. With the temperature hovering near ninety degrees, vendors sold thirty thousand bottles of soft drinks to the crowd of more than forty-seven thousand, about twice as much as beer. Normally, the sales of beer and soda were fairly close. Moreover, the stadium patrons ate twenty thousand hot dogs, eighteen thousand ice cream cones, and seven hundred pounds of bratwurst. Yerxa assumed the Ladies Day games led to increased souvenir sales, as some of the mothers wanted to bring something back for their children in the seats or at home. Anecdotally, these special days led to more visits to first aid stations. First aid director Marian Leonard contended that the "women have their children with them and then they're not used to ball games and all the excitement as men are."[21]

A four-game series with the St. Louis Cardinals in August nearly exhausted supplies at the concession stands. Yerxa said if the team had hosted one more game, the fans would not have been fed inside County Stadium; only sixty pounds of hotdogs and ham were left after the series. So much meat was sold at the Friday night game that it was jokingly referred to as Protestants Night. The only item that did not set records was beer because fans brought an estimated fifty-eight thousand to sixty thousand cans of beer into the ballpark. Yerxa noted that two fans sold beer from two garbage cans full of ice they'd set up right next to a concession stand—most likely Budweiser produced out of state, for fifteen cents, about half the stadium price. Eventually authorities chased away the two entrepreneurs. There was concern that the ongoing Wisconsin State Fair had increased demand for products sold at the stadium, and all of Yerxa's suppliers were out of "bratwurst, hot dogs, hamburgers, cornbeef, and barbecue beef." He was able to secure some products from other suppliers who made deliveries during the games. Yerxa said the fans "were buying sandwiches without knowing or caring what was in them." The only items that the team did not run out of during the last game were ham and cheese sandwiches.[22] All of this was good for the Braves and the community, as Yerxa said that 99 percent of all food and 90 percent of the merchandise sold at County Stadium were sourced from local suppliers.[23]

Demand for Braves goods led some unscrupulous individuals to sell pirated or outdated Braves merchandise outside County Stadium to unsuspecting fans, such as souvenir pennants with 1957 pasted over the previous year's 1956. Not employees of the Braves, most were from Chicago, according to the police who arrested several of them. While this is not an uncommon story, even today, it demonstrated the fervor of Braves fans to purchase items in support of their club. Anything with a Braves logo could sell out or be given away surprisingly fast. The Milwaukee Civic Progress Committee prepared "official" posters and streamers that local merchants grabbed up within thirty minutes of their release.[24] The Braves were big business, but the future of the team would arguably hinge on who was entitled to make money off of the fans, the Braves or Milwaukee County.

Finding a Second Milwaukee

During the summer of 1957, fundamental changes came to baseball as a result of the success of the Braves in Wisconsin. Seeking greater riches in new communities, both the Dodgers and the Giants were playing out their last seasons in New York before they transferred to the West Coast. Lou Perini was asked about what would become one of the greatest transitions in professional sports in American history. Dodgers owner Walter O'Malley could not make it anymore at Ebbets Field, said Perini, because it was "antiquated, has not sufficient or desirable seats and above all, has extremely limited parking facilities." The Braves' owner was pragmatic about the situation and said that the other owners "can't be selfish about the matter" and if "O'Malley wants to move we should let him do it." He added, "Suppose it does cost each club another $25,000 or $35,000 in additional transportation? As I said before, O'Malley can't live here— at Ebbets Field, I mean." Perini believed that the National League should keep a team in New York, especially if a rumored third major league was formed.[25] Some Dodgers fans hoped that a prospective new ballpark in Flushing Meadows could have been the answer to the team's problems, but it never came to fruition. As for the Giants, very few mourned the loss of a team that had been in New York since 1883. Even today, while many baseball fans remain nostalgic about Ebbets Field, the Giants home at the Polo Grounds is not missed.

Warren Giles said that his National League had abandoned "all of New England to the American League when the Braves moved to Milwaukee and we don't regret that." Perini, a lifelong Bostonian, countered Giles, saying the situation was different because "New York is the greatest sports town—the greatest baseball town, I think—in the country. We should keep a franchise here. I'd certainly insist on it in any National League meeting on the matter." He also believed the Dodgers would do well in Los Angeles, but "the folks out there want to see champions all the time. The Dodgers would draw well, sure. But they'd have to be champions to do it all the time" and it "might be the same in San Francisco" for the Giants. Regardless of what happened with the departure of the Giants and Dodgers, Perini said, the National League "ought to have a club here, no matter what sort of expansion takes place."[26] Regardless of what happened in New York, the move to California made major league baseball a truly national sport. The response by California fans to both teams and their financial success led other owners to seek new riches in new markets. Unlike the previous franchise shifts, existing losses or a decaying fan base didn't trigger the Dodgers' move. The quest for more money and parking spaces led the Dodgers to truly abandon fans that had loved them.

In mid-June 1957, in a piece for the *New York Times*, sports reporter William Furlong compared the situation in Milwaukee with what was happening in New York as the Dodgers and the Giants prepared to leave. Furlong believed that the furor that developed around the Braves since their arrival in 1953 "must be pardoned on grounds of temporary insanity." It had been so good in Wisconsin that "a good many owners have dedicated themselves less to finding a second Mantle than to finding a second Milwaukee." The inferiority complex of fans in the Beer City had virtually disappeared. After all, when "the Braves defeat the Giants we're showing that we can battle the world's greatest city" and sometimes win, according to a local brewery president. He added that in "a few brief years we've become a big city. The team is the symbol that we've become a big city in every way."[27]

In Milwaukee, wrote Furlong, fans were willing to spend money inside and out of County Stadium to support the club. Milwaukee fans "not only streamed into the ballpark in record-breaking throngs but, once they were there, spent twice as much money as fans in other cities spent inside the gates." Businesses that benefited included those selling transistor radios and transporting fans to the stadium (a remarkable one-third of the fans were believed to come from outside Milwaukee). The only businesses that seemed to suffer were those that competed with the Braves for entertainment dollars, such as movie theaters. Moreover, he noted that you could not just "take forty thousand people off the streets every day—besides the thousands and thousands who listen to the games at home—and expect to do business." The few commercial endeavors that prospered because of the Braves were hotels, bars, restaurants, taxis, and other transportation. Furlong argued that the success of the Braves in Wisconsin meant that in Los Angeles "the sheer exuberance of finally winning recognition as big-league could carry even a mediocre team for several years. In San Francisco, where there is less concern for this type of prestige, the Giants might well be regarded as mere immigrants instead of Bearers of the Word."[28] Major league baseball in California could be the midcentury gold rush that the Dodgers and Giants were hoping to reap and other owners would try to emulate.

To Telecast or Not

In early October the Milwaukee Common Council passed a resolution that allowed the implementation of "toll TV" through Skiatron TV Inc. in the Milwaukee media market. Skiatron, one of the primary reasons for the Dodgers' move across the country, attempted to create a new market for fans through pay television. While pay-per-view television is well known in the twenty-first century, it was a frightening prospect in the late 1950s. The spokesman for the American Federation of Television and Radio Artists told reporters that he hoped the aldermen "enjoy what may be their last free TV World Series; that they further realize that the hundreds of thousands of Milwaukeeans who have spent millions of dollars on their television sets may have to pay to see the next World Series on TV, as well as other events of national interest." Although it opened the door to pay television, the Common Council in the end did not authorize or set specific franchise rights to any company. Several other companies were interested in pay TV, and the Federal Communications Commission was already looking into what ultimately became the future of American television.[29] There is a bit of irony in this action, as the Common Council claimed to represent the blue-collar worker of southeastern Wisconsin who now might be priced out of pay television.

The Common Council also voted in September to set aside $10,000 for celebrations if the Braves won the pennant, such as fireworks, bunting, and images of the screaming Braves image that was the team's primary logo. Alderman Richard Nowakowski said he could not see "why a municipal fund should be used to fete a team that will draw two million people into the stadium this year." Despite his opposition, the measure passed 17–3, and a gigantic lakefront fireworks celebration was scheduled for the night the Braves clinched the National League pennant. Ben Barkin, a strong supporter of civic celebrations, was named chair of the World Series Party Planning Committee. It was also recommended that the county be asked for additional funds if the celebration exceeded what the city was prepared to pay.[30]

Bushville Wins

As the regular season came to an end, and after only five seasons in Wisconsin, the Braves won the National League pennant and their first trip to the World Series since 1948. Along the way they had won ninety-five games, a franchise record, and set another National League attendance record of 2,213,404. Opposing the Braves were the defending champion New York Yankees, at the apex of the Casey Stengel years. The 1957 World Series was one of the few in the 1950s that was not entirely encapsulated by the city of New York, and it was the first since 1946 that played games in the Central Time Zone. Robert Creamer of *Sports Illustrated* wrote that in the last decade, forty-nine of fifty-four World Series games were played exclusively in New York City and the series "had deteriorated into just one more Sight To See in New York, ranking well ahead of Grant's Tomb but slightly behind the Empire State Building."

As a result, Creamer argued, the most appealing element to the 1957 Fall Classic was "the fact the Brooklyn Dodgers aren't in it." He added that with the Dodgers moving to Los Angeles for the next year, the "New York Yankee— Brooklyn Dodger World Series routine is over, done with, finished, as dead as vaudeville."[31]

The first two games were played at Yankee Stadium and telecast across the country. During Game One, few people were on the streets of Milwaukee, particularly Wisconsin Avenue, which appeared to be almost deserted. Large groups of fans gathered at taverns, office buildings, stores, or anyplace a television set could tune in the game. Customers at bars were not afraid to order beer or cocktails, regardless of having to return to work when either their lunch break or the game ended, whichever came first. City and county parks were also noticeably abandoned during the game, and many of the side streets witnessed "all but a handful of pedestrians, some of whom broke into a fast trot to get inside to the nearest TV set when the roar of fans already gathered, indicated a high point in the game." Some Wisconsin schools "arranged their television sets for student use during noon-hour and study hall periods though no students were released from regular class periods to view the contest."[32]

When the Braves returned to Milwaukee after the first two games, more than 7,500 fans greeted the team at Mitchell Field. The crowd roared when Lew Burdette, the winning pitcher of Game Two, led the team off the plane. Braves shortstop Johnny Logan, a Milwaukee baseball institution, said it was "good to be back in Wisconsin." Mayor Frank Zeidler referred to the gathering at the airport as "the biggest spontaneous celebration" in Milwaukee history. Fans had arrived at the airport a few hours before the plane arrived and cheered as the team rode the eleven miles from Mitchell Field to County Stadium. Players and coaches interacted with rabid, screaming fans whose noise drew additional fans out onto the streets. The impromptu parade gathered an estimated 175,000 to 200,000 Milwaukeeans. Police escorted the vehicles at a slow pace in the cool evening, and it was readily apparent that Milwaukee truly loved the Braves. In fact, some fans paid nearly ten times the face value of the tickets to see a World Series game at County Stadium. Ticket director Bill Eberly said the club had done everything possible to prevent tickets from falling into the hands of scalpers, but it could not prevent a season ticket holder from selling because it did not "have any control over what the mail order customers do with theirs."[33]

The World Series game played on October 5, 1957, in Wisconsin was a historic first. Five years of high expectations and tremendous fan support had rewarded the Milwaukee governmental and civic planners who had supported the construction of County Stadium. Two thousand Wisconsinites and a local band greeted the American League champions when they arrived on Friday, October 4. The Yankees refused to get off the train and acknowledge the warm reception because they had to get to County Stadium for batting practice.[34] One of the Yankee representatives referred to the gathering and greeting as "strictly bush"—a city that was hopelessly stuck in the minor leagues, a hick town with a bunch of rubes rather than the big league city that was now Milwaukee. Soon picked up by the local media and fans, the rebuff and the slur went national fairly quickly. The *Milwaukee Sentinel*'s Lloyd Larson addressed it head on and said if the Yankees had simply clarified the team's wish to be excused and have "no part of anything that could possibly interfere with the job at hand" the locals would have understood. Larson added that if "the electrifying Miracle of Milwaukee, the biggest shot in the arm of all time for baseball, is bush, so be it." Furthermore, all of baseball should "start praying for more bush, more Bravelands, more hopped-up baseball followers." With local pride, Larson wrote that the "alleged bushers in this neck of the woods have turned out ten million-plus strong over a stretch of five seasons, enabling the Braves to outdraw every other team in the big leagues, including the Yanks."[35]

"Them's Our Boys!"

The series went back and forth between two great clubs like a heavyweight fight. After splitting the first four games, the Braves won Game Five, the last to be played at County Stadium before the Series headed back to New York. The Yankees took Game Six, and the Braves, behind the World Series Most Valuable Player Lew Burdette, won Game Seven and realized Milwaukee's dream of being the baseball capital of the world. Burdette had won three games, the last one on two days' rest. For many across the nation, the Braves became the symbol of the underdog against the might of the Yankees. Tiny, blue-collar Milwaukee battled the mighty megalopolis of New York. It was brewers against businessmen, Wisconsin Avenue against Wall Street, southeastern Wisconsin versus the five boroughs of New York. Several Braves players were interviewed on national television the following day, and congratulations poured into Braves offices from across the United States. New York mayor Robert F. Wagner sent a telegram to Frank Zeidler: "We New Yorkers don't lose very often, but when we do, we are good losers. My heartiest congratulations to you, the Milwaukee Braves and your fellow townsmen who have so inspiringly supported your team every inch of the way right up to this afternoon's splendid victory." Cook & Dunn Paint Corporation of Newark, New Jersey, shipped paint to Zeidler so the people could "paint the town red." Minneapolis mayor P. Kenneth Peterson informed Zeidler that he was naming all people of Milwaukee as honorary citizens of his city. A restaurant ran a special on "bush leaguer" dinners. National media covered the crowds that exploded out of homes and bars across Milwaukee and throughout Wisconsin. NBC reported, "There were so many drunks on Wisconsin Ave. that it took one man ten minutes to fall down."[36]

All across Milwaukee, Braves fans took to the streets in a sea of humanity that "shoved, drank, sang, kissed strangers and jitterbugged. They did things they never normally would think of doing." Milwaukee sanitation crews did not start cleaning the streets until "the last drunk had downed his final bottle of beer and the last sailor had embraced a pretty girl." The celebration was the biggest since the end of World War II and probably in Milwaukee history. At its height, more than 225,000 celebrants were on the streets of Milwaukee at 9 p.m. Fans grossly outnumbered the police, who made arrests only for serious violations. Signs read Bushville Wins and Welcome Bush Leaguers You're Tops.[37] The *Walworth Times* ran an extra edition headlined "Them's Our Boys! They Gave the Yanks BUSH LEAGUE TREATMENT." The Braves took out full-page ads in the local papers to thank the faithful for the celebration that had "surpassed any previous reception in the history of Milwaukee." Joseph Cairnes said the Braves regretted that the scheduled parade for the victors was altered because "the turnout of more than seven hundred thousand people made it impossible for the parade to follow the original route."

Two days later the victory celebration began to wind down, and local fans began to sober up. Taverns that "were full of unfamiliar faces" during the seven-game series "resumed their preseries look." Television retailers that had offered free viewing when the games were on "now could go back to their more customary role of selling sets." Many of the signs were removed and the "odor of spilled lager which had hung over the downtown area" blew away. Cans and bottles were swept up, and Milwaukee began to resume its usual look and routine. Celebrating was "fun while it lasted, but it's great to know we don't have to do it soon again," said the *Journal*. Seventy city workers, many of them on overtime wages, worked around the clock to clean up more than two hundred tons of paper and other refuse, at a cost of about $4,000. Unfortunately for the Wisconsin Telephone Company, much of the paper that rained down on the parade came from their phone books, and new ones would not be released until January 1958. Thirty-five people were sitting in jail for public drunkenness, two for weapons charges, eight for disorderly conduct, and one for resisting arrest.[38]

Shortly after the World Series win, the team began to shake things up for 1958. Fred Haney would be back to manage the club, but three of his coaching staff were fired in late October. First and third base coaches Johnny Riddle and Connie Ryan were let go, along with pitching coach Charlie Root. A former Milwaukee Brewer, Whitlow Wyatt, immediately replaced Root, and John Fitzpatrick was named as first base coach. Haney made it clear to the higher echelons of the Braves that he wanted to make changes to his staff before he signed a new, one-year deal, to lead the Braves into a defense of their World Series title.[39] No one could have anticipated that this was the apex of the Braves experience in Milwaukee or that only eight years later the team would be gone. The World Series was the last time that the county, the Braves, and the local officials really worked together for the good of the fans and the future of baseball in Wisconsin. Previously, most members of the county board and civic leaders were willing to accommodate the Braves, but now Milwaukee County prepared to maximize the return on their investment in the stadium they had built in the Menomonee Valley. From this point forward, the county and the Braves front office would be at loggerheads over who was entitled to make money from the four-year-old stadium. Braves fans who lived in Wisconsin but outside Milwaukee County had no effective voice in these negotiations. Worse for all of the Milwaukee Braves faithful, some in the Braves organization now began to question their future in Wisconsin. The Milwaukee Miracle began to unravel.

"We run along in the red"

With the glow of the world championship still evident on the faces of baseball fans across Wisconsin, the Milwaukee County Board moved quickly to raise stadium rental fees for the Braves. The existing contract expired on December 31, 1957, and, with both sides eager to get the best deal possible, negotiations were contentious. Walter Bender, chair of the county park commission and responsible for getting "the best contract, for the county, moneywise," months earlier had made it clear that the county wanted greater returns from gate receipts and concessions. Raising the annual rent from $196,000 to more than $331,000 was presented as a way to offset increasing maintenance costs for County Stadium. One supervisor said the proposal was fair and equitable to all parties, and the new costs, including higher parking fees, would return to the taxpayers about 10 percent of the cost of the ballpark and its upgrades since 1953. Supervisor John L. Doyne, later elected county executive, wanted to make sure Milwaukee County was getting its share of television revenue generated at the stadium by the visiting teams. Currently the Braves received nothing from these telecasts, but Doyne thought it was "an area that at least ought to be discussed."[40] Cairnes said the team felt that any stadium rent increase was unreasonable and if higher rates were demanded, the team would have to make adjustments, including ticket prices. The Braves also wanted a percentage of the parking revenues, which currently went solely to Milwaukee County, although the team was responsible for maintenance of the lots and its lights.

Cairnes contended that the team had averaged $366,000 in profits during the first four years in Milwaukee, but the "profit we made has not been excessive." With all operating costs included, Cairnes argued that Milwaukee County "should not make any lease that will provide less profit than the club has made." Nailing the issue dead on, Cairnes pointed out the supervisors "felt that the Braves have been a success and shouldn't have been, and you want to take this $366,000 profit from us?" Even worse for future operations in Milwaukee, the Braves would have to pay more rent than "any other club; even the Yanks paid less."[41] The average major league baseball team paid approximately $400,000 per year for salaries in the front office and administrative operating costs. Additional expenses included $250,000 for spring training, equipment, and travel; $250,000 for annual stadium rent and maintenance; and $600,000 for player development and procurement, including minor league operations.[42] Successful teams like the Braves certainly spent more and required more to maintain the existing team and build for future pennant runs. If the county was successful in raising the stadium rent, the Braves would have to find other sources of income to remain competitive, including raising ticket and concession prices and selling off players or some of their minor league operations. If the team was not as successful afterward, fewer fans would have interest in going to games, which would reduce team revenues even further.

"Sir, I don't think you know much about baseball"

Regardless of the Braves' position, Milwaukee County remained adamant throughout the negotiations that they expected a much higher return from the stadium. Cairnes expected the existing deal that required payment of 5 percent of gate receipts and another 5 percent of all concessions would simply be extended for another five years. The supervisors countered with an offer of 8 percent of the gate and 20 percent for concessions, which could provide an estimated $330,000 in additional revenues to Milwaukee County. Not happy with the response by the Braves and their negotiations, Doyne contended that the Braves president appeared to think that the County Board of Supervisors was "a bunch of bush leaguers." If you are "paying $1,000 a year flat rental," asked supervisor William H. Hintz, and if things worked out well for the club, "don't you think we ought to get a little more" in revenues? Cairnes replied that with "all due respect to you, sir, I don't think you know much about baseball."[43]

Cairnes had argued back in 1953 that baseball was not a profitable business and "we run along in the red." The justification for the low rent of $1,000 per year was to allow the Braves to get settled financially in Wisconsin. When attendance exceeded expectations in 1953, the team voluntarily raised the rent to $25,000 for the first year and $250,000 for 1954. Cairnes estimated that Braves losses could be as high as $2 million under the new proposal and the team had to attract at least $1–1.2 million per year to break even. There was no thought from the supervisors "on the part of Mr. Perini to make a profit out of it." County officials were dubious about how much money the Braves had actually made during their time in Milwaukee because the team was not forthcoming. Cairnes pointed out that Milwaukee County's promise of forty thousand permanent seats in the stadium had still not been fulfilled despite a stadium expansion in late 1953 that added more than eight thousand seats. In the championship year of 1957, capacity remained at thirty-six thousand with an additional seven thousand bleacher seats.[44] He argued that if the current deal offered by the county were signed, the Braves would be forced to raise ticket and concession prices.[45] Regardless of the Braves' position, county officials clearly feared that the taxpayers would accuse them of "subsidizing baseball" in Milwaukee if they did not get a better return on the ballpark.[46]

Contention and distrust between the Braves and the county became more problematic and more of the norm as the years progressed. The county dispatched stadium manager William Anderson to visit other cities to see how they handled the leases for their municipal stadiums. Although he was not personally involved in the discussions, Anderson was still tasked with compiling, analyzing, and reporting information to the Milwaukee County Park Commission, which was responsible for negotiations.[47] Frustrated with the progress made between the parties, Clifford Randall, an attorney who represented the citizen groups that funded the stadium and lured the Braves to Milwaukee, publicly urged the county board to prevent its members from participating in negotiations with the team. He argued that it was in Milwaukee County's best interest to get a fair return on the stadium and sufficient funds to maintain the facility, but he also understood the "desirability and necessity that the baseball club operate successfully." Randall was sure that the rent needed by the county to manage and preserve the ballpark "can be computed rather quickly." Furthermore, if the Braves are "unable to pay this rental, I believe that they should explain why and I also believe that the management of the ball club will be willing to do so." He felt it was regrettable that the entire board was participating in negotiations.[48]

As relations between the county board and the team deteriorated, the local media became more critical of the club as it negotiated the new stadium deal. An editorial in the *Milwaukee Journal* said that as a "profit seeking business, the Braves baseball club is of course entitled to bargain for the lowest rent it can get at County Stadium," but Cairnes's attitude struck "a sour note right at the outset." It criticized the team and its president for not letting the supervisors have a full accounting of what the team could afford to pay and for believing that rental price went only one direction: down. To the Braves' argument that other municipal stadium deals were lower than Milwaukee's, the editorial pointed out that the "Braves do more than twice as much business as any of them, and nearly as much as all three put together." The Braves did not understand that the county was "duty bound as any other management to insure a full return on its investment." And as much as the taxpayers loved the Braves, they were "not giving away any stadiums." Therefore, any number that was reached had to be in favor of the county because the "stadium is the indispensable key to the Braves' being so well set up in business" in Milwaukee and they "are not going to burn the house down because the landlord wants more rent." The editorial concluded by stating that the "park commission and county board are in the driver's seat, and surely will not be blustered out of it. Mr. Cairnes will be back—in a more reasonable frame of mind."[49]

Such an attitude would be corrosive to the relationship between the county and the Braves in the years ahead. The problem remained that the elected officials of Milwaukee County had an obligation to maximize the return on the stadium and the Braves needed as much revenue as possible to remain competitive. Many citizens of Milwaukee now sided with the county board and felt that as long as the team was making money, the county was justified in raising the rent at the ballpark.[50] Combined, this would be the worst case scenario in the years ahead.

The Braves' president again spoke of his concerns on November 26, 1957. He had met with the park commission in late October to address the county's original proposal back in June, which the team believed was unreasonable because the rates initially projected as a basis for negotiation were "much higher than those ever included in a major league baseball rental contract." He said that the Braves were "most anxious to continue as tenants of Milwaukee County Stadium" and he hoped that "you gentlemen, as representatives of the people of Milwaukee County, share our desire that we continue to use these facilities." He added that the team had been fair with the county and "we should like to be treated fairly." The Braves had paid more in rent than any other club since

1956, and he was quite sure that this held true "for the other years we have used Milwaukee County Stadium as well." In addition to paying higher rent than their competitors, the Braves had to supply many of the services and utilities that were provided to other teams at "no expense" and spent almost $42,000 per year on stadium cleanup, unlike other teams. Therefore, in comparison with other teams that used municipal stadiums, the Braves spent between $75,000 and $100,000 more. Moreover, other teams got a percentage of parking fees and scoreboard advertising, which was denied to the Braves at an estimated loss of $140,000 per year. Cairnes pointed out that the ballpark, according to Milwaukee County, had not been built to turn an operation profit but rather to attract a professional baseball club and give the region major league status.[51] The Braves had fulfilled this goal.

Cairnes also pointed out that the team, in its first five years, had paid Milwaukee County $800,000 in rent while the county made an additional $770,000 in parking fees from Braves games alone. This did not incorporate other revenues generated from stadium usage outside of baseball games, which would increase the county's take to more than $2 million. Furthermore, Milwaukee County received additional "national and international advertising" that greatly increased the county's revenues. Cairnes felt that the Braves should not "be penalized because they were good" and had "brought a first division team and subsequent pennant winner and World's Champion to this wonderful community." What the Braves front office wanted was a lease deal similar to the one between the City of Baltimore and the Orioles. That agreement was for three years and had a club option for five three-year extensions. There was a final option for an additional two years, which made the Baltimore agreement a twenty-year lease if all options were exercised. The Orioles could vacate their lease after any three-year period, but retained "the privilege of remaining at the same rate for twenty years" without renegotiation.[52]

The Braves proposed a two-year lease with a club option to extend it for four additional two-year periods. Ideally, if accepted, this would permit the Braves to use County Stadium for a total of ten years and keep the team in Milwaukee at least through 1967. If, however, there were "some good reason for limiting the terms of the lease to five years, we would be agreeable to it." Cairnes said the stadium remained a moneymaker for Milwaukee County and the entire region had benefited from the Braves being in Wisconsin. People who "previously shopped in Chicago and the Twin Cities are now making their purchases in Milwaukee, not only during the baseball season, but their year-round buying habits changed in favor of Milwaukee." He further contended that "the Braves have been good for Milwaukee and Milwaukee has been good for the Braves. We hope this mutually advantageous relationship continues for many years."[53]

"Only under our conditions"

Ultimately the Braves and the supervisors did not find much in each other's position to agree upon, and when the county offered a contract the Braves rejected it outright on December 13. The county remained intractable on several issues, and Cairnes felt that the Braves needed better options. He objected to the county's clause that permitted renegotiation at the discretion of the county if the Braves decided to televise home games. County officials feared that telecasting games would hurt attendance and thereby reduce the revenue the Braves would owe the county. The county wanted a guaranteed minimum written into the contract, while the Braves felt this "condition is not contained in any other major league contract. We have no present intention of televising— in fact, we have been the outstanding opponent to televising." Still, Cairnes acknowledged, "None of us can foresee what the future may require." He further considered it very important that "our rental contract assure us of occupancy for a definite period of time. No such assurance is provided by a contract which may be reopened before its expiration date."[54]

The county offered a five-year contract, unless television forced renegotiations. It raised the Braves' rent an estimated 80 percent and required the team to pay for maintenance of the entire electrical infrastructure, including the parking lots, while still receiving none of the parking revenues. Cairnes said that the Braves "certainly do not want to take advantage of the wonderful people in this county, and we are sure they do not want to take advantage of the Braves." He said the team wanted to work out a deal as quickly as possible because their radio contracts expired in 1957 and "we have been unable to discuss a new broadcasting contract although budgets of prospective sponsors are frequently set up in November." With no deal in place, the Braves were not able to sell Christmas gift certificates because ticket prices for 1958 were not yet established. The team had even discontinued season ticket sales because an agreement had not yet been reached. County supervisor Eugene Grobschmidt, soon to be a thorn in the side of the Braves' owners, said he "voted for the contract and I'm going to stick to it." Milwaukee County acted to protect the interests of the taxpayers of Milwaukee and many believed that the Braves were attempting to get the board to compromise on this principle.

Robert P. Russell, first assistant counsel for the county, said that if a deal was not done by December 31, the Braves would stay at the ballpark "only under our conditions."[55]

Doyne proposed that the county and the Braves consider a ten-year lease, but it was not approved because the supervisors "apparently didn't feel that way about it."[56] Stadium manager William Anderson later clarified that the proposed ten-year contract was actually a two-year contract that gave the Braves an option to renew for a four-year term at the same rates and then for another four.[57] This left the length of the lease solely in the hands of the Braves and the county with limited options. The uncertain ten-year lease was dismissed in favor of the leverage of a single five-year pact that kept the Braves at County Stadium through the 1962 season. The supervisors hoped that the shorter lease meant they would soon be able to renegotiate if the Braves continued to be successful. This guaranteed the county would not miss out on additional sources of baseball-generated revenues if the Miracle of Milwaukee continued into the future.

"The bier that made Milwaukee famous"

After long negotiations the team and the county finally agreed upon a contract that was formally approved by the Milwaukee County Board on January 7, 1958. Under the terms of the deal, the county was annually guaranteed a minimum $400,000, with an escalator clause of $25,000 if the Braves played in another World Series. The contract did not exclude telecasting games, but it gave the Braves the option of renegotiation for television if they chose not to pay the minimum allocated to the county. The new compact raised the total the county received from the Braves to a higher level than the previous five years, and even more than in 1957 when the team paid $216,000, including $10,000 of additional revenues from the World Series. The Braves were required to turn over 7 percent "of the gate receipts after deduction of admission taxes, league and visiting team shares" and an additional 15 percent of concessions; make rental payments and its shares of "gross paid admission receipts and gross sales of merchandise" on the fifteenth of every month; and "keep such reasonable books and records as directed by and in the manner and form approved by the County." During the baseball season the Braves had to maintain the field, including for nonbaseball events, and provide all "labor, services, material, supplies and equipment necessary to maintain a clean, orderly and inviting condition" at County Stadium. They were to keep the walkways, concourses, and areas around the ballpark clean, and not make any "alterations, improvements or additions to any part of the stadium" without the consent of Milwaukee County through its park commission.[58]

Because expansions at County Stadium had eliminated the view of the field from the hill above the facility, the Braves had to reserve five hundred seats inside the ballpark for "purchase by members and patients of the Veterans Administration" until twenty-four hours before each game. They also had to provide "at its own expense, its own tickets of admission, ticket sellers, ticket takers, ushers and other employees necessary to the proper use and occupancy of the Stadium" as well as "watchmen service" to provide security to the facility. For this latter clause, the team was reimbursed two-thirds of the cost by the county. Milwaukee County was not to schedule football games at County Stadium within thirty-six hours of a listed Braves game without permission from the club. Both parties would split any revenues generated from advertising on stadium spaces, including the scoreboard and the fence that separated the field from the stands, but only the county could sell those rights.[59]

Concern over strained relations between the Braves and the county led Cairnes to host the entire Milwaukee County Board at a luncheon at the Wisconsin Club on May 27, 1958. The press was prohibited from attending, causing one elected official to leave in protest. Cairnes presented the supervisors with world championship lapel pins and a framed cartoon that featured a dead Yankee player in a casket surrounded by a trio of dancing Indians and labeled it "the bier that made Milwaukee famous." The Braves president told the board that he was prepared to host such meetings every month or so as needed in the interest of good relations between the Braves and the county. If the supervisors had any issues with the team and their operation of County Stadium, they should come directly to him rather than spread it around.[60]

4

The Beginning of the End

1958–1961

> If the Braves can't win with him, they might just as well start all over again.
>
> Arthur Daley, *New York Times*,
> March 11, 1960

Baseball Goes National in 1958

The future of the Milwaukee Braves and the overall landscape of baseball were inextricably changed in 1958 when, after eighty-one years in New York, both the Brooklyn Dodgers and the New York Giants left for riches of new markets on the West Coast. Many baseball owners, like the Dodgers' Walter O'Malley and the Giants' Horace Stoneham, believed that the Milwaukee Miracle could be replicated in other cities. In return for the investment in a municipal stadium, expansive revenues could be generated from concessions, parking, taxes, and other baseball-related items. Community leaders, politicians, and members of the media therefore linked new big league stadiums with civic pride. For some cities, stadium construction was sold as the only way to attract an expansion franchise or, like Milwaukee, the transfer of an existing team. The Milwaukee formula created this new era of franchise mobility, and the Dodgers and Giants maximized their opportunity.[1]

When teams began to leave for new stadiums in new markets, municipalities that currently had a team did everything in their power to retain the big league status that baseball offered. Regardless of the economics of the times, even as manufacturing went into decline and many were left looking for jobs, cities spared no expense to save their teams. Owners quickly learned that they held

71

the economic leverage to get a new stadium, either in their existing market or in another city desperate for professional sports. The owners could exhort favorable leases, expanded revenues, and new ballparks from civic leaders who were terrified they would be left behind like the fans of the Boston Braves, the St. Louis Browns, or the Philadelphia Athletics.[2]

The National League benefited from the Dodgers' and Giants' moves because the advent of television made their game truly national. Commissioner Ford Frick said the move of the Dodgers and the Giants was most likely only the beginning of what could be radical changes to baseball. There was now a National League void in New York City that needed to be filled with either a relocation or expansion. Frick was strongly in favor of healthy expansion to former minor league cities that were really "big league—like Milwaukee or San Francisco." He cautioned against strong markets that might simply be abandoned because there were not enough franchises to meet demand. After all, several cities much larger than Kansas City or Milwaukee did not yet have major league baseball. Pursuit of the next Milwaukee or Los Angeles prompted the baseball owners to come up with a plan for expansion. Frick added that major league expansion must come "either through a third major league" or the already-approved ten-team leagues. It was certain the majors would show growth of either type within a decade. Concern remained over the quality of baseball, as player drafts could strip strong teams of some of their great players and teams could not protect their entire rosters from an expansion draft.[3]

In May, Lou Perini met with officials in New York about possible expansion or a National League franchise transfer to a city that was now missing two teams. When asked about the trip, Perini refused to confirm or deny that he had met with New York parks commissioner Robert Moses and William Shea, chair of the mayor of New York's baseball commission.[4] The future of baseball was still unfolding; a certain level of fluidity remained with franchises and their host cities, sports telecasting was out of its infancy, and new cities and markets wanted to cash in on the popularity of professional sports. Perini thought that it would take up to $3.5 million to purchase a franchise, outside of any arrangements for a ballpark that would have to be constructed. In the event of an expansion draft, the owners of the new National League franchise would have to compensate the teams that gave up players. The *Milwaukee Sentinel*'s Red Thisted, who was also the official scorer at County Stadium, said this was just "another scheme to enrich unfairly the men who now control the game." When asked if there was any substance to the rumors that Perini might put a team in New York and the Yankees might move to California, Perini said he had to stay in Milwaukee. Thisted ominously noted that even though business was great in Milwaukee, "The Braves are feeling the pinch; the stadium they got practically free in 1953 costs $450,000 a year in rent right now."[5]

This financial pressure on the Braves led to rumors that the team might be looking for a better deal in another city. In fact, since the Braves arrived in Milwaukee in 1953, they—and every other major league team—were alleged to be on the move. Even the Red Sox, now alone in Boston, were rumored to be looking for a new home, possibly in California.[6] Into this potentially volatile situation came Lou Perini, a leading backer of major league expansion. Perini supported the proposed ten-team leagues with new franchises in Minneapolis, Toronto, Houston, and a National League team in New York for starters. It seems unlikely that Perini wanted to move the Braves to New York, but there was the possibility that he could sell the team and use the money to purchase the New York expansion franchise. This would put his new team much closer to his home in Massachusetts. One wonders if Fred Miller, were he alive then, would have purchased the team, leaving Perini with a new franchise in a much larger market and a great deal closer to home.

At a news conference at County Stadium in late July, Perini said the Braves would "have to make some sacrifices. We may have to divest ourselves of some of our talent." He reminded all that the Braves had not been for sale since he bought the team and he did not plan on moving the club to New York or anywhere else. He said that if Cubs owner Phil Wrigley owned the Braves and wanted to move, "I'd vote against it. Leave it alone." Perini made it clear that he had "waited fifteen years to win the world's championship and now do you think I'd want to start all over again and build a new organization? In a pig's eye. I haven't got that much stamina." Moreover, if he ever sold the Braves it would not be to start another team and "if we ever sold stock, it wouldn't be to one man." And then he said something that all Braves' fans wanted to believe: he hoped this ball club remains in the Perini family for generations.[7] For the future of the Milwaukee Braves, it is truly too bad that within four years, Perini would sell the team and end his family ownership. In 1964, when given an opportunity to vote against the team leaving Milwaukee, Perini voted with the majority to abscond to the Land of the Pecan. Perhaps someone should have reminded him of what he said in 1958.

"That's my job"

George "Birdie" Tebbetts, manager of the last-place Cincinnati Redlegs, resigned in August and, in a somewhat shocking move, was hired by the Milwaukee Braves as executive vice president. Braves president Joe Cairnes introduced

Tebbetts at a press conference and said, "Maybe in a matter of years Birdie will be president of the ball club." Cairnes was currently heavily involved in projects for Perini's company that took time from the day-to-day management of the Milwaukee Braves, such as working at a new construction project in Florida that was projected to take up to a decade. "Birdie'll head up the organization in my absence," he said, and will provide the on-site leadership critical to a successful baseball team.[8] The new vice president eventually transitioned to the president's job while John Quinn remained the team's general manager through the 1958 season. Manager Fred Haney said he had Cairnes's personal assurance that there would be no interference from Tebbetts, who would work only "in the front office and will not have anything to do with the way I run the ball team."[9]

Many in the local media did not understand Perini's decision to hire Tebbetts, who had clearly been very unpopular with the fans in Cincinnati. Furthermore, it was still not clear why Perini had even turned the club over to Cairnes in the first place because he assigned Cairnes to other projects only a year later. Haney could not have been very comfortable in his position. Despite winning the World Series the previous year, he would have Tebbetts looking over his shoulder, and Tebbetts was continually rumored to want to manage again. The college-educated Tebbetts was described as intelligent, with "enthusiasm, perspicacity and personality to do an excellent job with one of baseball's most progressive organizations. He's far better off than he ever was as manager. That is something he never should permit himself to forget."[10]

On the field, the Braves had another successful year in 1958, again winning the pennant. They faced off against the New York Yankees again, but this time, the series started in Milwaukee. All year their strength had been pitching that was consistently better than all the others in the National League. The Braves won three of the first four games of the Series, but lost the last three games in a row, the last two at County Stadium. The Braves struggled to hit in the Fall Classic and score runs, and the loss in Game Seven was certainly disappointing to Milwaukee fans who had been celebrating only one year earlier.

The team was first in attendance in the National League for the sixth year in a row. Ominously, this was the last time the Braves paced the senior circuit, and their home attendance was down 244,000 from the previous year. This was only the second time that Braves attendance went down, yet it would decline every year—with the exception of 1964—the Braves remained in Milwaukee. It was evident that the attendance was settling in Milwaukee, as it did in every other city with a new franchise. Unlike the others, however, Milwaukee carried fan interest far longer than that of any other team that moved, including the Atlanta Braves, whose attendance declined in five of their first seven years. From this point forward, the Braves struggled in Wisconsin because of limited promotions, declining performance, unpopular managers, and the loss of players who were fan favorites at County Stadium. Despite the decline of attendance at the ballpark, the Milwaukee Braves actually outdrew the neighboring Chicago Cubs twelve out of the thirteen years the team was in Wisconsin. Unfortunately for the Braves' fans, the owners believed Chicago was a great baseball town and Milwaukee no longer was.[11]

"I've lost an awfully good friend rather than an employee"

After the 1958 season, the front office saw additional upheaval. John Quinn, who oversaw three pennants and one World Series title, left the organization for a similar position with the Philadelphia Phillies in January 1959. During his years in Milwaukee he had dealt with strife in the front office and extremely high expectations from the owner and the fans. As the general manager, Quinn said his only concern was to "put the strongest possible team on the field and win as many games as possible" and there was "only one place to finish and that's on top. That's my job." It was apparent that Quinn was on the outs with the Braves front office when they hired Tebbetts the previous summer.[12]

Despite his success in building the entire Braves baseball operation, including the farm system, the popular Quinn would not be part of Milwaukee's future. It was reported that with the Phillies, Quinn "will have security, a much larger paycheck than from the recession-minded Braves and a chance again to prove he knows how to build a baseball club." Perini told the papers that the resignation made him feel "as if I've lost an awfully good friend rather than an employee." He said he was surprised by the decision to leave and hoped Quinn was doing the right thing. Perini "didn't have a chance to discuss anything" with Quinn, but believed that if he had, the former GM would still be with the Braves. He denied that Quinn had not received a raise in a couple of years; if he had wanted a raise, he would have said something to Perini, and he had actually "received a raise recently." Perini also said that in the meantime, Cairnes and Tebbetts would recommend a replacement for Quinn as general manager. Tebbetts was "pretty much running the show and I'm going to give him a chance to express his views."[13]

John McHale Arrives

The Braves moved into a new era when John McHale, the former general manager of the Detroit Tigers, was introduced in the same capacity to the local press at a luncheon in Milwaukee on January 27, 1959. McHale, who would later be blamed in Milwaukee for his role in the Braves' departure, was initially tasked with dealing with players and, according to Cairnes, whatever "Birdie Tebbetts wants him to do."[14] Cairnes also said that he was moving out of operational authority and Tebbetts and McHale would now run the club. Lloyd Larson reported that McHale had "made a mighty favorable impression on all meeting him for the first time" and described him as hard working and intelligent. McHale appeared to be the choice of Tebbetts, who was excited that McHale joined the organization.[15]

McHale acknowledged that he knew he had "joined a strong baseball organization and I am going to do my utmost to keep it that way." It would not be easy following Quinn, but "I can only add I am going to do my best here so as not to let down the persons who have placed so much confidence in me." McHale was tasked with player personnel, stadium management, and dealing with the county board.[16] Perini pointed out that hiring McHale meant that Tebbetts was "not intended to be general manager. He is executive vice president and sometime in the near future he will be president. You certainly wouldn't expect him to step down to general manager."[17] Perini also said that Cairnes had accepted the presidency of a Florida real estate development company and was expected to devote his full time to that position in the near future. This would mean that the Milwaukee Braves would be controlled by an owner in Massachusetts, run by an absentee president, and built by a new general manager, at least for a while.

As the 1959 season unfolded, attendance at County Stadium continued to drop. In a letter to the park commission, Tebbetts attempted to minimize the problem, saying that Milwaukee and Wisconsin fans had, through their history, witnessed great attendance. It was "no accident and I have every reason to believe that when we reach our norm, it will be one of the highest attendance figures in all major league cities." Tebbetts noted that attendance was down across almost all cities, but the percentage of decline appeared greater in Milwaukee than elsewhere. Many chartered buses that had run from clubs and restaurants discontinued service to the stadium in 1959, and streetcar lines that had brought several thousand paying customers to the ballpark closed. The Braves would have to "assess the value of an advertising program" and intensify salesmanship to boost attendance, with the team assuming the costs. It was noted that under the current stadium deal, higher attendance was beneficial "for us and good for our landlords."[18]

Stadium improvements would enhance the game time experience and encourage attendance, said Tebbetts. A major problem was the current setup of the bleachers, where attendance was down by about sixteen thousand after the first twenty-five home dates. The experience out there was described as "most unsanitary and unsatisfactory because of flies and mosquitoes" that pooled in water and garbage that was strewn beneath the bleachers. Because this area was not yet paved, it was difficult to keep clean. Viewing was also problematic because fans walked in front of the stands. Combined, these issues caused a loss of "most of our women bleacherites." Constructing permanent bleachers across the outfield would help solve those problems. Another improvement concerned paving the area where buses park to make it easier to walk up to the stadium. Braves fans who used public transportation had to walk in from Bluemound Road or pay ninety cents to be dropped off at the stadium—an insignificant amount, perhaps, but more than a Ladies Day ticket to the game itself. Tebbetts also felt that there was "an urgent need" for large escalators to move fans who now had to walk up long ramps to the upper grandstand. Particularly on hot days, too many older patrons had had "cases of illness and fainting" because of the walk.[19]

In addition to alleviating all such issues, the Braves wanted the county to finally complete the stadium to its proposed capacity of forty thousand seats and replace the railing on the upper deck that was "obstructing the vision of our box seat fans." Facility improvements would "make it easier and less costly for patrons to reach the ballpark and to permit them to witness ball games in greater comfort." Combined with a great team and an aggressive sales campaign, they would restore attendance to the two million mark. Finally, Tebbetts was grateful for the "friendship and cooperation which has existed between the County officials" and Braves since he arrived.[20] Regardless of the outcome of these suggestions, the Braves were beginning to feel the economic impact of higher rental fees and lower attendance. No one seemed to understand if this downturn was temporary or the new norm, but something had to be done to secure baseball in Wisconsin.

In mid-September the Braves authorized the ticket office to begin sending out World Series ticket applications to their season ticket base. Any tickets that remained would be offered to the general public. The Braves indefatigable ticket director, William Eberly, said season ticket holders had until September 21 to purchase or pass on the tickets. Each holder was entitled to buy a strip of three tickets at a cost of twenty-one dollars for a reserve seat and thirty dollars for a box seat, plus a dollar for postage and handling. Eberly expected good sales for the two-time defending National League champions once the team got closer to locking up its third pennant in a row. Three of the games for the 1959 Fall Classic were scheduled in the National League town, and hotels and restaurants were again ready for the rush. They did not anticipate a shortage of rooms in

Milwaukee for the weekend the Series would be in Wisconsin. Local officials were also getting ready for another major celebration if the Braves won it all again in 1959.[21]

As the season neared the end, the Braves remained the presumptive favorite to win the pennant as, according to Roy Terrell of *Sports Illustrated*, they were "the superior ball club, not great but very good, the best in the league." They had tremendous power in their lineup and "some of the best pitching in baseball." They were not, however, "very inspiring. They won the pennant the last two years simply because they were far better than anyone else" in the league.[22] Unfortunately for the Braves faithful in 1959, they would lose again in their last game of the year. The team had wandered through most of the season, and it was not until a late season hot streak that they were able to tie the Los Angeles Dodgers on the last day of the season. The Braves boasted two twenty-game winners, and their power hitters, Henry Aaron and Eddie Mathews, combined for 236 runs batted in and 84 home runs, yet the Dodgers swept the Braves in the best-out-of-three playoff. To make the defeat even worse, the Dodgers scored three times in the bottom of the ninth before winning the game and the pennant in the bottom of the twelfth. What no one knew was this would be the last postseason appearance for the Braves in Milwaukee and they would never get as close to a pennant again while they were in Wisconsin.

Noticeably absent during the Braves' late season run, as the team fought back into pennant contention, were fans in the stands. After forcing a three-game playoff with the Dodgers, the Braves hosted the first game at County Stadium on September 28. In the stands for the last game in Milwaukee were 18,297 fans, whom Arthur Daley described as a "disgracefully small gathering" and apathetic. He argued that no one "seemed to care much and the players responded with the routine job that the uninspired surroundings appeared to demand" as the Braves lost 3–2. Daley said the game-winning home run by Johnny Roseboro went into the right-field bleachers where, upon landing, "The ball startled the two sparrows and five fans who were dozing peacefully out there. Then everyone went back to sleep." Daley pointed out that in the very recent past, Milwaukee was the most "rabid baseball town west of Flatbush," where fans braved all the elements to see their teams finish strong. In 1959, however, something was different, as Milwaukee was now "assuming aspects of a baseball tragedy." Rain certainly impacted the crowd, but the bleachers were sparsely populated and vast "spaces in the grandstand were vacant. This could have been a run-of-the-mill Monday in the August dog days with the Phillies as the opponents and nothing obvious at stake." Maybe "the Braves shouldn't have given their followers the bonus of two pennants and one world championship. They have nothing left for an encore."[23]

Fred Haney Departs

In a postseason postmortem, Red Thisted argued that there really was not one thing that doomed the team that lost a playoff game with the Los Angeles Dodgers and just missed going to its third straight World Series. The team had started 1959 very hot, and then, over the next three months, had lost more games than it won but still remained in the pennant hunt. Despite a big push toward the end of the season, it was too late to win the pennant, or perhaps save the manager's job.[24] In a sign of further change for the Braves, Fred Haney resigned as manager after four years, one World's Championship, two National League pennants, and two last-day second-place finishes, in 1956 and 1959. At the Ambassador Hotel in Los Angeles, the former Braves skipper said the end of the season had nothing to do with his resignation; even if the team had won the National League pennant, he still would have left. He said he had "been in baseball over forty years and I feel that at this time I owe some time to my family." He said before he made his final decision he spoke to Perini, who tried to get him to reconsider. His decision had nothing to do with his pay or contract, and there was nothing to the idea that he and Tebbetts or McHale had differences. They cooperated with him, according to Haney, "and they did all they could to help me. I wouldn't want anyone to think my quitting was in any way connected with them." Perini said that this "came as a thunderbolt out of the blue" and we "figured win or lose in the playoffs, Haney would be back to manage the Braves in 1960. We hadn't even given thought to a successor."[25]

Perini later said that the new manager would be someone with knowledge, character, and the ability to lead a successful team. He added that the team would "start from the top and work our way down" but the Braves "won't go down too far." It was rumored that Tebbetts was in line for the job, along with Leo Durocher, who had won a World Series with the New York Giants and won pennants for them and their crosstown rival Brooklyn Dodgers. Braves second baseman Red Schoendienst was also on the short list to replace Haney.[26]

Instead, McHale hired Charlie Dressen to replace Haney as team manager for 1960. Dressen was described as a firebrand and the type of manager needed to coax an aging team to excel, as he had led the Brooklyn Dodgers to the World Series twice during his reign. Arguably, he was most famous for being replaced as the Dodgers manager after his wife, Ruth, wrote to owner Walter O'Malley and asked for a multiyear contract starting with the 1954 season. Under Dressen, the Dodgers had won back-to-back pennants, but O'Malley made it clear in front of the press that the Dodgers used only one-year contracts for managers. Dressen resigned, and his replacement, Walter Alston, signed the first of what became twenty-three consecutive one-year contracts with the

Dodgers.[27] Now with Dressen at the helm, the Braves deviated from their recent established policy of one-year contracts, put in place when Grimm was fired near the end of his three-year deal. Given a two-year contract, he was confident that he could return the team to the World Series.

The Continental League

The fluidity of baseball franchises since the Braves moved to Milwaukee in 1953 remarkably altered the landscape of professional sports in the United States. While it seemed completely irrelevant to Milwaukee when the discussions were taking place, the future of baseball in Wisconsin ultimately depended on further expansion. Attempting to cash in on what appeared to be a growing interest in the national pastime and a refusal by baseball's owners to expand, a new group spearheaded by Branch Rickey and William Shea wanted to create a third major league. Announced by Shea in late July 1959, the new league was to introduce four new cities to baseball and return another team to New York. The proposed new markets included Houston, Toronto, Minneapolis–St. Paul, and Denver. Other cities expressing interest were Miami, Indianapolis, Dallas–Fort Worth, San Diego, Portland, Seattle, Montreal, San Juan, and Atlanta. It was hoped that new markets would enjoy the same enthusiasm for baseball as shown by the Milwaukee Miracle and the transfer of the Dodgers and Giants to the West Coast.[28]

The creation of a new league faced enormous challenges from the existing structure of baseball, which had enjoyed legal protection for its monopoly since 1922, when the United States Supreme Court upheld a lower court decision in a lawsuit brought by representatives of the defunct Federal League. Rickey and Shea, after four months of discussion to get recognition and access into the major leagues, formally discussed congressional action to get the ball moving. Unfortunately for the Continental League, its movement triggered a new drive to expand by the existing leagues. American League president Joe Cronin said expansion was unavoidable, but there was no "indication at this time, that the American League intends to expand in 1961, 1962, 1963, 1964, or 1965." Cronin added that he "made it clear that the AL will not delay the Continental League from going forward with the completion of its organization." Commissioner Frick said that he was not opposed to the new league and when "they get eight teams, I'll be behind them 100%" and it was impossible to say that the existing leagues were not going to expand.[29]

The two existing major leagues voted for expansion in July 1960. Perini served on the committee that voted to add new teams to the senior circuit. No cities were initially mentioned in the vote, but it was clear from Frick that New York would get a new National or Continental team.[30] But on August 2, the eight prospective Continental League owners watched their dream of a third major league pass into history. Four of the owners were given unanimous approval from the expansion committee of the National and American Leagues to officially join the existing two circuits, while the others were relegated to the ashbin of history. The new teams would bring the two leagues to a total of ten teams each by 1962, and the possible locations for the new teams included Minneapolis–St. Paul, Houston, Toronto, and of course New York.[31] Baseball now became far more of a national sport than before, and new franchises and innovative stadiums as well as a few transfers made baseball much different than it had been only a decade earlier.[32] Ultimately Georgia and Florida were left out of the formal expansion plans, continuing the absence of major league baseball in the Southeast until further expansion or transfer of a franchise.

The expansion plan was formally revealed in December, as was the increase in the number of games played, from 154 to 162 per season. The new schedule would impact the American League in 1961 and the National League in 1962. It was previously announced that the National League would add expansion teams in New York and Houston, the Mets and the Colt .45s, respectively. The American League was expanded to ten teams after a franchise was added in Los Angeles and another in Washington, DC. The new Washington team resulted from another franchise shift when Calvin Griffith, the owner of the original Washington Senators, was given permission to move his club to the Minneapolis–St. Paul market. Rechristened the Twins, they would begin play in Minneapolis in 1961.[33] This was further bad news for the Braves because a new team nearby would impact attendance and broadcast revenues.

The Minnesota Twins

The American League had suffered a decline in attendance for years; the National League had annually outdrawn the junior circuit, thanks largely to the Braves. In 1958 every AL team witnessed a decline from the previous year. Some blamed the dominance of the New York Yankees. Rather than exciting pennant races that went to the end of the regular season, as witnessed in the National League, in some years it seemed the American League race was already over by May. The Yankees dominated road attendance, and it was estimated that "the other clubs aren't drawing much more than enough to make expenses." The result was a virtually permanent second-division status for most of the American League, and hammered very hard were the Washington Senators.[34]

Not only did they suffer from declining interest, they were also now competing with a franchise located in nearby Baltimore.

The original Senators had suffered from poor attendance for years leading up to their transfer to Minnesota. As discussions over the proposed Continental League ebbed and flowed, sports fans in Minnesota attempted to bring professional baseball to their state. Griffith, who had negotiated off and on to move to the Twin Cities, resumed talks when it looked like the Continental League might put a franchise in Minnesota. He had asked for permission to move his floundering club to one of four cities in 1958, but the American League refused to discuss the proposal.[35]

As a result of his previous attempts, Griffith faced increased personal hostility in the nation's capital and finally sent a representative to Minneapolis to continue discussions. His seeming vacillation on whether the team would relocate led to litigation from the Senators' board of directors and consternation among his fellow American League owners.[36] In October 1959, Griffith refused to say if he was going to move the ball club but an offer he had received from Minnesota was tremendous and anyone "who might get a contract like that would be fortunate." He was informed that if he truly wanted to leave, he should personally recommend that an expansion franchise be immediately given to Washington, DC. This meant the nation's capital would not be abandoned, unlike Milwaukee a few years later.[37] The Senators' owner signed a fifteen-year lease to play in Minnesota's Metropolitan Stadium that provided 90 percent of the concession sales for all events there, including, eventually, Minnesota Vikings football games. The Twin Cities Sports Area Commission received 7 percent of net ticket sales, but the Twins would get free rent if they did not draw at least 750,000.[38]

Their final year in Washington, the team drew around 750,000 and there were hopes that this number could be doubled in their new home. Even more, there was optimism that the team might equal the success of the Boston-to-Milwaukee Braves. The existing stadium in Bloomington, where the Twins would play, was expanded from twenty-two thousand to more than thirty-four thousand. An additional expansion was planned to bring the stadium to forty thousand by 1962. Herb Heft, the Twins publicity director, announced in late March 1961 that the number of tickets sold had already tripled from the previous year and the year would begin with "more money in the bank than Washington grossed all of last year." In addition, Heft said, the "way fans have been clamoring for tickets, a million attendance our first year in Minnesota should be a snap. Some of our people are envisioning a million and a half." The fans in Minnesota were truly excited to have baseball and treated Griffith with respect and gratitude.[39] As a result, his franchise led the American League in attendance for most of the next ten seasons, although numbers dwindled after their pennant in 1965.[40]

One should not presume that every fan who went to a Twins game between 1961 and 1965 was a former Braves fan or would have traveled to Milwaukee in the same numbers to catch major league baseball in person. In fact, during the 1957 championship run, the Braves' records indicated that just more than fifteen thousand fans out of approximately 2.2 million who saw a game at County Stadium came from the Twin Cities. Moreover, Eberly later testified that the creation of the Twins was not a factor in the attendance decline in Milwaukee.[41] It cannot be doubted, however, that a significant number of people who traveled to see the Minnesota Twins came from western Wisconsin, Iowa, Minnesota, the Dakotas, and Illinois, and might have gone to Braves games if there were not a team closer to home. The Twins broadcast network also most certainly cut into territory once dominated by the Milwaukee Braves.

As discussions took place about expansion of baseball into new markets and an old one, New York, the cost of municipal-built stadiums came under scrutiny. A nationwide survey determined that while new parks make money, it was often not enough to cover their initial cost to the community. George Weiss, general manager of the New York Yankees, believed that public stadiums represented a "white elephant" to every city where they had been built, though that was actually not the case in Milwaukee. It was reported in 1960 that County Stadium and the Braves generated more than $643,000 against an operating cost of slightly more than $306,000. The Braves paid Milwaukee County $186,703 in rent plus $196,167 in concession revenues and $200,648 in parking lot fees. The Green Bay Packers added another $19,960 in rent. Further money was paid to the county in advertising and other events held at County Stadium during the year. All of this was set up against the cost of building, expanding, modernizing, and maintaining County Stadium, which by 1960 was estimated to total more than $7.4 million.[42]

"They know where they're supposed to sit"

In hopes of reversing the attendance decline of the previous two seasons, in late November season ticket notices went out to four thousand individuals and companies. Eberly said that the hiring of Dressen had triggered "a most encouraging response from the fans" and the team had "already received a large number of new season ticket applications" and many more inquiries. The Braves' target of matching the record 12,567 season tickets sold in 1958 (12,086 in 1959) seemed possible because the team did not raise prices for the 1960 season. Season tickets in the upper grandstand cost $85 per seat, $120 in the lower grandstand, $165 for box seats, and $220 for mezzanine boxes. In addition, Braves tickets were, according to Eberly, the lowest in the major leagues and "13.5 percent below the average of the other fifteen clubs."[43]

Within a week, more than half of the 1959 season tickets had been renewed. One woman wrote to Eberly that she would renew her tickets only if "the Braves do not trade Warren Spahn away for a second baseman." The Braves planned to keep the tickets available until December 16, when they would be released to the rest of the fan base or those who wanted to upgrade their seats.[44] By January 1960, the Braves had sold 714,000 tickets for the upcoming season. The figure represented more than 9,700 season tickets and more than 5,500 single game tickets for the seventy-seven home games on the schedule for 1960.[45] Shortly thereafter, it was reported that Braves Field, the team's old home in Boston for forty-six years, was in the process of being demolished. The old ballpark soon joined Ebbets Field as just a memory and the symbol of a team that abandoned its home for riches in a new market.[46]

In contrast to the excitement and cooperation from stadium staff since 1953, July 1960 brought an usher strike to County Stadium. Braves front-office employees were brought in to replace the 150 regular ushers who were demanding a raise of a dollar a game: from six to seven dollars for a single game and up to nine for a doubleheader. Braves officials, including McHale and Tebbetts, led fans to their seats for a Fourth of July doubleheader against the Pittsburgh Pirates. Others in the front office worked to minimize any confusion for patrons, and Tebbetts said the fans had "been coming here so long they know where they're supposed to sit. About 75 percent don't need anything except directions." Some striking ushers punched in to work but walked off the job when the gates were opened and failed to notify the team. They also set up picket lines in front of the box office windows and appealed to fans to support their cause. Tebbetts told the media that the team's offer was fair and Milwaukee's ushers were "paid above average for the sixteen teams in the major leagues."[47]

Other unions that served the Braves at County Stadium considered making a "united effort" to support the ushers. There was the real possibility that the strike could impact Braves fans away from County Stadium, as the American Federation of Radio Artists could join and, in effect, silence the voices of the Braves, Earl Gillespie and Blaine Walsh. Despite some delivery trucks' being turned away, there were no reports of food or beverage shortages at the stadium.[48] After five days, the ushers ratified a new contract. It provided the ushers with a fifty-cent raise per game, retroactive to the beginning of the season.

The Braves also agreed to increase their pay for the following year after negotiations. Cairnes and Tebbetts committed the Braves to continue to purchase products and merchandise from vendors who had refused to cross the picket lines.[49] While many inside and out of Milwaukee County supported their union brethren in this unfortunate strike, it should be noted that the settlement represented an increased cost to the Braves that would have to be made up with higher prices for tickets and concessions or cuts in other areas of operation. It happened at the same time that attendance was declining. Higher prices would not encourage people to return to County Stadium.

Ongoing restructuring of the ball club continued throughout 1960 and 1961. In October 1960 the club unconditionally released Red Schoendienst, a key component to the Braves pennant runs in 1957 and 1958. Schoendienst was a fan favorite in Milwaukee since his trade to the Braves in June 1957. After three years, he said, the Braves had informed him that they "had no further use for him." McHale offered him a nonplaying position with the Braves, but Schoendienst turned it down. For the Braves faithful, his loss was simply one more in the transition from the glory years to a younger team.[50] It was the start of a rebuilding movement that strained the relationship between the fans and the club, and it was another step in the failure of the Braves to survive in Milwaukee. Another fan favorite, Billy Bruton, was traded in December, triggering further fan discontent. In late November, the Braves announced that all ticket prices for the 1961 season would go up between fifteen and thirty-five cents, except for bleachers and children's seats. The Braves made it clear that the increase was to offset the "greatly increased over-all operating costs" of baseball in Milwaukee.[51]

"Accused of padding the books"

In 1960 the Milwaukee County Board's Parks and Recreation Committee looked into several of the practices of the Braves front office. One of the supervisors asked the Braves about the practice of issuing passes to games at County Stadium. McHale refused to disclose how many were actually dispersed and stated it depended upon promotions that the team was conducting. There was pressure put on the Braves to give a full accounting of these practices to the Milwaukee County auditor, Robert Boos. They wanted to make sure that the Braves were being truthful in their attendance records, which impacted the rental fees the club paid to the county, and whether "the Braves payments were based on the amount of money it received on tickets sold at reduced prices to supervisors and other pass holders, or on the face value of the tickets." The Braves' secretary and assistant treasurer, Francis X. Leary, upset that the team had previously been called "cheats, thieves" and "accused of padding the books," noted that the county was reimbursed on the basis of the actual amount paid, not the face value of the tickets. He added that the "contract says our payments are based on gross sales" and the Braves paid "the county 7 percent of gross gate receipts after deduction of federal admission taxes, visiting club and league shares, and 15 percent gross receipts from most concession items." These totaled $186,073.38 in tickets sales, more than $200,000 in parking, and $206,215.26 in concessions. Because the Braves were responsible for all concessions at the ball park, included in the totals was an additional $10,300 in sales from Green Bay Packers games played in Milwaukee during the 1959 National Football League season. The committee was concerned it was not getting a full accounting, and McHale tried to make it clear that the Braves were being forthright. He added that the ball club wanted "to maintain a cordial relationship. If there are any questions about the operation we would like to be able to sit down and talk it over with you." McHale hoped to settle any differences "privately and without interferences."[52]

"Rather slow compared to the good old days"

To Milwaukee restaurateur Ray Jackson, something was clearly different in 1961. During the peak of the Braves hysteria, players and fans gathered at Jackson's place, located fairly close to the stadium, when the team was in town. Eddie Mathews, the Braves' Hall of Fame third baseman, later wrote that the owner originally brought food down to the team's clubhouse after a game and had a "real nice place, so our wives could wait for us there." According to Mathews, Jackson's bar was the place to be "for Braves fans."[53] Although his business saw continued increases since opening in April 1953, by 1960, for the first time, there were no increases. In the past, he served dinner and drinks to an average of 175 people on game nights, but now that number was down to thirty.[54] The decline in baseball patrons impacted businesses like this across all of southeastern Wisconsin and, in fact, across most major league cities in the 1960s. Milwaukee was not the only city to see this type of downturn, but it would become perhaps the most infamous, as the decline later became a reason and an excuse for the team to leave the city that had embraced it like family just a few years earlier.

The 1961 Braves were projected to finish in the top three, as they had every season since arriving from Boston. There were some holes in the lineup, but it was felt that solid pitching and great hitting would carry the Braves to "the pennant if the outfield holds together and the pitching staff comes up with a stopper in the bullpen. Even if that parlay doesn't come off, the Braves should be close to the top all year." The team's front office was still intact, although *Sports Illustrated* noted that Perini continued to devote more time to his construction business than to running the team. McHale and farm director John Mullen were praised for building a team "with talented youngsters" that "should be near the top of the league for years." Improvements at the ballpark included the Braves Reservation, located at ground level between third base and left field, which catered to families and other groups who wanted to eat and drink while watching the game. Perini's Woods, the famous natural barrier in the batter's vision in centerfield, was replaced with green bleachers. County Stadium still had the best "grandstand eating in baseball": familiar items like cheeseburgers and bratwurst, as well as "two kinds of hot dogs, grilled cheese sandwiches, combination sandwiches" and plenty of beer. Hopes were high for 1961.[55]

Ticket sales lagged from previous years, and Eberly reported sales of around 4,500 tickets for Opening Day 1961, short of a sellout in the reserved sections of the ballpark. In addition, approximately five thousand bleacher seats remained available. In comparison to 1960, the current season ticket sale was far behind the previous year, but Eberly said the team was "very pleased" with sales to date. It had been "rather slow compared to the good old days" but "Milwaukee still is one of the greatest baseball cities in America." He was also excited that the Braves had doubled the number of tickets sold by the Twins, and they remained well "ahead of the Giants—and San Francisco is only in its third year in the majors." The Braves had sold more than 8,300 season tickets, which trailed 1960 by more than 2,500. Eberly saw the economic recession across the nation and poor weather as primary reasons for the ongoing attendance slide. The team looked forward to "renewed interest with the advent of pleasant weather" and a favorable schedule. All would be well if "the Braves are in the thick of things" and the Braves would be "packing them in as we have in the past. There are very good seats available for all games, incidentally, and I would advise the fans to make reservations now" to get the best seats.[56]

Eberly later testified that attendance declined primarily because of the team's on-the-field record, which was "the most important factor in its ability to attract fans" to the ballpark. He acknowledged that sometimes winning a pennant and then dropping to "third, fourth and fifth [place] has a much more serious consequence on attendance than does a club that is in tenth place moving up to seventh or eighth." He believed, therefore, that attendance at County Stadium resulted from "the club's performance on the field," which was not as good as it had been at the beginning of the Milwaukee Miracle. He also felt that the trading away or criticism of popular players negatively impacted the team, as well as the lack of television broadcasts of Braves games in Milwaukee. Increased ticket prices also damaged the team's gate receipts.[57]

Beer, Rowdiness, and Petitions

A legendary tale of Milwaukee Braves lore was the infamous beer ban imposed on the County Stadium faithful in 1961. At a time of competing franchises and ongoing needs to maximize revenues, it is hard to believe that fans were allowed to carry in beer as late as 1960 and even later, after the ban was repealed. Eight years previous, when the Braves first played in Milwaukee, stadium manager Frederic M. Mendelson saw the ballpark as a "public facility where beer is sold," so how could "you stop people from bringing their own?" Some complained about drunkenness as "groups of fans are bringing in as much as a case or two of beer." Mendelson said the biggest problem was "vandals pouring beer or water from the runways leading to the upper deck. For the most part, this has been the work of teenagers. I don't see that stopping fans from bringing their own beer would have any effect on this." There was no real history of throwing beer bottles at umpires or players, even dating back to the Borchert Field days, according to Mendelson. Finally, no ban by County Stadium officials would hold up without an ordinance passed by county officials.[58]

Originally proposed in 1955, 1957, and again in 1959, the ban on beer would dramatically impact attendance in a city known for frugality and free beer to brewery workers. When county officials proposed an ordinance in 1955, it was joined by proposals to prohibit people from throwing objects in the ballpark and to reduce the price of beer from thirty cents to twenty-five cents for a twelve-ounce cup. The former ordinance was obviously a safety issue, and the latter reflected a belief that the current price of beer created a "financial hardship for the average consumer of liquid refreshment."[59] Some suggested that only fans who could not afford thirty cents for a beer should be allowed to bring their own. Another reason for the ban was the refuse that beer created. At one doubleheader in August 1957, stadium workers cleaned up nearly sixty thousand beer cans and bottles. Bottles also presented a safety concern, versus the paper cups in which beer was served at stadium concessions.[60]

In February 1961, the county board discussed implementing the beer ban as well as beer and liquor consumption in the Teepee Room. The Parks and Recreation Committee again recommended a ban on carrying beer, booze, soda, or any other bottled and canned items into the ballpark. Questions also

arose about whether the Braves' beer license covered serving cocktails to reporters and other media who use the Teepee Room when covering the team.
Tebbetts and McHale responded they would most likely stop serving it if that
practice were determined to be illegal. In regard to carry-ins, Tebbetts said he
and other club officials believed it caused "much of the rowdiness" witnessed at
County Stadium and noted that Milwaukee was the only major league franchise
that allowed it. Eliminating carry-ins would limit drunkenness at the ballpark,
as did the prohibition of concession workers to sell beer to drunken patrons.
Some area tavern owners opposed the ban because many of their customers
bought beer at their bars to take to County Stadium. No matter how this issue
was resolved, the fans in the stands would be paying more to drink beer at
County Stadium.[61]

Before Opening Day in 1961, the County Board passed an ordinance that
prohibited fans from carrying beer or other products in glass or cans into the
ballpark. Some fans were upset enough to organize the Committee for Beverage
Carry-Ins at Milwaukee County Stadium, which appealed the decision to no
avail. County Stadium was now like other ballparks in banning carry-ins. The
Milwaukee Journal editorialized that there was no more of a right to "carry six-
packs into the Stadium than into a theater, for instance." It stated that "organized labor's plea for repeal of the ban has nothing to do with public policy; its
interest is beer sales promotion." If the ban were sustained, perhaps there would
be some uniformly aroused people to go to work "on open housing or completion
of expressways or urban renewal."[62] Milwaukee police and county sheriff's
departments were tasked with enforcing what would become one of County
Stadium's most fan-unfriendly moves. Police patrolled inside County Stadium
while the sheriff's deputies covered the parking lots. Patrons seen carrying
banned items toward the gates would be warned. If the contraband made it to
the turnstiles, ticket takers would say that the items were not allowed in the park
and would have to be checked at a station. Uncooperative patrons would be
refused entrance to the stadium. Ushers were to keep on the lookout for banned
products and to call police if necessary.[63]

Some intrepid Braves' fans took legal action to get the ban repealed and,
bearing petitions, crowded the Milwaukee County Courthouse for a hearing.
While the Parks and Recreation Committee voted to indefinitely postpone any
discussion on a repeal, the movement transcended the committee's ability to
control the issue. One county supervisor argued if County Stadium were
"properly policed, there will be no need for this ordinance." Since the ban, he
said, busloads of patrons were no longer coming to the games, and many could
not afford to purchase beer at games. In effect, it appeared that the sole purpose

for the ban was to get County Stadium patrons to pay inflated prices at concession stands.[64] The case against the ordinance ended up in Milwaukee Circuit Court before judge Ronald Dreschler. The baseball patrons argued that the ban was unconstitutional and a personal invasion of their rights when they attended baseball games at County Stadium. Dreschler ruled that the ordinance violated no property rights and Braves fans had no "inherent right" to carry beer into the stadium. He noted that the risk of injury from bottles or cans thrown around the stadium seemed negligible because there had been only 442 recorded injuries among more than fifteen million fans who had attended games at County Stadium since 1953. Dreschler added, "At times the many must be limited because the few cannot otherwise be controlled." The demand for cheaper beer did not sway the judge.[65]

"Maybe they thought I didn't know that"

The Braves were no closer to a pennant than they had been when Dressen was hired almost two years earlier. On September 2, with twenty-five games remaining in the 1961 season and the Braves seven games out of first place, he was fired. Dressen was caught off guard and on the verge of tears when informed that he was no longer the Braves' manager. With the team near the top in the standings, at 71–58, Dressen was shocked to no longer be at the helm. Talking with a sportswriter in the manager's office at County Stadium, he said that they "just told me I was through" and even worse, they "didn't even tell me why or who the new manager was. They didn't have to tell me who it is going to be. Tebbetts has wanted the job for some time. Maybe they thought I didn't know that."[66] McHale told Dressen that the firing was timed "to ensure him sufficient time in the event other Major League managing jobs become available." Dressen said that "these things happened before and are part of baseball."[67]

The most surprising move regarding Dressen's dismissal was Tebbetts's resignation as executive vice president in order to take the position on the field. Contradicting previous statements in regard to Tebbetts's role with the club, McHale said that Perini had wanted him as the manager for a while. It was when "Birdie let his availability known, we acted" and the team "can hardly say, in view of our decision, that we were entirely satisfied with performance of the Braves under Dressen." Responding to the announcement of Tebbetts as manager, Dressen said the Braves "had so many vice presidents, what were they going to do with them?"[68]

In 1966, when asked why he had been fired five years earlier, Dressen still did not know but said he was "going to find out the real story about it some day." If Tebbetts did not want the job, "I might still be there." He said he was liked by Perini, McHale, and Tebbetts and was told by the Braves general manager that his firing was "the toughest thing he ever had to do." He added that Tebbetts was "supposed to become president" but when it was apparent that was not going to happen, "He had to have somewhere to go." Tebbetts "was sure he was going to be the manager the following year" and therefore change was inevitable. Perini later told him "he'd made a mistake firing me. Some day I'll find out why."[69] Most likely he never did before he suffered a fatal heart attack several months later, in August 1966.

Personnel Changes

The move to replace Dressen was perhaps not without merit. The team had made some significant changes in personnel to make a playoff run in 1961, and coming up short had impacted attendance. Dissatisfaction with the team's on-field performance led to an angry front office and ongoing second-guessing by fans. Dressen had a hard time dealing with some of the players and coaches, and the team had some troubling personalities. Oliver Kuechle wrote that these personalities were "slobbered over when the Braves came here in 1953," and they were the ones "who got so many things for nothing from fans that they really thought they were making a contribution to civilization, personalities who in many instances didn't know what to do with this adulation." Therefore, how could any manager "ever be popular with men who have been conditioned for eight years in this way?" McHale said he "never bought the idea that a manager should be judged by his popularity with his players. I have seen too many good managers and coaches who were not unanimously liked by the players, and too many of the other kind who were." The front office expects the team to "do as well, if not better, the rest of the season. It means that, rather than giving up in the pennant race this year, we are trying to improve our chances."[70]

For his part, Tebbetts said Perini had told him his "work in the front office was completely satisfactory," but he missed the game as it was played and wanted to be in the dugout rather than the Braves' offices.[71] With that, he became the fourth manager in nine years in Milwaukee. Tebbetts knew that people found it difficult to "understand how a man who had an executive position with the Braves and could have had the presidency at any time he wanted would give all that up for the insecurity of being a manager." He added that he and McHale were too often doing work together "that one man could have handled" but "I am not eliminating myself from another executive job in baseball by taking this job." The only concern appeared to be getting a uniform big enough to fit Tebbetts before their scheduled doubleheader against the Chicago Cubs. He did not plan on utilizing a curfew to keep his players in check and would let the players themselves "set a time after night games, say two hours after they get back to the hotel. Of course, it's always midnight after a day game or a night off." Furthermore, he said, he would not personally check to make sure the players were in, but he did "get around town quite a bit and if somebody's out, they're liable to run into me." This was the opposite of Dressen and his approach to handling players.[72] The club won twelve of their remaining games under Tebbetts and finished fourth in the National League.

Three weeks later, after more than four years as the president of the Milwaukee Braves, Joseph Cairnes was replaced by John McHale. Lou Perini came to Milwaukee to formally announce the change and said Cairnes would remain with the Perini Corporation as the vice chairman of the board. McHale had actively led the team since Tebbetts resigned and left the day-to-day operations to the general manager. Cairnes had moved to Florida shortly before Tebbetts was hired in August 1958 as executive vice president.[73] McHale later announced that there were some substantial changes to the front office, although he would retain the responsibilities of the general manager. Bill Eberly was promoted from ticket manager to business manager, Austin Brown was named director of ticket sales and customer relations, and Ralph Delforge was named comptroller and assistant secretary.[74] Delforge, also an officer in the parent Perini Corporation, would also serve as the club's auditor. McHale stated the moves would allow the president to "circulate on all sides of the team operations" and this would make the front office a "more successful and stronger" operation.[75]

Milwaukee County Stadium as originally designed is nearing completion in 1953. (Milwaukee County Historical Society)

Frederick C. Miller and his family at County Stadium. Miller was essential in the building of the stadium and bringing the Braves to Milwaukee. (Historic Photo Collection / Milwaukee Public Library)

An early game for the Milwaukee Braves at County Stadium. The grandstands feature temporary chairs and the bleachers are not yet completed. (Milwaukee County Historical Society)

A night game at County Stadium in the mid-1950s. The parking lots are full and there are temporary bleachers along the outfield and baselines. Fans stand in a line around the bullpens near the scoreboard. (Milwaukee Journal Collection / Milwaukee Public Library)

Fans welcome Braves players and officials. (Milwaukee County Historical Society)

The 1956 Braves began a streak of four great seasons that included two National League pennants and the World Series championship in 1957. They also finished in second place twice to the Dodgers. (Historic Photo Collection / Milwaukee Public Library)

By April 14, 1959, the grandstands and the bleacher seating at County Stadium had been expanded. Perini's Woods can be seen in straightaway centerfield. The parking lot in the foreground is where Miller Park stands today. (Historic Photo Collection / Milwaukee Public Library)

Former Brave's owner Lou Perini (*left*) with traveling secretary Donald Davidson (*center*) at the press conference announcing the sale of the team to William Bartholomay (*right*). (Milwaukee Journal / Bob Buege Collection)

The new owners of the Milwaukee Braves (*from left*): Thomas Reynolds, James McCahey Jr., John Louis Jr., Daniel Searle, William Bartholomay, and Delbert Coleman. Team president John McHale is seated in front of the group. (Journal Sentinel Inc.)

Milwaukee County Board Chairman Eugene Grobschmidt (*left*). While he may have been difficult to work with, Grobschmidt's passion for Milwaukee County never waivered. (Milwaukee Journal Collection / Milwaukee Public Library)

Milwaukee County Executive John Doyne with his "Back the Braves" card. (Milwaukee County Historical Society)

The team heads on to the field for the last home game of the Milwaukee Braves, September 22, 1965. (Milwaukee Sentinel / Dave Klug Collection)

The Milwaukee Braves Booster Teen Group displaying their disdain for the team's decision to move to Atlanta. (Dave Klug Collection)

A fan steps on a program at the last home game of the Milwaukee Braves. Perhaps no photograph displays better the anger Milwaukee fans felt over the team abandoning them for Atlanta. (Milwaukee Journal / Dave Klug Collection)

Edward Tuchalaski, a Milwaukee County employee, points to the scoreboard that was ready for Opening Day 1966 in the event the Braves were ordered back to Milwaukee. (Ernie W. Anheuser of the Milwaukee Sentinel, Journal Sentinel Inc.)

Judge Elmer Roller (*center*) with a copy of his decision regarding the Braves. While it temporarily made Milwaukee fans happy, his decision was ultimately overturned on appeal to the Wisconsin State Supreme Court. (Journal Sentinel Inc.)

This photo collage was hanging at Turner Field in 2016. It indirectly puts the blame on the Milwaukee fans for the team's relocation to Georgia. The caption reads, "The Braves' young talent included Hank Aaron and Eddie Mathews. They won the World Series in 1957 and followed it with a NL pennant in 1958, but attendance had already begun to drop somewhat. This trend was accelerated when the team failed to contend in the early 1960s, and by 1966 Milwaukee had lost their team to Atlanta, the team it had greeted so enthusiastically in 1953."

5

Something New

1962–1963

There is every reason to believe the Braves and Milwaukee
were meant for each other.

Lloyd Larson, *Milwaukee Sentinel*,
April 10, 1963

The Beginning of the End

For almost a decade, baseball fans across Wisconsin and a good portion of the
Midwest had embraced the Milwaukee Braves. There were record attendances,
stadium expansions, unforgettable nights at County Stadium, a world championship, and two National League pennants. Braves fans were willing to travel to
see their beloved team play, even when on the road. But changes were coming
for the Braves in ways that no one could have predicted when the team first arrived from Boston. Lou Perini, once hailed as a hero for bringing his forlorn
and virtually unloved Boston Braves to Milwaukee, sold the team on November
16, 1962, and a new ownership group promised a positive direction for the ball
club. Seemingly dedicated to keeping the team in Wisconsin, it indeed offered
something new.

In early February 1962, Braves president John McHale announced that for
the first time since the team left Boston, the Braves lost money. During the 1961
season, the team needed to draw about 1.5 million "to break even and we only
drew 1,100,000. If it hadn't been for the expansion draft, we would have lost a
lot more," as the money they received from the New York Mets and Houston
Colt .45s did not "quite make up the difference." McHale believed that the
Braves had the highest priced team in the National League. Expenses included

103

travel, a farm system that encompassed eleven teams, twenty-six scouts, public relations, and player salaries. They also spent an unprecedented amount on promotions, fireworks, and other displays on behalf of the Braves. The team would do better in 1962, but McHale reminded all that when they "were drawing two million fans a year, we were spending tax dollars for players. Now that we're down to one million, we're spending operational dollars." This meant that the Braves would "probably spend about one-third as much for players as we did last year." Radio broadcast rights enhanced revenue by an estimated $275,000 per year, although this would not cover the estimated shortfall. As usual, WTMJ and WEMP would broadcast all regular season games and many of the spring training games, with play-by-play by Earl Gillespie and Blaine Walsh.[1]

"The most controversial item in the stadium"

Relations between the county board and the Braves continued to be contentious at best, if not toxic, even over a peripheral matter within food safety. The Parks and Recreation Committee had recommended an ordinance that required all individuals who handled food for the county to have a physical examination once a year and to report any communicable diseases. In proposing the ordinance to the full county board in mid-March 1962, supervisor Marty Larsen argued that "the county is doing everything to provide sanitary food handling." The ordinance impacted any employee who served food for the county, including the House of Corrections, the jail, parks, and, of course, County Stadium. Concessions manager Earl Yerxa noted that of his 535 employees, many work only once or twice during a year, most likely Opening Day, when crowds were expected to be enormous. Getting some of these workers might be more difficult if they were required to have a physical to work a single game.[2]

Prices of items sold at County Stadium, as established by the team and the county board, was another area of contention. McHale argued that the sales tax was difficult to enforce and collect, especially when "unit prices are small," and turns County Stadium into a "penny arcade" with a "slowdown of service, customer irritation, and employee frustration." Consequently, he wanted to roll the tax into existing ticket prices, even though it would cost the team a significant amount of revenue and reduce "our gross profit margin on ticket sales." Also, because the Braves were "committed to the idea that we offer the community a wholesome brand of family entertainment" and wanted to "serve the youth of Milwaukee," the team wanted to raise the price of beer, most likely to reduce drunkenness at the stadium.[3]

The price of beer was also in response to a 3.5 percent sales tax on all items sold at the stadium, including tickets. Ralph Delforge, Braves secretary and assistant treasurer, reasoned that raising the price of a bottle of beer a nickel would cover the tax, keep prices the same for other concessions, and spare concession workers from handling pennies. The team also said it planned to sell "shorty" beers for twenty cents and regular beers for thirty-five cents. The Parks and Recreation Committee pounced on Delforge's suggestion, one supervisor saying the Braves picked "the most controversial item in the Stadium. . . . Couldn't you pick something else?" Another supervisor threatened that if the team raised the cost to thirty-five cents, a repeal of beer carry-ins would be in front of the county board by the following week. Another issue concerned whether the team was contractually obligated to sell only Milwaukee-based beer. Selling other Wisconsin beers at County Stadium might lower the price to twenty-five cents. The Braves would not be obligated to promote the outside beer, but fans should have the choice. The Milwaukee Arena was currently selling beer for thirty-five cents, with minimal complaints or objections. Delforge said that he did not think this issue would "create that much of a furor." The Braves also seemed to back a partial repeal of the carry-in ban.[4]

In the end, beer was priced at thirty-one cents per bottle, and a movement to repeal the carry-in ban remained strong. Prices of other concessions were adjusted in an effort to absorb the recently enacted Wisconsin sales tax. Concession manager Earl Yerxa said the team adjusted all of its prices about five minutes after the county board refused to roll the sales tax into a higher beer price, which would have made up for a tax increase on all other items. He added that he was "going to be a stinker about this" as prices went up on all items: thirty-six cents for bratwurst and hamburgers, twenty-six cents for hot dogs, and twenty-one cents for a cup of soda. Parks and Recreation Committee chair Marty Larsen said the Braves' price hikes on popular items appeared to be retaliation for the county's refusal to authorize the beer increase. County supervisor Cornelius Jankowski announced that he would reintroduce a repeal of the carry-in ban at a scheduled hearing before Larsen and his committee. Supervisor Edward Lane said that the team made $1.54 profit per case of beer and had sold about seventy-five thousand cases in the last year. But, he did not want to suggest the Braves were "profiteering" on beer sales.[5]

On June 5, the Milwaukee County Board voted 14–10 to repeal the carry-in ban on cans of beer but bottles remained prohibited at County Stadium. The Parks and Recreation Committee opposed any repeal on the grounds of safety for fans, although there was no record of a fan at County Stadium having been hit by a flying beer can.[6] It did not take long for the repeal to impact the ballpark experience in Milwaukee. June 29, 1962, saw a brawl between Cubs and Braves fans that was triggered when John Meroni, police chief of Hainesville, Illinois, threw a cup of beer in the stands. Two others joined in the fray, and three Illinois men were arrested. Milwaukee police said it was now apparent that the repeal meant more beer was consumed at the park. Were people bringing more beer to games just to spite the ban? Despite the problem at this game, police believed that they had a sufficient presence at games to prevent future incidents from escalating.[7]

No More Joy in Beertown

An article by Walter Bingham of *Sports Illustrated* in July 1962 highlighted the attendance decline in Milwaukee that was now evident to the rest of the nation. In the heady days, players could not "spend a dime" because the local merchants "gave them food, wristwatches, cars, beer, anything they wanted." The town of Cedarburg, Wisconsin, "with a population of 2,500, ordered 3,000 tickets to one game and filled every seat." Since their World Series win in 1957, however, and peak attendance, Braves fans had been dwindling—not "surprising since fans seem to lose some of their interest when their team becomes an overdog." The crowds at County Stadium went from 2.2 million in 1957 to 1.7 million in 1958 and 1.1 million in 1961. The gate at County Stadium probably would not even break eight hundred thousand by the end of the 1962 season.[8]

This situation was, of course, a real concern in the Braves hierarchy. Some believed it was simply "a return to normalcy," and while it was not good, several other baseball teams were struggling through worse declines. Bingham noted that in the nine years since the euphoric entrance of the Braves down Wisconsin Avenue, it was now "almost as if the town, stuffed full with the Braves and baseball, decided to give them up completely." A local hotel clerk said that they "used to be packed tight on weekends" and now they "never fill anymore. And tickets! I saw $1.80 tickets go for $10. Now you can't give them away." Bingham cited such reasons for the decline as Wisconsin fans' going to Minnesota for Twins games, the trading away of popular players, and the rise in ticket and parking prices. But perhaps the "unkindest cut was last year's law prohibiting fans from carrying in their own beer into the park. The law, now repealed, was a master stroke of public relations ineptitude in a town that likes to think that it invented beer." The team's position near the bottom of the National League also contributed. Worse were the rumors that Perini would move the team again. Bingham thought this was unlikely despite Perini's complaint that you "can't compete in the market for players with clubs that consistently outdraw you, as Walter O'Malley said when he took the Dodgers from Brooklyn to Los Angeles."[9]

Milwaukee had proven it "could support a major league team in grand style when it wants to and, perhaps more important, there are no longer many places left to go," said Bingham as he pondered what Perini could do to rectify the situation. He could sell the team, "and he probably will, despite statements" made to the contrary. It is also possible that he "may be urged by the board of directors to unload the Braves purely for business reasons. The team is part of the vast Perini Corporation that deals in construction and real estate, among other things." When the company had gone public in June 1961, the Braves had reportedly been "an outstanding financial and competitive success," but by the end of the year the team had lost money and was likely to do so again in 1962. This was not good news as the price of Perini stock had dropped by half along with dividends. If Perini was to sell the team, Bingham said, whoever purchased it "must face the problem of coaxing people back to the ball park." McHale was puzzled that "so many people just don't seem to care anymore" and the team was now down "to our hard-core fans."[10]

"If I thought it were some disease affecting us locally"

Renewal of the Braves' stadium lease was the subject of a special meeting of the Milwaukee County Park Commission in late July 1962. The prospect of television revenues and their financial impact on the team and its use of County Stadium was of particular interest. Some county board members fretted about money the county would lose, including its percentage of ticket sales, concessions, and parking if fans watched the games from the comfort of their own homes or the local tavern. Televising even a few home games would negatively impact future attendance and should be prohibited within a fifty-mile radius of Milwaukee. The county would also have to be compensated for the losses of parking revenues. County Stadium manager William Anderson stated that the Braves originally "were dead set against televising any road games and that has changed now." He said he had no knowledge of the team wanting to telecast local games, "but that doesn't mean they might not be considering it."[11]

There was considerable discussion about the falling attendance and what it meant, particularly in light of the negative article in *Sports Illustrated*. Park commissioner Walter Bender commented, "If I thought it were some disease affecting us locally or something that has affected all teams—that will be raised as a talking factor by the Braves themselves, there is no question about that." Another concern was liability to Milwaukee County for incidents occurring in parking areas around the ballpark. The team was responsible for incidents during games, but the county had paid for damage caused by fresh paint in the stadium and mud in unpaved sections of the parking lot. Concern persisted over handling of food and other products sold inside the stadium. Under the existing contract, the county was responsible for inspecting all items, and one staff member asked, "Why should we do it?" After a series of discussions, the commission recommended that the Braves begin the process of reworking the stadium lease for the best interests of both parties.[12]

"The mouthy type of manager"

After slightly more than one season with the manager who could have been president, the Braves were forced to look for a new skipper when Tebbetts, somewhat expectedly, resigned in early October 1962 to take the same position with the Cleveland Indians. Unlike a year earlier when Dressen was fired, McHale said there was no one in mind yet. Several names were mentioned as possible successors, but Bobby Bragan was most likely to get the head position, Tebbetts said, because the Braves had already offered him a coaching job. McHale said he barely had time to inform Perini before the announcements were made. He added that the team regretted "seeing Birdie leave. He did a fine job for the rebuilding job that had to be done. But we wouldn't want a man to stay with us if he wanted to be somewhere else."[13] The next manager should "be a man young enough to have the necessary fire but mature enough to have acquired the necessary experience." Speculation swirled around several prospective candidates, including the current catcher, Del Crandall. However, all signs seemed to point to Bragan, a former manager and a current scout for the Houston Colt .45s.[14]

As the Braves moved forward, unbeknownst to all, the selection of the next manager would turn out to be the last in a line that had started with Charlie Grimm. Over the past ten years, the Milwaukee Braves had experienced the Grimm, Haney, Dressen, and finally Tebbetts eras of management. Each brought his own style, and all won more than they lost. But the concern that the team was drifting under Tebbetts was dealt with when Bragan, the former Pittsburgh Pirates manager, replaced him. McHale introduced the extroverted Bragan on October 17, 1962, and said that he liked "the mouthy type of manager." Bragan said that he was "on cloud nine" and the "players and fans will know when I'm around. I'll be in sight a good deal of the time." He felt that the team was in good shape because it "has a lot of experience, a lot of good ball players. I have seen the club's personnel for some years now and I think we all can get the job done."[15] Bragan added, "I don't know a better place to manage than in Milwaukee. I'm convinced the Braves have the nucleus to be a contender again."[16] Bragan later said that he "had never been as well received in all my life" and everyone "has been wonderful to me" in Wisconsin. Growing up in Alabama made him familiar with "southern hospitality, but it has nothing on Milwaukee." He promised that the organization would "do things about making this club a contender again" and put "Milwaukee back where it belongs as a great baseball city."[17]

Bragan was well received by local sportswriters, who were later accused of belittling Braves decisions and engendering hostility toward the ball club. Oliver Kuechle wrote that Bragan appeared to fill the need of the club, as his experience as a player, coach, manager, and scout would help him develop the young players that were the Braves' future. Lloyd Larson "had the definite feeling that the Braves had picked wisely" and "had come up with the man who has what it takes to get the club back in serious pennant contention." Red Thisted acknowledged that Bragan was "sometimes rash, usually brash" but now seemed to have matured. The team "has experience, a lot of good ball players and I am certain we will all get along real good" and "can get the job done." Thisted noted that the fifth-place finish in 1962 did not help attendance, which "dropped to a new low," and a "shot in the arm is what is expected from Bragan." He also believed, like Kuechle and Larson, the "Braves are in good hands."[18] All seemed to embrace a manager they would later come to question.

"I've never said I'd sell the Braves at any time"

Speculation that Perini would either sell the team or relocate had persisted ever since the team arrived in Milwaukee. It was reported in June 1954 that "the Perinis may sell the Braves after this season and have placed a $4,500,000 price tag on the club." It was reported that Perini's wife wanted him "to get out of baseball because he is away from home too much." Speculation that he was preparing to sell the club to Fred Miller (before his death in 1954) bothered Perini. He later testified he was not considering selling it to Miller or anyone else, although he had said publicly after Miller's death that he would have sold the team to the local icon. He continued to deny the club was for sale to "anyone else in the foreseeable future. I have repeatedly told you that the ball club is not for sale, and perhaps now that I put it in print it may be more convincing to you."[19] During the World Series in 1958, Perini said he had an unexpected offer from Hal Roach Jr., the son of a Hollywood producer, who "said he understood that win or lose, I was ready to sell the club, and he asked that I promise to give him the first chance at buying it." The Braves' owner replied that "I couldn't make any such promise" and "I don't know where people get those ideas, I've never said I'd sell the Braves at any time."[20]

In June 1962 friends of Perini were telling the media that his health was a concern and he was now in position to sell the team. The asking price for the Milwaukee Braves was projected at $7 million, although some in baseball thought the asking price might be a bit too high because the team did not own its stadium.[21] Along with rumors of selling were ongoing stories that the club was going to move. Reports of declining attendance coinciding with the team's struggle on the field were hard to ignore. After all, in four consecutive seasons attendance hit more than two million; in the other five years, it was more than a million. In 1962 the team was running more than 136,000 behind the previous year over twenty-seven home dates. There was ongoing concern over whether the club could handle all of its expenses, including salaries. McHale clearly stated that Perini had not discussed the possibility of moving the team because of Milwaukee's history. He said that baseball "is a game of peaks and valleys. It's a pure and simple fact that the performance of a ball club determines crowds. You've got to have a competitive club—one in the race. When we do, the fans will come out in force."[22]

Some blamed attendance on baseball itself, as games got longer. And after all, after nine years, it was hard to sustain past levels of enthusiasm. The Braves' concession to telecast a limited number of road games back to Wisconsin was hoped to increase existing fan interest in the team and engage new supporters. New advertising aimed to develop a stronger fan base across the region, such as knot hole promotions for children, ladies days, and special days for teenagers. Civic organizations and other groups were encouraged to take outings to County Stadium. The team did not oppose lifting the carry-in ban so that fans could take their own beer into the stadium. The front office worked aggressively to revamp the team, increase its competitiveness, and make a run at another pennant.[23]

One can only guess that Perini feared the Milwaukee franchise would go into the same death spiral that it had in Boston between 1948 and 1952. In 1966 Furman Bisher, a sports reporter for the *Atlanta Constitution*, wrote in *Miracle in Atlanta: The Atlanta Braves Story* that McHale approached him in the summer of 1962 and made it clear that Perini was interested in the Atlanta territory and thought it would make a good market for major league baseball. He further stated that Perini was considering moving the Braves again and Georgia was a potential destination. Kuechle of the *Milwaukee Journal* later testified that he believed a meeting between Atlanta and McHale took place.[24] There is no reason to doubt the veracity of Bisher's story, and it does match the pattern

Perini used to move the Braves from Boston to Milwaukee. Whether Perini, as the principal owner of the Braves, would have moved the team to Atlanta is not clear, as the team was sold weeks after the proposed meeting between Bisher and McHale in September. In late October 1962 a broker notified a group of investors that the National League Baseball Club of Milwaukee might be up for sale.[25]

William C. Bartholomay and Thomas A. Reynolds, both of whom were previously minority owners and on the board of directors of the Chicago White Sox, spearheaded the group that purchased the Braves. The current team president, John McHale, joined the new group as a fellow owner, as did John Louis Jr., Daniel Searle, Delbert Coleman, and James McCahey Jr., a nephew of the late Fred Miller. While most of the men lived and worked in Illinois, all had connections to Wisconsin.[26] For the next three weeks, the broker worked on behalf of Bartholomay to complete the purchase. Bartholomay's consortium was not given the Braves' fiscal records to examine, nor was it apparent that they asked for "information concerning the financial history of the Braves." The decline in attendance was presumed to reflect the Perini ownership and could be corrected in the near future.[27]

The group who purchased the team from the Perini Corporation designated their new holding company the Milwaukee Braves Baseball Club Inc. and named the operating club the Milwaukee Braves Inc. The latter was formally incorporated under the laws of Delaware on November 15, 1962, and eleven days later, November 26, they obtained all the stock from the previous corporation. The final cost of the acquisition was $6,218,480, including brokers' fees, and the team was purchased primarily on credit. The syndicate made a down payment of $500,000, borrowed from the First Bank of Chicago on short-term personal loans. They also secured a $3 million loan from the First Wisconsin National Bank and an additional $1.5 million from the First National Bank of New York.[28] The group made up for the remainder in personal loans. Perini retained the largest single block of stock, but it was only 10 percent of the voting stock of the new team.[29]

At the time of the sale, half of the Braves' income came from receipts from home games, a percentage of road games, and spring training games. Radio and television rights added an additional 20 percent to the coffers, almost equal to the revenues generated from "the sale of food, beverages and merchandise" at County Stadium. There was also the prospect of additional monies if the team reached the World Series. With the sale of the team to the ownership group, a new legal entity rose from the ashes of Perini's Milwaukee Braves. The old company was liquidated and all of its assets were transferred to the new team.

At the time of the sale, the team had "ownership of or working agreements with seven minor league clubs," and beyond the major league roster there were "approximately 160 additional player contracts."[30]

"Never expected to sell"

On November 16, 1962, Perini hastily called a press conference at County Stadium. He arrived twenty minutes late and then shook up the baseball community with the announcement that he had sold the team to a syndicate of owners from Chicago. The timing of the sale seemed to strike the local media as somewhat expected, although there had been virtually no speculation about the immediate sale prior to its announcement.[31] Implying that his various construction endeavors and other commitments had prompted the sale, Perini stated that he "never expected to sell" but "the members of our corporate family, particularly myself, have found it more and more difficult to participate as fully as we would like in the affairs of the club" and to give the Braves front office "the backing" it deserved.[32]

Perini argued that because the Braves would remain "a Milwaukee-Wisconsin franchise, its continued success depends substantially on the loyal support of local organizations and top, active baseball men from Milwaukee and Wisconsin." Additional "civic minded fans from Wisconsin" would be part of the ownership group.[33] The team was in good hands, as the new owners lived nearby and were "vital, imaginative young men with baseball experience who will add much to baseball's leadership" and its future.[34] Having an absentee owner had been problematic, as had the direction, or lack thereof, of the team for several years. In addition, fifty-eight-year-old Perini's health was reportedly not as good as it should be, and it was time for him to slow down a bit.

Bob Wolf of the *Milwaukee Journal* speculated that another reason for the sale might have been the previous two seasons, 1961 and 1962, which had witnessed a tremendous decline in both attendance and results. Perini estimated that he had lost between $200,000 and $300,000 in revenue the previous year.[35] Whatever his motivation for selling the Braves, for the first time in two decades, there would be a new ownership group to lead the franchise. Perini remained as chairman of the executive committee and as a member of the board of directors.[36] A few years later, Perini said he had perceived a familiar pattern of failure, which prompted the move to Milwaukee in the first place: the Braves' fan base had soured on the management of the team and "there were wounds that could never be healed."[37]

Declining attendance concerns would have to be addressed by the new owners, as well as stadium lease negotiations for the immediate future. McHale later said it was unfortunate that "about that time the team ownership got restless with Milwaukee attendance-wise. They even lost our major television sponsor, Miller Brewing Company. Several seasons before the fact, rumors started circulating that the team would eventually move to Atlanta. It had to be a terrible distraction for anybody, a manager or a player."[38] Imagine what that did to the fans who had poured their hearts and souls into the team since 1953.

A Welcome to the New Braves Owners

The local community, including the press, welcomed the fresh owners and new direction for the Braves in Milwaukee. The owners released a prepared statement that called the Braves franchise "the finest in professional baseball," one that "already has a great baseball tradition and we are tremendously pleased to become part of it." They recognized the hard work and devotion of Perini, who had "championed baseball in Milwaukee, and we only hope that we can continue to build on his efforts." The local media granted authenticity to the new owners' statement that they wanted to "maintain" major league baseball in Milwaukee. They seemed to understand the "necessity for promotional innovations, solid management and public forthrightness required to maintain a successful operation in Milwaukee."[39] After "abominable public relations originated by former President Cairnes," baseball in Wisconsin was now refreshed. The syndicate was described as "young, enthusiastic, intelligent baseball buffs" who understood the situation in Milwaukee. It was presumed these men would have better relations with the county board, which had been in a long, public dispute with Cairnes during the stadium lease negotiations. There was optimism despite the lack of local connections of most of the new owners. They could relate "to Wisconsin people" because they "are not distant Massachusetts cousins" but from the Chicago area.[40] They could attend games at County Stadium more easily and more often than Perini did.

According the Kuechle, a hearty welcome was extended to the new owners because they had "restored my confidence in baseball and they will yours." Lou Chapman referred to this as "Phase 2" of the Braves experience in Milwaukee. The first was the Milwaukee Miracle under Perini; now it would be under "young executives, who average under forty years of age. They're dyed in the wool fans, with one important difference. They can hire and fire the ball players, although this responsibility they have thrust solely into the hands" of John McHale. None of the new owners would "be involved in the baseball operation," as that is the "quickest way to kill a franchise—letting the boys from the front office in the clubhouse," according to Bartholomay. The new Braves leadership was within fifty miles of Milwaukee and had some business-driven ideas for running the club. They were "interested first of all in creating a favorable image of local ownership. The Milwaukee franchise, in our opinion, has slipped in attendance and performance—and we believe this has roots in the former system of absentee ownership." They also wanted to "put into effect an expanded television program. We felt the fans were entitled to more TV and have worked out with county officials a change in terms of the lease." Additionally, the owners had "taken a hard look at the whole question of attendance and we're going to let a substantially larger number of youngsters into the park." They personally would take "no salary whatsoever, because our interest is developing a championship team and an enduring franchise rather than a quick income." Bartholomay said the owners would purchase their own tickets for games and, if they could not attend, would make their seats available to fans. He was optimistic about the future of the team and its attendance.[41]

"Milwaukee fans are still there and there are none better"

The decline in attendance at Milwaukee was not unique to Wisconsin or baseball in general. It did not mean that Milwaukee fans had soured on the team or that the special relationship that had been forged since 1953 was solely in the past. Instead, it meant that Americans had other ways to spend their time, as well as other sports and entertainment options. Even teams like the New York Yankees, the dominant team in the American League in wins, championships, and attendance, had seen their gate drop "sharply since the early 1950s." Arguably television bore much of the blame for the decline across all of baseball, and many believed that "televising home games kept people from coming to the park." Some teams thought they could increase attendance by eliminating home broadcasts and expanding coverage of road games.[42] But the Braves did not telecast home games and had only a limited road schedule. Television grew more popular, and telecasts of other sports, including professional and college football, could diminish interest in the Milwaukee Braves.

When Bud Selig retired as the commissioner of baseball in 2015, he recalled a statement in a speech by Oliver Kuechle at the Associated Press Managing Editors Association in December 1961. Kuechle called baseball a moribund sport because "it wasn't attracting the younger generation." Selig took great delight in pointing out that more than fifty years later, "baseball's more popular than ever."[43] Kuechle's speech came at a time of significant and disturbing drop in major league attendance and rising interest in professional and collegiate football. Televised football games were arguably easier to follow and more exciting than baseball. A viewer at home could see most of the football players during any given play, but, in baseball, only close-ups of a pitcher or hitter or a distant ball in play on the field. Conversely, some argued that it was the lack of baseball telecasts that allowed football to transcend baseball as America's game.

Whitey Gruhler, sports editor of the *Atlantic City Press*, said that if it had not been for the 1961 home run race between Roger Maris and Mickey Mantle in the American League, attendance would have been even worse. But he believed that football still had far too many limitations, such as a limited schedule, difficult rules, and a lack of modern stadiums. Baseball would remain on top because it "was easier to learn, requiring less intricate coaching and less monotonous rehearsing" and was far ahead of football in the development of young players.[44] Therefore, according to Gruhler, it would be "extremely difficult to shatter a long standing tradition" of the supremacy of baseball because it was well established and nationally understood. It had adhered "strictly to one set of long established rules, is as much a symbol of our nation as Uncle Sam or the American Eagle."[45]

The issues Kuechle raised were highly significant during this transition from baseball to football on the American landscape. Despite his personal belief, "the Milwaukee fans are still there and there are none better." After nine years when Braves' fans bought more tickets for home games than any other team, interest was still strong. Even when they were fourteen games out of first place in late June 1962, said Kuechle, this was "not bad when you consider the prosperity we have enjoyed and that eight other clubs are off" in attendance and "all but one of them, the Chicago Cubs, for less reason." He then struck at what he considered to be the heart of the matter: Many of the problems the Braves faced could be "traced to the front office." Cairnes "had the worst possible public relations" and often got belligerent with Milwaukee County officials. When the supervisors won the battle to raise the rent at the stadium, Cairnes "raised admission prices within twenty-four hours." Even worse, when the "federal government reduced the admission tax from 20 to 10 percent, the Braves had sold more than ten thousand season tickets. The purchasers had paid the 20 percent tax. Cairnes refused to refund the money."[46] Ultimately, all of these events contributed to declining numbers at the stadium.

21–3: The 1962 Stadium Lease

The stadium lease that the Braves negotiated turned out to be its last with Milwaukee County. Present for the preliminary discussions in the summer of 1962 were stadium manager William Anderson; Richard Falk of the Park

Commission; Park Commission general manager Howard Gregg; Gregg's delegated assistant, Bernie Memel; team president John McHale; and team secretary and assistant treasurer Ralph Delforge. Anderson later testified that over the course of five or six meetings, he "felt we should talk about at least a fifteen-year contract." According to Anderson, however, McHale wanted a three-year deal and was not interested in a lease of any other duration. Anderson acknowledged that it was probably "a mistake to consider more than a one-year lease."[47]

The new lease that emerged after a marathon session with the board, in December 1962, resolved several complex issues. The Braves could televise up to fifteen games at County Stadium if the team believed it would be advantageous. In an effort to protect the county's stadium investment, the previous agreement called for a punitive rental payment if the Braves telecast a single home game. Supervisors in opposition to the new agreement to televise games wanted more substantive stadium-driven revenues from the Braves. There was a failed attempt to amend the deal with an escalator clause that could have netted Milwaukee County an additional $38,000. McHale successfully argued that the amendment would materially change the agreement; the whole equation was "based on the fact that we don't begin to approach the break-even point until we draw one million people in any season." Under the new lease, the ball club would pay Milwaukee County 5 percent on the net receipts from the first one million fans, 7 percent on one and a half million, and 10 percent for any more than that. Supervisor Gerard Skibinski fought against telecasts of Braves games from County Stadium but was voted down 16–8. The Braves could now try out promotional broadcasts of home games over the next three seasons.[48] The final vote was 21–3 in favor of the new deal.

It's worth noting that the Parks and Recreation Committee's original proposal calling for a nine-year lease, which would keep the Braves in Wisconsin through 1971, was voted down. The deal also reduced the revenue that Milwaukee County would receive from gate and concessions, especially if attendance was low. The board met three times on December 11, 1962, to hammer out the contract. There was a strong concern that failure to complete an agreement by the end of the year would endanger the Braves' right to utilize County Stadium going forward. The county wanted a sliding scale on admissions, including a share of the gross sales of all merchandise. The old contract called for 15 percent of sales of most items sold at Braves games and 20 percent of receipts from other events held at the stadium. Under the new terms, the Braves paid the county 10 percent of sales under $800,000 and up to 16.5 percent if sales exceeded $1.7 million. County executive John Doyne was expected to approve the deal.[49] As a bonus for the region, Pabst, Miller, Schlitz, Blatz, and Gettleman could sell beer at County Stadium. The Braves, however, were not limited to just these local labels.[50]

The new lease was for three years instead of five years as previously; the county had legal leverage to keep the team locked in County Stadium until December 31, 1965. The Braves retained an option to extend the lease for two additional three-year periods, which could keep the team in Milwaukee until December 31, 1971. Among other changes was a clause, at the request of Anderson, that the Braves furnish the services of ushers, ticket sellers and takers, as well as other employees for football games, wrestling matches, concerts, and any other events. The Braves would pay them and be reimbursed by sponsors of the events. The Braves were granted the right to "review the Stadium projected maintenance and operation budget and any capital improvement items considered necessary to the stadium structure." Except for one hundred parking spots set aside for Braves employees, the team and the county would charge twenty-five cents per car. Parking and other financial terms were subject to renegotiation during the lease. Milwaukee County was responsible for first aid equipment at County Stadium.[51]

It is apparent in reviewing the negotiation process that the supervisors saw the Braves primarily as an additional revenue source for the county. Robert Russell, corporate counsel for Milwaukee County, later wrote that while the stadium was "a public facility in one sense" it was operated "as a proprietary function rather than a governmental function."[52] County officials sought to maximize receipts from the ballpark, while the Braves had to pay rent and fees at a time when attendance was down, not just in Milwaukee but across all of baseball. This three-year deal was acceptable to both sides but really beneficial to neither.

The Stock Sale

Concern over the team's immediate future in Milwaukee had prompted its owners to address falling revenues. Following the public ownership model of the Green Bay Packers, the Braves were prepared to offer a stock sale to raise operating capital. The team even appointed Vince Lombardi, the Packers' head coach and general manager, to the Braves board of directors. In February 1963, the Milwaukee Braves Inc. offered 115,000 shares of stock in the club at a price not to exceed $11.50 per share, in hopes of raising about $1.15 million, $900,000 of which would "be used to pay a bank note incurred to finance in part the acquisition from Perini Corp., and the balance will be used to provide working capital for operations of the baseball team."[53] Any unsold stock would be "purchased at the Subscription Price" by Milwaukee Braves Inc.[54] When the sale was completed, the current owners retained more than 50 percent of the ownership with the Perini Corporation holding 9 percent and the remainder went to the new stockholders.

The ownership group restricted the sale of the stock to Wisconsin residents in an effort to create a community-owned team atmosphere and new excitement for the Braves. So strong was this incentive that the team rejected international investors. Bill Bartholomay, the Braves' principal owner, later testified the team had targeted forty or fifty Wisconsin residents who might be in a position to purchase stocks "equal to the investments we made," but no one bought more than five hundred shares. Worse for the stock sale, Bartholomay said that only about thirteen thousand or fourteen thousand shares of the 115,000 were sold.[55] Approximately fifteen hundred people purchased stock, but most only a few shares. Thomas Reynolds, the Braves' executive vice president, said it was not "a question of raising money. The purpose was to rekindle local interest in the ball club. As per the prospectus, the remaining 85 percent of the stock was purchased by the "investors who own a controlling interest" in the team.[56] Willard S. Stafford, the special prosecutor for the State of Wisconsin, later said the stock sale was disappointing because it offered no voting interest in the operation of the team.[57] The Packers' five stock sales over the years were far more successful in drawing fans into the limited ownership of the Packers. Perhaps in Wisconsin, football had already transcended baseball, particularly at the height of the success of Lombardi's teams in the 1960s. One cannot help but wonder if the Braves would still be in Milwaukee if there had been more interest in purchasing stock.

Milwaukee and the Braves were a peerless match in baseball until 1961 when attendance was only half of that in 1957. Signs were abundantly evident that the fan base was losing interest in the team, a situation, according to the *Sentinel*'s Lloyd Larson, that could lead to separation and still later, divorce. But it appeared that all sides were working to reconcile and "there is not the slightest doubt that sound thinking people are hoping against hope that the Braves and Milwaukee will patch up their differences." He added that the Braves had benefited the entire region since arriving in 1953 by giving the city and state some nationwide and even "world-wide advertising and promotion" worth millions. This contribution to the economy across the region, including the fringes of neighboring states, "has been considerable." For Larson, the ten-year attendance total of 17,312,396 told the story. Furthermore, there was every reason to believe that "the Braves and Milwaukee were meant for each other. May they live happily together for years and years to come."[58]

It goes against popular interpretations, but it does seem apparent through the lens of time and distance that the new owners were originally dedicated to keeping the team in the Midwest. From their previous minority ownership of the White Sox and other business interests in Chicago, it is fair to say that, at least at first, the owners tried to solve the financial issues in Milwaukee. McHale later said that they "never had anything in mind but making the most of what we had in Milwaukee. We went in there determined to go full blast toward making it work to the best interest of the Milwaukee people and us. After all, that made good business sense."[59]

In May 1963 the Braves and Milwaukee County cleared up a shortfall in revenues owed by the team from the years 1959 to 1962 when a deficit of $1,396 had accumulated from rain checks. McHale wrote that "we feel that this whole matter has been inflated beyond its merits and are most concerned that the matter does not drag on any further." He added, "To dispose of it to our mutual satisfaction, we are enclosing our check covering the indicated deficiency." The check went to county supervisor Rudolph Pohl, chair of the county board's finance committee. It was a small matter—spanning four baseball seasons!—but it exemplified the frugality and assertiveness of the county board in protecting its interests at the ballpark. This state of affairs would get progressively worse as the next two seasons unfolded in nightmarish fashion for Wisconsin's Braves fans.[60]

"We plan to start moving rapidly in all directions"

In the early 1960s civic leaders in the city of Atlanta and Fulton County, Georgia, embraced what Glen Gendzel later called "Competitive Boosterism" when they looked to sports to enhance their region in the fledgling New South. Atlanta mayor Ivan Allen Jr. encouraged the business community to spend advertising money to promote Atlanta because "whatever was good for Atlanta was good for them." Highlighting his view of a new Atlanta was a sports stadium that, once it attracted a major league franchise, would give Georgia the big league status that Wisconsin had gotten in 1953. In June 1963, Atlanta officials and community leaders dedicated themselves to realizing Allen's dream of a modern municipal ballpark as part of an aggressive effort to get baseball and football to migrate to the South. Allen had appealed to Kansas City Athletics owner Charles O. Finley to bring his floundering club to Atlanta. Encouraged by Finley's interest, Allen began to push for the stadium when the goal of becoming a big league city seemed truly possible. The Atlanta stadium would, according to Allen, be "a Southern project, built on Southern soil, by Southern architects and contractors" and add big revenues to the local economy. Critics said it would provide entertainment for the wealthy and the middle class at the expense of education or other social spending in a decaying city.[61] To the contrary, said Allen's supporters, a stadium would benefit all citizens by providing jobs, entertainment, and that status of big league baseball. Allen asked if there was "any other area of activity where a city gets as much national publicity as sports?" He believed that the local minority population would embrace an Atlanta-based professional sports team. Sports were "a by-product of equal rights" and would add to the numbers of fans in the stadium built in a city that was "too busy to hate."[62]

After sitting relatively idle for almost four years, the Atlanta–Fulton County Stadium Recreation Authority (hereafter, Stadium Authority) was revitalized under the leadership of Coca-Cola president Arthur Montgomery Jr., who had pushed for a new stadium as part of Atlanta's urban renewal plan. The new stadium would have not only easy access to the new interstate system but also a downtown interchange, to be completed in mid-1964. It could draw fans from across the South; more than twelve million people lived within a four-hour drive of Atlanta. When they arrived, the new fans would find more than twenty-four thousand parking spaces currently in the downtown area, not including parking on the forty-seven-acre site of the ballpark. More parking could be added by clearing land through condemnation of existing properties. This would be the perfect spot to introduce professional sports to the South because Atlanta had a growing population, it was the financial center of the region, and it was one of the "great communications centers of the world," with nineteen radio and five television stations that carried all of the network affiliates. In addition, there were five daily newspapers and twenty-four community papers. Atlanta was more than a major sports town, it was "a great baseball town. It was a major league city in every category. It is completely ready for major league baseball."[63] Montgomery said that they would "plan to start moving rapidly in all directions" and "in making site and architectural studies and institution talks with major league baseball and football franchise owners." There had been quite a bit of talk about a municipal stadium in Atlanta over the years, "but we are past the talking stage now." He had been assured of cooperation from officials and leaders in the city, county, and state and we "mean business now." Montgomery also noted that several baseball team owners had already been in contact with him and asked when the stadium would be ready.[64]

"Atlanta is interested in a big league franchise"

The perceived failure of the Braves to attract fans in Wisconsin at the same pace as in their pennant winning days of 1957 and 1958 opened the door to many possibilities, including another shift of the franchise. Mayor Allen later testified that he had met with representatives of the Braves in July during the 1963 All-Star break to discuss the stadium and his attempt to land a franchise for the new ballpark. He denied that a deal was in place with Finley to move the team to Atlanta, so Allen and the Stadium Authority continued their efforts and were inviting all major league teams, "from the Yankees to the Dodgers." His meeting with the Braves was not to entice them to come to Atlanta, he said; the talks were more about baseball in general, but he and his group "spoke glowingly of its advantages and its attributes and its growth and development" and what was happening in Georgia. By early 1964, said Allen, the Braves' owners were severely disappointed with the response in Milwaukee and "were considering other places and Atlanta was foremost in their minds, yes sir, I don't think there was any doubt about that."[65]

Lou Chapman later wrote, and testified, that he had interviewed a Coca-Cola official who said that the Braves' owners had contacted him within two months of purchasing the team. Supposedly the Braves wanted to "become the first tenants of the new Atlanta Stadium."[66] In the middle of July 1963, the new ownership group was forced to deny reports by Bob Broeg, sports editor of the *St. Louis Post-Dispatch*, about meetings with Allen. Broeg said the Braves would most likely end up in Georgia if attendance did not rebound. He further insisted that he had learned of this possibility during the All-Star Game in Cleveland on July 9. Soon after this report went public, Bartholomay and McHale denied there had been any meeting between the Braves and Atlanta officials.[67]

Bartholomay did say Atlanta was "interested in a big league franchise" and "did have a delegation including the governor and mayor" at the All-Star Game to "explore possibilities." However, he said, "they did not approach us" and there "has been talk, of course, that the Cleveland franchise might be moved." Furthermore, the Braves "had a rebuilding job to do" in Milwaukee, which the owners believed past attendance showed was possible, and it was "up to us to stir it up again."[68] McHale told the press that the Braves still had a "three year lease in Milwaukee and many other commitments," were currently "rebuilding and didn't expect any miracles" in 1963. Low attendance was believed to be only "a temporary condition" and the "miracle of Milwaukee is expected again— but not this year."[69] Kuechle, however, later testified that the new owners "indeed had an unwavering interest in Atlanta since July of 1963."[70] Throughout the rest of the 1963 season, unconfirmed reports persisted that the Braves had already committed to move to Atlanta, possibly as early as the 1964 season, and new contracts for television and radio broadcasts awaited them there. Concern over this very real possibility prompted Wisconsin governor John W. Reynolds to threaten a congressional investigation if the team relocated.[71]

The Decisive Factor: Television

As rumors about the Braves leaving Milwaukee intensified, Arthur Daley, a Pulitzer Prize–winning sportswriter for the *New York Times*, addressed the subject. He opined that it was "disquieting" to hear that the team wanted to leave "from what was once a land of milk and honey for newer, but not necessarily greener, fields in Atlanta." It was distressing to see the "growing restlessness in the big leagues" as teams that witnessed attendance drops, including the Kansas City Athletics and the Cleveland Indians, were rumored to be looking for better, brighter homes. Daley cited three cities in particular that wanted major league baseball: "Atlanta, Oakland, and to a lesser extent, San Diego." He argued that the "quick success" the Braves had in Milwaukee made "the fast-buck guys eager" to cash in on the rewards. Teams rapidly moved in the aftermath, and nothing in baseball "was sacred." Expansion across baseball had "curbed the trend momentarily, but the restlessness has begun anew." Daley then added some concerning statements from Bartholomay. The Braves owner said that his group was going to "sit down at the end of the season and examine not only the past year, but where do we go from here? I would be less than honest if I told you we weren't disturbed by our attendance in Milwaukee." He added that while the team on the field finished strong, they drew only thirteen thousand to a heavily promoted Labor Day game. Daley wondered if "this newfangled game of musical chairs is the solution to baseball's attendance problems." He did not believe so, because it made baseball owners look like "marauding troops living off the countryside" who then moved on "after they have ravaged it and laid it bare. It is a cynical surrender to mercenary expediency that destroys the appealing image of what was once propagandized" as the "Great American Game."[72]

Television was considered to be the driving force behind the rumors of the Braves' transfer. The Associated Press reported that unless Milwaukee business and civic leaders could find a way to double existing revenues, the Braves were "a virtual certainty to be transferred to Atlanta before the start of the 1964 season." The front office did not have much hope of turning things around in Milwaukee, and although there was no commitment yet to move, only a complete change of heart by the owners would "keep the Braves from moving to Atlanta next season." The owners were sold on the idea of the fastest growing metropolis in the United States and lured by a five-year radio and television network deal that was worth at least $1.5 million annually. It was a deal the Braves could not turn down and Milwaukee could not match, said the AP, because of geographical limitations from neighboring franchises. If accepted, the deal would be the second highest in baseball behind only the New York Yankees. Despite the AP report, McHale said the Braves had made "no commitment to any city," including Milwaukee, for 1964. Bartholomay added that the ownership group would "sit down to discuss the future when the season is over." Officials of the Stadium Authority also denied the rumor the Braves were going to relocate for the upcoming season.[73]

Addressing the issue of money from radio and television, Kuechle wrote that ultimately the team would remain in Milwaukee because the market was still competitive compared with Atlanta. Geography—the Great Lakes and the neighboring Minnesota Twins and Chicago's Cubs and White Sox—limited broadcast revenues to $525,000 compared with the Houston Colt .45s, who got $1.5 million for their multistate deal. The Houston arrangement included money from the Schlitz Brewing Company, as did Milwaukee's deal. Milwaukee's populace was significantly larger than Atlanta's, 741,324 versus 487,455, while Wisconsin's and Georgia's were almost identical. Milwaukee also had a larger per capita income than Atlanta, $2,194 versus $1,652. Kuechle understood that Atlanta had a much higher upside in future broadcast deals. It had the entirety of the Southeast and no Lake Michigan or competing teams to impact revenues. In fact, baseball in Atlanta could "give the Braves the kind of money that Houston got. It is this which has caused the Braves' owners pause," in view of their investment in the team. As for the future of baseball, attendance was no longer the "decisive factor in whether a city has big league baseball or not—television and radio money are, mostly television."[74] Therefore, while Milwaukee could outdraw Atlanta in physical attendance, it ultimately could not compete with the riches of the entire American South.

"There are always rumors of a franchise shift"

On September 10, 1963, the Braves finally announced that they had been approached by several cities, including, in particular, Atlanta. Vice president Reynolds said they have "all been after us, but we're going to take a long, hard look before we do anything." Furthermore, any time a team had attendance problems "there are always rumors of a franchise shift." McHale acknowledged what many feared when he said they had "been approached by Atlanta. That group is persuasive. But the Atlanta people also have approached the Cleveland and Kansas City teams. They are persistent and they have big plans," but nothing had been discussed during the baseball meetings. It was also reported that the Atlanta group had lost hope of landing the Indians or the Athletics, and it was assumed the American League would block any move other than one to the West Coast. If Atlanta landed a team, it would spend 1964 in the minor league Ponce de Leon Park and move to the new stadium in time for the 1965 season.[75] In late September, multiple media sources reported that the Braves' move was almost definite unless things changed dramatically in Milwaukee and the team had a complete change of heart about the move. Still, team officials had already inquired about support within the National League if they chose to relocate.[76]

Advertising revenues for radio and television broadcasts remained critical in Milwaukee. Unless the Braves made at least $1.2 million on the next contract, they would most likely be on their way out of Milwaukee. Local business leaders remained optimistic that something could still be done to keep the team in Wisconsin. Lester Brann, executive vice president of the Association of Commerce, said he had not "accepted the fact that a decision has been made and there is no turning back."[77] Complicating the financial situation in Milwaukee was another downturn in attendance, which declined for the fifth year in a row since the record-setting 2.2 million in 1957. Despite all efforts to promote the team under the new owners and reports that the Braves might leave, fewer than eight hundred thousand crossed the turnstiles in 1963. It went "practically without saying that a change for the better is vital as other cities with big league ideas continue to cast covetous eyes on the valuable Milwaukee franchise," wrote Lloyd Larson. Rumors of Atlanta continued to swirl, and the new ownership "said nothing about being committed to Milwaukee, win or lose." The failure of "solid promotions designed to win new friends and influence the old" and a rebuilt team had resulted in poor attendance. It was not implausible, said Larson, that the team could leave, which would be "humiliating, even tragic to an area that made history with the Miracle of Milwaukee." If attendance permanently spiked upward, the Braves might survive in Wisconsin; if not, "relocation could happen."[78]

"I'm glad Milwaukee can keep them"

On September 24, 1963, McHale issued a statement that haunts and angers Milwaukee Braves fans to this day. The new ownership of the Braves had listened to potential offers for relocation in response to declining numbers at County Stadium. It was "quite natural" for cities to seek out professional teams and to "solicit the interests of clubs whose attendance has declined, just as Milwaukee did in 1953."[79] McHale's statement was to "dispel confusion" over rumors that the team was leaving for better markets in search of temporary profits. He then made the most stalwart denial to date: "The Braves will be in Milwaukee today, tomorrow, next year, and as long as we are welcome." Normally "the results of a baseball operation and plans for the future are discussed at the end of the season. However, in this case, the Braves management feels that the air should be cleared."[80] Although the Braves board of directors had not met, Bartholomay "got in touch with all of them over the weekend. The decision was to do what was right not only to Milwaukee, but to the stability of baseball itself."[81]

McHale also said appealing "offers have been made to us by several cities, but our decision is to remain in Milwaukee." In Atlanta, Montgomery responded that they "gave it a good try" and the Stadium Authority had "hoped to get the Braves to come to Atlanta, but we found out that our stadium is inadequate for their needs." The owners "were nice enough to listen to us" and if "we can't have them, I'm glad Milwaukee can keep them."[82] Besides Atlanta, representatives from San Diego, Toronto, and the Dallas–Fort Worth metro area all expressed interest in attaining the Braves, but the new ownership group had bought the team as a "Milwaukee baseball club. We intend to keep it that way." The president acknowledged that offers from San Diego and Atlanta were well prepared and if the ownership group was "just looking for money, we weren't good businessmen in turning them down. We wanted to do what was right for Milwaukee and Wisconsin fans." Governor Reynolds said he hoped the team would remain permanently in Milwaukee, and that the state would do all it could to "assist them in building attendance" because the state had a tremendous investment in the Braves.[83]

Local officials received McHale's statement with much relief and excitement. Milwaukee mayor Henry Maier claimed it was "good news for the community and in my opinion an extremely sound decision." The threat of the Braves moving "may have been helpful in reminding Milwaukeeans of what an important asset they are." His office monitored "the situation closely from the very first rumor, and were in the process of preparing recommendations should the danger prove real." John Doyne responded that it had seemed more likely that the Braves would leave than remain. Their commitment to stay, he said, meant a lot to Milwaukee County and was worth about "a quarter of a million dollars" in baseball-generated revenues from County Stadium. Charles Wampler, president of the Greater Milwaukee Committee (GMC), said the Braves responded quickly and their "decision now places upon us an obligation to demonstrate that their faith in our city has been well placed." Moreover, the GMC advised McHale and his associates about the "enthusiastic efforts on the part of GMC members" that were available to the Braves "in any organized effort to sell season and individual game tickets and to promote special events." Robert Cannon, legal adviser to the Major League Baseball Players Association, said this was "the greatest news Milwaukee has had since the Braves came here. It's up to everybody now. And if the fans don't support them, no one can complain if they leave."[84]

The day after McHale's announcement, the Braves hosted the Cincinnati Reds to an intimate crowd of 4,744 at County Stadium. Officials closed off the upper grandstand for the game. "Considering the chilly weather and the fact that baseball interest generally wanes at this stage of the season" and the potential of a fourth-place finish, it was not as bad as it could have been. McHale said the team was not "looking for any miracles" and they understood the excitement of the season was over "except the fight for third and fourth place. You don't base your hopes on one night's performance. That is the beauty of baseball. It takes 162 games to make a season—not one." Tom Reynolds added that all of the Braves' efforts would be directed toward the 1964 season and the Braves would start "as soon as this season is over." The cold and mediocre performance of the club had more to do with the low attendance than an overall lack of interest in the team. Reynolds cautioned not to draw any conclusions about the poor turnout. Low numbers at late season games did not accurately reflect how the people felt about the Braves, who were no longer in contention, and the football season was drawing fans' attention. There was optimism that the last home stand of the year, against the Cubs, would draw between twenty-five thousand and thirty thousand, which might allow the Braves to exceed the previous year's attendance.[85]

But rumors about relocation of the Braves continued to percolate. National League president Warren Giles reported in November that expansion at this time was unwarranted. It "should not be seriously considered until the newest members of our leagues" are soundly organized and able to participate in future player allocation drafts. Giles did not believe that expansion would be feasible for some time to come and the existing owners were encouraged to remain a ten-team league. They currently had "sound ownership, new ball parks, good management, reasonably well balanced competition and all should strive for ways and means to increase attendance." This could, according to Giles, be accomplished by "jealously guarding the game's integrity, sound baseball promotions and making our games attractive and our fans comfortable." This meant the National League was not likely to expand in the near future. If Atlanta wanted a team in the senior circuit, an existing franchise, like the Braves, would have to transfer. For Milwaukee, if their beloved team left, it meant that no expansion team was on the horizon to fill the void of major league baseball in Wisconsin.[86] It was keep the Braves or lose baseball.

Go to Bat for the Braves

The attempt to build support for the Braves through the stock sale continued through the fall of 1963. On the day of McHale's announcement that the Braves were going to stay, the stock was selling at its best bid price since it had been released. Walter Wegner, the *Milwaukee Sentinel*'s business editor, wrote about an old Wall Street saying "that the market discounts what lies ahead and there may have been some premonitions early in the day that McHale and parties would not desert their loyal fans." To Wegner, the rising price of the stock could indicate demand and mean the Braves might stay and witness an upturn at the gate. He hoped that the "new and enthusiastic group of young businessmen" who ran the club would give the fans a contending team. However, Wegner noted, the sale was less than it should have been to date—approximately thirteen thousand shares of the original 115,000. The money generated would help the owners pay down the debt in the form of a bank note, "which was used to finance part the acquisition of the Braves from the Perini Corp." Again, the stock sale was designed to generate close to $1 million toward the debt accrued from the purchase of the Braves. The first payment to the First Wisconsin National Bank was paid on February 15; two payments of $500,000 were due on June 1 of 1966 and 1967; and the remaining $2 million was scheduled for June 1, 1968. Operating expenses for the team were escalating at a time when attendance was declining, putting the Braves in a precarious position moving forward. Milwaukee County also faced an economic loss as declining attendance reduced its revenues. Something had to give to either save the franchise in Milwaukee or make it economically competitive in a changing market.[87]

With the future of baseball in Milwaukee at stake, a group of civic leaders stepped forward in an effort to save the team and its Wisconsin future. The effort to generate more interest in the Braves was primarily aimed at the year ahead, through expanded season ticket sales, but at least two organizations attempted to boost attendance at the final home games. The Milwaukee Metropolitan Ford Dealers used radio spots to encourage fans to bring another person to a game to boost the final numbers "at least by one more person than last year's total attendance." Citizens Committee for the Milwaukee Braves, spearheaded by Richard Falk, promoted the team in newspaper ads, while the Mutual Savings & Loan dedicated some of its advertising on buses to the Braves with entreaties to "keep our Braves" and "buy season tickets now." The Chamber of Commerce was optimistic that its plan to work with organizations in other Wisconsin cities would substantially increase ticket sales for 1964.[88]

The indomitable Edmund Fitzgerald, a Milwaukee civic and business leader, led Go to Bat for the Braves, an organization launched to boost interest and ticket sales. Fitzgerald said the team management's commitment to Milwaukee as long as they were welcome showed a high degree of faith in it as a major league city. He understood the decision challenged all of Milwaukee and its neighboring communities to substantiate that confidence. Go to Bat for the Braves hoped to get three hundred volunteers to help send out ticket applications to potential buyers.[89] Fitzgerald pulled no punches in November when he said the effort to keep the Braves had to be successful, because so many cities were waiting for Milwaukee to fail. In addressing some 250 volunteers, Fitzgerald said that many cities were looking for major league franchises, particularly in the National League. Therefore the entire region was on trial in the national court of public opinion, and every city that wanted a team was going to sit back and wait to see if Milwaukee stumbled.[90]

McHale hoped that all such efforts would return the team to the "glory days" when the baseball world looked to Milwaukee. He praised his relationship with the Milwaukee County executive and other local officials and said their arrangements were "'second to none' among rental arrangements of any similar facility in the United States." He was grateful for the efforts made by Fitzgerald and his group to generate "tremendous interest and confidence in our ball club." He emphasized, however, that the team was not "looking for subsidies or handouts—just help from our friends." McHale viewed the future and the new ownership as chapter three of the Milwaukee story. The first was the Milwaukee Miracle, and the second was the melancholy of the recent years. He hoped that this new campaign would outline the future for teams facing financial difficulties in other major league cities. The Braves were going work with the local groups, said McHale, and together "We're going to do everything we can to bring you the best baseball club you've ever had." Public relations director Ernie Johnson said that the team had already sold more than 2,200 season tickets, considerably more than the five hundred sold for the 1963 season but down from the peak of 12,500 in 1958. It was also lower than the 1955–60 average of eleven thousand.[91] But, it was a move in the right direction.

In mid-December, the Braves announced that the team had lost more than $43,000 in 1963. At the first shareholders' meeting, it was announced that the team was optimistic about the future because the loss was $21,200 less than in 1962 under Perini.[92] Still, as 1964 dawned, the baseball landscape across America remained in flux. Numerous past issues directly impacted the outlook of baseball in Milwaukee and the Braves franchise. The arrival of the Minnesota Twins in 1961 impacted long-term radio and television revenues because their location in essence landlocked the Braves network primarily to Wisconsin. Professional franchises flowed from one market to another, hampering long-term commitments from teams and communities and hurting the fans of all sports affected, especially baseball as it underwent declining interest. The rise of professional football and its expanded, extensive television contracts altered the sports landscape as, for the first time ever, more Americans claimed to be football fans than baseball fans. Vince Lombardi's Green Bay Packers won five championships in the 1960s and were clearly the primary sports story in Wisconsin, displacing the Milwaukee Braves as the state's favorite team.

The Kentucky Athletics

Rumors still circulated that several teams were interested in moving to the greener pastures of a new market. However, desire to leave and an actual approval to go are two different things. Unlike the Braves' owners and organization, which had been given an easy green light to come to Milwaukee in 1953 and would again easily gain league approval to move to Atlanta, others were not so fortunate. Charlie Finley, whom many credited for triggering Atlanta to build a major league stadium, wanted to take his team out of Missouri. The reaction of the American League president and owners would be markedly different from that of the National League when it came to the Braves. Finley's plans appeared not to have been for a long-term location but perhaps merely one of many stops along the way. While it is important to note what happened to the Athletics in early 1964—and how other owners handled Finley and his team—their situation was not directly comparable to that of the Braves. Some Braves fans certainly held out hope that the National League would respond in the same manner to the Braves when it was announced they were going to leave.

On Monday, January 6, 1964, Finley signed a conditional contract between his club and the State of Kentucky to move to Louisville for the 1964 season. The team would play at the facility on the fairgrounds and play ball as the Kentucky Athletics. Finley hoped that "in two years the fans of Kentucky will demonstrate to us that we should stay here." Terms of the deal included 5 percent of gross gate receipts and a further 7.5 percent from concession sales. In return, Kentucky would spend upward of $500,000 to expand the seating capacity by about ten thousand. It was fairly evident, however, that the American League owners would not approve the move. League president Joe Cronin didn't want the American League to "make a checkerboard of this franchise by moving it from place to place from year to year." Chicago White Sox owner

Arthur Allyn excoriated the Athletics owner as "a fool, and his action is inexcusable. He has no right whatsoever to attempt such a move. He has an obligation to the people of Kansas City and he had better make it good."[93]

Cronin informed Finley in a telegram that he considered his "current activities unfair to the loyal baseball fans in Kansas City and [felt] they could result in disillusionment for the baseball public in Louisville, Ky." He added "I, therefore, as president of the American League, direct you from any further arrangements and await the determination of the American League concerning this matter." Finley responded by threatening legal action against the other owners if they vetoed the move.[94] McHale said he was glad such a state of affairs was not present in the National League.[95]

Several congressmen from Missouri and Kentucky planned to attend the owners' meeting that would determine the fate of the Athletics and which state they would play in next season. The federal government had considered baseball to be a sport rather than a business since 1922, when the Supreme Court ruled that the Sherman Antitrust Act did not apply to Major League Baseball. Owners had enjoyed this antitrust exemption, and it remained the one leverage that Congress had to keep Major League Baseball in check. This status, however, could change pending the transfer of the Athletics. Finley said that he was tired of being crucified and if the American League pulled "the rug out," the league would go down with him. He said there was "not the slightest chance of the league taking my franchise away from me." Moreover, not once did Cronin pick up the phone to call Finley and ask about the problems in Kansas City or offer to help. Finley said that the "future of baseball has been threatened by what is taking place."[96]

The American League owners voted against Finley and his Kentucky Athletics, 9–1. The only For vote was from Finley, who was told he had to sign the lease with Kansas City by February 1, 1964, or risk being removed as the owner. Finley said they do not "have the right to force me to stay in a city where I have been losing money." The American League was prepared to "act upon the termination of the membership and or expulsion of Charles O. Finley & Co., Inc." Finley knew the league was not bluffing and threatened legal action to preserve his ownership and the ability to move the team wherever and whenever he chose. He later said he was inclined to sign a one-year lease, but then said to those around him, "What is the difference if I sign a one year, a five year, or a ten year contract? Whatever it is, I'm going to sign it with the provision that it all depends on the decision of the court." If the court sided with him, he would declare his lease with Kansas City to be null and void, otherwise he would abide by it and the American League's decision. Cronin said the people from Louisville "made a fine presentation but through the years Kansas City has been fine for the American League."[97]

In contrast to the Kansas City situation, Milwaukee had been outstanding for the National League and consistently outdrew Kansas City. Yet the Braves' fan base would not receive the same treatment as those in Missouri. In 1967, at baseball's winter meetings, a new expansion team, the Kansas City Royals, was awarded to Missouri after the Athletics left for Oakland, California. The Royals entered the America League two years later with the Seattle Pilots. In the end, Finley and Bill Veeck were the only two owners who were prohibited relocation during this era of mobility. In an ironic twist, Finley and Milwaukee County officials had discussions about the possibility of moving the Athletics to Milwaukee after it was announced the Braves were going to leave.

6

Bringing Down the Curtain

1964

This is the darkest day for Milwaukee since Prohibition
was declared.

Milwaukee bar patron,
October 22, 1964

We Want the Braves

The movement of teams from one city to another, or even just ongoing rumors, was a vexing problem for American sports in the 1960s. Fans who had supported teams through winning and losing seasons were not important to the future success of franchises. After all, there were new fan bases to tap into as new markets embraced professional sports. Bill Veeck blamed much of this on baseball commissioner Ford Frick. He later wrote that Frick's reign was tragic because it covered a time when baseball needed resilient and resourceful leadership, which Frick lacked. Even worse, according to Veeck, professional football in two leagues saw attendance increasing in the same decade that baseball was in serious decline. Frick, he argued, "seldom uses his power to do anything that would help the game itself," and he often uses his power "as a tool to reward his friends and punish his enemies."[1] But soon none of this would matter to the fans of the Milwaukee Braves, whose team appeared to have the sword of Damocles dangling overhead.

For months, rumors of the Braves relocation had been circulating in the local and national press. In 1964 *Sports Illustrated* reported that despite assurances to the contrary, the Braves were on a fast track to a new home in Georgia as soon as 1965.[2] Team owners had previously met with Atlanta mayor Ivan

Allen, Atlanta Stadium Authority head Arthur Montgomery, and a representative of Georgia governor Carl Sanders to complete an informal agreement on a transfer of the franchise from Milwaukee.[3] Allen later testified that Atlanta officials were hoping to get a contract similar to the one the Braves currently had with Milwaukee County. Among the items negotiated were parking revenues at the new ballpark in Atlanta, which would be substantial, especially in contrast to the team's having received none from parking at County Stadium. Allen later said Thomas Reynolds, acting as the Braves' attorney, explained the team's disappointment with Milwaukee County. Reynolds made clear that the Braves were interested in moving to Atlanta but could not yet commit because any move had to be approved by the National League owners. Allen had wanted to get a formal agreement from the Braves, but at least he had a verbal commitment from the owners to move to Georgia after the completion of the new stadium. Bill Bartholomay and Reynolds met with Frick in July 1964 to inform him that the Braves were considering relocating to Atlanta and they wanted some direction to accomplish their goal.[4]

"We're going to stay in Milwaukee as long as we are welcome"

Despite the rumors of relocation, the Milwaukee faithful remained optimistic that things could still turn in their favor. Yet as the Braves prepared to head to spring training in 1964, a distinct lack of season ticket sales remained a deep concern. There was hope that some local interests might step up and help sell at least 7,500 tickets to keep the team economically viable at County Stadium. After all, the Braves had previously sold up to twelve thousand season tickets without any promotion. Ultimately about four thousand were sold, more than in 1963 but well off the expected pace. A promotion by the Milwaukee business community added a mere four hundred tickets. Oliver E. Kuechle noted that while that number was small, elected and community leaders' commitment to save the Braves created a much more favorable baseball atmosphere. Recent history had shown that season ticket sales constituted only 45–50 percent of the Braves' total attendance at County Stadium. Therefore, if nothing changed, the club could expect between 750,000 and 800,000 fans in the year ahead. Kuechle cautioned readers to remember the fear in 1963 that the team was going to leave. He wrote, "Milwaukee wants the Braves because they are good for the city and state" while the region had been good for the team as well over its eleven-year history. "But there must still be that wherewithal to operate at a profit."[5]

In April, about thirty thousand people came to an open house at County Stadium, which, to Lloyd Larson, felt like the fifties again. With other cities in the market for big league baseball, Milwaukee's fan base needed to return to the level of excitement and fan interest of the previous decade. Larson believed the large crowd at the open house showed the Braves' importance to the region and a genuine resolve to avoid losing baseball in the county. On the bright side, he contended that the Braves did not need thirty thousand per game in attendance but merely fifteen thousand to hit the one million mark. This had been the benchmark of profitability, and if the team performed well on the field, that number could go up. Larson did not envision the same level of complacency that forced the Braves out of Boston, and all of Milwaukee should "take our cue from Boston, which took the Braves for granted." If early season indications were anything, then "Milwaukee and Wisconsin won't let it happen. And that's mighty encouraging."[6]

Despite the optimism in the Milwaukee papers, reports continued to surface that Atlanta had already reached a deal with either the Cleveland Indians or the Milwaukee Braves. Although other teams were interested in the Atlanta market, many were convinced that it was the Braves who were most likely to go, as the new owners would need "a big boost this year or they're eager to shift."[7] In July C. C. Johnson Spink broke a story in *Sporting News* that, according to an irreproachable source, the Braves were definitely leaving and intended to play in Atlanta in 1965. Lackluster attendance in Milwaukee and a thriving metropolitan area in and around Atlanta were all the Braves needed for justification to move for the second time since 1953.[8] Others reported that a seven-state television and radio network was included in the package. Team president John McHale immediately denied the reports. It was ridiculous that this rumor was again in the news, he said, and owners should not have to continue answering the same questions about relocation and "have people draw possibly wrong conclusions." But he refused to clarify whether the Braves would remain in Wisconsin beyond 1964, and he was "not prepared to answer that in any way until the season is over."[9] This was just another in a series of stories appearing in the past year, and the Braves were "going to stay in Milwaukee as long as we are welcome."[10]

Kuechle clearly did not have confidence in McHale and wrote that the Braves were seriously considering a move to the Atlanta market and that "in all likelihood it will lead to marriage for the 1965 season."[11] He believed there was not yet a written agreement, but that did not mean one would not be forthcoming. By the summer of 1964, only two things could keep the Braves in Milwaukee: an attempt by Congress to investigate the antitrust exemption for baseball and a vote by the owners. The former was a threat, the latter not as much. Chicago Cubs owner Philip Wrigley, who had waived some of his territory to allow the Braves' move back in 1953, now said if "the Braves have a good reason, if survival is at stake, I would vote for the transfer." National League president Warren Giles, addressed the Atlanta rumors in a letter to Fred Russell, editor of the *Nashville Banner*, on July 18, 1964, saying that as of now, no such request for a franchise shift has been granted or given to move a team to Atlanta. He further suggested that under existing league rules on transfers there was no way "any club in our League could commit itself and so far as I know, no National League club has a commitment to move to Atlanta or to any other city." He understood that informal discussions may have already occurred between interested parties, including "officials of the Milwaukee Club" as well as Charles O. Finley of the Kansas City Athletics and representatives of the Cleveland Indians. These meetings, and any agreements reached between the city and a team, "may have given the Atlanta people the right to believe that they would move to Atlanta conditional upon receiving League consent or some other conditions, but I know of no such declaration or arrangement by any National League Club."[12]

"The specter of more money in Atlanta"

Arthur Montgomery later announced that they had a commitment from a team and expected to be playing baseball in the 1965 season. He did not name the Braves, but they were presumed to be the club despite their commitments in Milwaukee, such as the Schlitz Brewing Company's sponsorship of radio and a limited television schedule in Wisconsin. A spokesman for Schlitz said that they had been assured by all concerned that the Braves had no intention to leave "as long as Milwaukee wanted the club to stay." Weighing in, Shirley Povich of the *Washington Post* decried what was happening to Milwaukee and described Atlanta's tactics as "ruthless." It offered a newer stadium and an enticing rental arrangement, just as Milwaukee had when the Braves were still in Boston, and now "the specter of more money in Atlanta than Milwaukee has just raised its wonderful head" again. The Braves had profited $400,000 per year in Milwaukee but now were "guaranteed a $7.5 million TV contract for five years in Atlanta." Povich did not expect much resistance from baseball in getting permission to move, as the owners were not likely to stand in opposition. There "used to be a horror at this sort of thing and for fifty years in the majors no franchise was shifted, but they have been handed around recently like a floating crap game and the votes to move are easy to come by." In fact, the only two owners who were denied were Bill Veeck and Charlie Finley, whom Povich described as "an abrasive pair whom the other owners have preferred to starve out of baseball." There was no hope that the commissioner would stop this and "protect the fans of Milwaukee from losing their team." Finally, Povich argued, the "Milwaukee story is the simple one of too much that was too good too quickly." The Braves had not finished under .500 since arriving from Boston, but in 1962 finished near the bottom of the league. Performance impacted attendance and left Milwaukee in a "futile bidding match against Atlanta, an eager city that has never known major league baseball as its very own. Milwaukee knows how that is."[13]

Arthur Daley of the *New York Times* editorialized on the fluidity of baseball franchises, initiated by the Braves themselves in 1953. He argued it had triggered moves from "all the other money-grubbers" to new destinations. Baseball had once been a game "involving sportsmen who gloried in their profitable years and suffered through bad ones" as the teams remained in the cities where they belonged. These teams and owners had "roots that were deeply embedded in the loyalties of their fans" but Daley felt this no longer was the case. After all, the "Great American Game has become as commercial as General Motors." Daley liked the Braves president and believed the other men in the ownership group were "all likeable men," but he had to take them to task, expressing outrage that "baseball has degenerated to the level of musical chairs." It was not realistic to think that Milwaukee could permanently remain as excited about baseball as it had been in 1953 when "adoring fans gave their heroes clothes, groceries, and furniture. Every day was Christmas. This was fantasia mit sauerbrauten and gemütlichkeit" but it could not last. It was amazing that "it lasted as long as it did, nine glorious years." Nevertheless the times had changed and the fans had been irritated by "front office" decisions. Milwaukee baseball fans could be brought back to the ballpark, but waiting for that "might put too much strain on the limited financial resources of the current owners." The new owners would probably still move the team, believing that new riches could be found in Atlanta, but that did not "mean that the move is right. Nothing is more destructive to the image that baseball pretends to have than this carpetbagging all over the map" once a town had been milked dry.[14]

"The best interests of the county, the fans, and the ball club"

On July 21, 1964, the Milwaukee County Board of Supervisors established a sports committee to find a long-term solution for the Braves in Wisconsin. At this juncture, relations between the team and the county were toxic. That the bombastic county board chair Eugene Grobschmidt served on the committee created a problem for the Braves. In fact, Bartholomay said he would not meet with any committee of which Grobschmidt was a member because of statements Grobschmidt had publicly made about manager Bobby Bragan and the performance of the team. A meeting was arranged between Grobschmidt and Bragan to discuss his public criticisms, but Bragan canceled, saying McHale had told him not to get involved in this dispute because he might make statements about a move of the team. Only when he was given assurances that relocation would not be discussed did McHale approve the meeting. When the two sat down, Grobschmidt apologized to Bragan and offered to do the same with the players, although Bragan declined. Only after the meeting and Grobschmidt's apology did Bartholomay finally agree to meet with the sports committee.[15]

Days later, Milwaukee county executive John Doyne met with Bartholomay to discuss the reports about Atlanta. Most of the conversation dealt with the existing stadium lease and what could be done to help keep the Braves in Milwaukee. Bartholomay told Doyne the team was satisfied with the existing contract, a sure sign that something was amiss. Doyne asked Bartholomay directly if the Braves were going to leave Milwaukee and was told that the Braves "had not made up their mind that they were going anyplace, and at the end of the season they would re-evaluate their situation and make a decision." When asked if the Braves and Atlanta had reached any agreement, Bartholomay responded that there was no commitment to anybody, including other cities such as Seattle or Oakland. Bartholomay assured Doyne that no deal was in place and the county executive would be informed of any decision after the Braves examined their position at the end of the season. Doyne also reached out to McHale, who was not present at this meeting, to clarify the direction of the team and its future. In their conference in Doyne's office, Doyne asked directly if the Braves were going to leave. McHale assured him that they were not and the team had not taken any steps to move in that direction but they would re-evaluate their situation at the end of the year. Like Bartholomay before him, McHale said the Braves were content with their existing contract with the county.[16]

Meanwhile, Atlanta's big league aspirations were set back in mid-July when the St. Louis Cardinals football team announced that it was, in the face of several lawsuits, staying in Missouri. According to reports, that left the Braves as the only professional franchise expected to come to Georgia.[17] Eventually the National Football League granted a franchise in Atlanta, beating out the American Football League's attempt to grant expansion for the new stadium.

The NFL also planned on cashing in on Atlanta's potential for television because it was a major city of the Deep South and would command a territory throughout Dixie.[18] Meanwhile, Richard Cecil, then the Braves' farm director, was sent to Atlanta to meet with local officials and work with the architects who were planning the early stages of construction. According to Cecil, only the basement stages of the stadium were done at this point, and the Braves wanted to make sure that the stadium met their needs.[19]

On September 30, Bill Bartholomay's Chicago office received a letter from attorney Richard Cutler on behalf of a group of Milwaukee businessmen who wanted to purchase the Milwaukee Braves. Spearheaded by Robert A. Uihlein Jr., president of the Joseph Schlitz Brewing Company, the primary sponsor of the Braves' radio network, the group included Richard D. Cudahy, president of the Patrick Cudahy meatpacking company; Elmer Winter, cofounder of Manpower Incorporated; Wallace Rank, president of one of the largest car dealers in Wisconsin; Walter Schroeder, president of Schroeder Hotel Enterprises; Charles Nelson, president of Waukesha Motor Company; and Allan H. "Bud" Selig, vice president of Knippel-Selig automobile dealers. Selig was reportedly one of the largest minority stockholders among the owners of the Milwaukee Braves. Cutler wrote that the Braves remained an important asset to metropolitan Milwaukee and Wisconsin and their loss would represent immense financial damage to the community if they left. He hoped that this group would negotiate with Bartholomay and understood that a "reasonable offer for the purchase of the Braves would relieve you of any concern which you may have about an insufficient return on your investment in Milwaukee."[20]

Bartholomay's response on October 3 was clear and to the point. He informed Cutler that they had received many other inquiries since purchasing the club but the Braves were not for sale. If a written proposal for the majority interest was presented, he would be "obligated to submit it to my associates for their consideration." Cutler responded that the group he represented would have to analyze the Braves' financial structure, and "an early meeting between our group and yours would be an essential prerequisite to a written offer." He insisted that there was a basis for discussions that constituted a realistic approach for a local purchase of the Braves. It would be at a price that was fair to the current ownership and allow them to preserve and protect "a community and state asset for the area they call home."[21]

The Home of the Braves?

Perhaps seeing the writing on the wall, the Milwaukee County Board raised the possibility of renegotiating the stadium lease in September. It would give the

Braves more than $125,000 in concessions and the right to set prices at the ball-park for all items sold, including beer, and it banned ticket scalpers on stadium grounds. The county board asked the team to respond within five days if they were interested in bargaining for a new deal. McHale replied he was thankful for the offer and impressed by it, but he did not feel that it was "in the best interests of the county, the fans, and the ball club to have a free ride on concessions rental." In addition, McHale said that Braves had "never complained about the concession rental percentage."[22] Bartholomay issued a statement that the board of directors would analyze the proposal as part of the long-range plans for the Braves in Milwaukee. He said the club appreciated the gesture, although it raised many more questions and represented a considerable alteration from previous negotiations between the Braves and Milwaukee County.[23] In the end, nothing would come of this proposal.

The news for the Milwaukee faithful got worse when Lou Perini Jr., the son of the former owner of the Braves, declared in September that major league baseball was going to Dixie in 1965. Perini, a significant shareholder in the Milwaukee Braves Inc., also told reporters that the team had already made a deal to move to Georgia and would make the formal announcement after the season, most likely in December. At the same time, the county board passed a resolution that encouraged the Braves to stay in Milwaukee and overcome the differences between the team and local officials. It asked the Braves to reply by the end of the month.[24]

A special report attached to the resolution, from Marty Larsen, chair of the Parks and Recreation Committee, and Howard Gregg, general manager of the Milwaukee County Park Commission, highlighted some problems. Included were a series of proposals that, if enacted, could keep the team in Milwaukee and solvent. The county was willing to negotiate the right of the Braves to operate their own concessions and establish prices for food, beverages, and merchandise, possibly without sharing the profits with the county. The board also supported a new ban on carry-in canned and bottled beverages, other than milk. If the Braves ownership felt that other operational areas or "Irritants to Successful Operation" remained, the board was amenable to further negotiations.[25]

Additional ways to make the Braves financially stable included a reduction in the stadium rental fee and an increase in broadcast revenues: $1.575 million for television and radio broadcasts over three years, through the 1967 season, to bring the total to $525,000 per year. This was $125,000 more per year than the existing deal in place with the Braves. Schlitz remained willing to raise the payments "to underscore our most strong and sincere desire to keep the team in Milwaukee." Uihlein said the offer was made for all baseball fans in Milwaukee and throughout Wisconsin. If fans continued to display great support of the team in the few remaining home games, 1964 attendance would exceed one million and keep the team profitable.[26] The Braves declined the deal.

On September 30, hoping to derail any attempt by the Braves' owners to leave Milwaukee, county officials asked to address the American and National League presidents and the major league owners. They also appealed to Wisconsin's two senators and ten congressmen to support their fight, which might indeed turn into a federal case. Frick called on the Braves to reexamine their problems and attempt to work out a solution that would keep the team in Milwaukee. He reiterated that he was in favor of orderly expansion of baseball into new markets and, at least in early October, was "opposed to shifting franchises from one city to another." Many baseball officials who had gathered in St. Louis for the 1964 World Series believed that the Braves could be pressured to stay in Milwaukee and that permission to transfer the franchise was not guaranteed.[27]

If the owners had a verbal agreement to move, said Frick, he would first insist that they give Milwaukee an opportunity to keep the team. Furthermore, if they asked the league for consent to move, the Braves had to give him "every figure on their Milwaukee operation." In a meeting with Bartholomay the previous week, Frick said, he told him to make sure that they studied the situation again, then a second time, and a third time, but he did not think "we can order anyone to conduct a losing operation." Bartholomay maintained that the team would reexamine it at the end of the season and would make a recommendation to the board at their meeting on October 16. To the chagrin of the Wisconsin faithful, Frick added that if the team had already given its word to another city, they would have to "honor any such word."[28]

Milwaukee fans continued to hope that fear of the Braves relocating was unfounded and perhaps it was another team that would move. According to rumors, the Cleveland Indians were also considering a move to Georgia because their stadium was antiquated and interest in the team was dwindling. The Indians front office announced that they would make their decision on the same day that the Braves board of directors was to determine the fate of the Milwaukee franchise, but the timing was "pure coincidence." Some hoped the Indians would relocate to Wisconsin if the Braves vacated County Stadium.[29]

Hopes for a positive resolution dwindled after October 7, when it was reported that Atlanta was spending an extra $750,000 to expedite the construction of its ballpark in order to complete it in time for the 1965 season. Mayor Allen said that public officials who had sponsored the construction of the stadium would be in serious political jeopardy if major league baseball did not come by 1965. He reiterated that he had had a commitment from an existing franchise since March, but he refused to identify the team. To Atlanta sportswriters, it was evident that the Braves would be in Georgia in 1965. State, county, and local officials appeared ready to support the agreement that was in place, and they were not impressed by any threats emanating from Wisconsin.[30]

"Not been exactly as we hoped"

It is not clear if anything could have prevented the Braves from exiting Wisconsin and crushing the hopes of their faithful. Up to the last minute, Milwaukee County and the business community attempted to improve the Braves' financial standing by offering more money for broadcast rights and better terms for the stadium lease. When these efforts appeared futile, only threats of legal action remained. Some believed that aggressive litigation would either convince the Braves to change their minds, prevent other owners from supporting the move, scare Major League Baseball into preventing the move, or, best-case scenario, provide Milwaukee with another team. The county board appeared ready to file suit as soon as an announcement was made. Wisconsin congressmen were ready to act at the federal level, as were their counterparts in Georgia. Therefore, extensive harm to the franchise and major league baseball could occur if Milwaukee County did not give in to the inevitable shift to the south. Financial damage would also be massive if the Braves were forced to remain in Milwaukee.

With a sense of inevitability that the Braves were going to leave, it should not have come as a surprise when the team transferred its main offices to Chicago just days before the board of directors meeting in mid-October. While some lesser offices remained at County Stadium, club executives said that they planned to commute to the new offices in Chicago. No specific property was removed from the stadium, but some officials said they were not sure if they would have jobs when the move was completed. Bartholomay said the relocation would lift much of the "business burden off McHale's shoulders," including concessions and broadcast contracts. The plan had always been to move the main offices during the offseason, as most of the team's fiscal affairs had been conducted from Bartholomay's Chicago office since 1963 and now McHale's office would be in the same building.[31] When asked if the business operations would return to Wisconsin for the next season, Tom Reynolds said he assumed they would. When asked to clarify if that meant that the Braves were staying in Milwaukee, Reynolds backpedaled a bit and responded, "I suppose I spoke a little quickly." Regardless of what happened, he said, the Braves' main offices would remain in Chicago.[32]

At the time of the office move, the owners acknowledged that a Milwaukee group was interested in purchasing the team but had made no formal offer and the owners were not interested in selling the club.[33] Bartholomay reiterated that his group did not "buy the club to sell it, and we didn't buy it to move it, either. If it works out that way, it will be a personal disappointment." He did not say whether he had decided, or would present to the board, an option concerning the long-rumored move to Atlanta. When asked if he and Reynolds determined such policy, Bartholomay confirmed that they did, "but we have others to consider, too—other directors, other stockholders, the ball club, the fans, the league, and baseball." He added that he was not happy with how things had developed since they had bought the club. Perhaps worst of all, it seemed as though things "in Milwaukee have not been exactly as we hoped. We feel we have gotten the season ticket sale up to a maximum, and only after a concerted drive last winter in which a lot of people worked hard" on behalf of the team. The owners had "injected a local flavor into the board of directors and offered stock for sale" but this had ended unsatisfactorily. Worse, of the 910,000 people who had come to County Stadium to see games, he estimated that there were about twenty-five thousand diehards who could have purchased stock for themselves or family members. Yet, only about sixteen hundred shares were sold, including seven hundred to minors. While season ticket sales were disappointing, the "game sale was the most encouraging feature we had."[34]

On October 14, Bartholomay acknowledged that after meeting with Montgomery and Allen in Atlanta, the Braves were indeed debating leaving Milwaukee. He said that the offer on the table "may amount to millions of dollars" and did not deny that an agreement was reached. All that was needed was approval from the Braves board of directors and from seven National League teams, including the Braves themselves. Despite the longstanding rumors, this was the first commitment from Atlanta, he said, and he did not yet know if the offer was satisfactory.[35]

Bartholomay's statement that "we can no longer ignore the vast areas of this country" that do not have baseball must have struck Milwaukee fans as ominous. He said the "stadium authority has given me a firm contract offer for consideration of the Braves." Still, he believed that the team recognized the "responsibility and public trust involved in even considering the moving of a professional sports franchise from one area of the country to another." The offer would be presented to the board of directors as they debated "whether Milwaukee is the right place" for the Braves. Bartholomay would not comment on how long the negotiations had been ongoing, despite statements from Allen for months that a team had already committed to move to Atlanta.[36] It was also reported that if the Braves' owners pursued the move, the National League owners would not prevent it from happening. Private conversations among the owners indicated that they had enough votes to approve the move and had the right to do so as long as the destination had a reasonable ability to support the franchise.[37]

Doyne responded to the Braves' announcement with a personal letter to Bartholomay. Clearly upset that he had trusted Bartholomay's denials of relocation, Doyne saw that Bartholomay's Braves had always planned to leave Milwaukee before the lease expired in 1965. Doyne was compelled to take legal action to require the Braves to play out their existing deal, but there really was little else he could do.[38] Doyne might have rallied more support across the region, but it most likely would not have made a difference at this point and the end game was finally in sight.

Forward Atlanta

By October 17, Richard S. Falk of the Milwaukee County Park Commission had hired an attorney to prepare several lawsuits in the likely event the Braves would attempt to leave. One suit was on behalf of the stockholders who had bought into the team with the understanding that it would stay in Milwaukee.[39] Another suit on behalf of taxpayers sought financial damages for Milwaukee County and its business community if the Braves left before the end of their lease. There was also the specter of an antitrust suit against Major League Baseball and even the Braves franchise. Falk warned the team that the minute they announced they would leave Milwaukee, these suits would be filed and carried "to the highest court in the land." Any officials in Atlanta who had negotiated with the Braves would also be named parties in the lawsuits. Moreover, Falk intended to contact the Securities Exchange Commission to determine whether the stocks that were sold in Wisconsin on behalf of Milwaukee Braves Inc. conformed to existing regulations.[40]

In a letter to Frick, Richard Cutler outlined the process of his group's effort to purchase and keep the team in Wisconsin, one without economic damages to the present owners. The relocation of the Braves was bad for baseball and Wisconsin fans, he said, and the short-term gain from the move would disregard the record-setting support of the Braves in Milwaukee and Wisconsin. According to Cutler, it would "seriously threaten the future potentials of teams continuing to be focal points of state and local pride in any momentary location." History showed that fan identification and pride generated by baseball gave it the long-term economic support it needed. Cutler did not believe that the new Braves owners understood this, and he asked for help in arranging an opportunity to meet with them "for the purpose of arriving at the best solution for the sport as a whole without sacrifice on the part of the present owners."[41] Cutler said his group was prepared to make an offer once they had a full accounting of the team's financial status.[42]

The Braves owners reminded Cutler's group that they were not really interested in hearing offers to purchase a team that was not for sale, as Cutler was well aware, said Reynolds. Frick responded that the syndicate's request was a "very serious matter" and he would "give them the courtesy of an answer." Bartholomay had previously said there were no offers and if "he were to receive a definite offer, he would present it to his board of directors at their coming meeting." Cutler stated that there had been no response to his group's request for the financials necessary to make an offer.[43]

"Malicious inducements and solicitation"

The Milwaukee County Board, through its corporation counsel, in a letter on October 17, laid out the course of action the county would take to keep baseball in Milwaukee. It was addressed to Mayor Allen, Fulton County manager Alan F. Kiepper, and Arthur Montgomery. Copies went to Ford Frick, Warren Giles, the presidents of all major league teams, and U.S. deputy attorney general Nicholas Katzenbach. In clear language, George Rice stated that Milwaukee County had consistently been informed that Atlanta officials had "for a considerable period of time . . . been actively soliciting the principal officers and majority stockholders" of the Braves to breach their contract with Milwaukee. These activities could become grounds for legal action under the laws of Georgia and Wisconsin. It was an official notice to "cease and desist" from this illegal activity or Milwaukee County would be obligated to seek relief through the courts. While the county commended the Atlanta officials for their hard work in attempting to land a team for their new stadium, there would be legal action if the contract offered to Bartholomay on October 14, 1964, were not rescinded. If this warning was ignored and the offer remained, the "malicious inducements and solicitation of breach of contract must inevitably subject" the Atlanta executives "personally to a substantial liability for damages."[44]

Among the responses that Milwaukee County received were two from baseball owners in Chicago that reflected frustration with Milwaukee's attempt to keep the Braves in spite of their owners' desires and resentment of the possibility of being dragged through the courts. Chicago Cubs owner Philip Wrigley said he believed in free enterprise and that "the people engaged in any particular business probably know their business best." He outlined his past support for the Braves, including going against his advisers to allow Perini's move to Wisconsin in 1953. Having supported the original move, Wrigley felt it would be inconsistent to object to the Braves moving now if they judged it to be in their best interest. Wrigley hoped for understanding of his support for the Braves at the expense of Milwaukee because it was "in the over-all interests of not just one team or one city" but all of baseball. Chicago White Sox co-owner Arthur Allyn Jr. said that he did not have a voice in the affairs of the National League because the White Sox were in the American League. The White Sox would not receive legal threats with equanimity and any legal action against Allyn's franchise "would be most improper and ill-advised."[45]

Congressman Clement Zablocki of Milwaukee asked the Federal Communications Commission (FCC) to investigate whether it was in the public interest to allow sports teams to continually move in search of larger broadcast revenues. Clearly Zablocki's request was aimed at getting any kind of ruling that might prevent the Braves from moving to Atlanta. He informed the FCC that the main reason for this move was to reap "huge income" from broadcasting that would benefit not only the team but also the radio and television stations that would "derive considerable revenue from such a transfer." Such use of advertising revenues, to prompt a team to abandon one metropolitan area for another, might "not be in consonance with the intent and purpose of the federal communications act." Zablocki argued that the FCC's regulatory power revolved around "what is in the public interest," and "how could it ever be argued that the public interest is served by dangling best advertising sums before a sporting attraction to induce it to move from one city to another?" Furthermore, he did not believe that the "expenditure of large sums by radio and television" to induce relocation "is an appropriate use of a public grant."[46] Apparently Zablocki did not appreciate the future of electronic broadcasting, not just in Atlanta, or even just baseball. It now transcends almost all sports, professional as well as collegiate, and, to a growing degree, even high school.

Milwaukee fans who held out hope that the Cleveland Indians and not the Braves were headed to Atlanta soon faced a bitter reality. Fear of losing the Indians had prompted Cleveland officials to offer a new ten-year lease that reduced stadium rent from 7 percent to 6 percent of gross receipts. It also provided a credit of $32,400 for operating costs of Municipal Stadium and an additional allocation of $1 million for stadium and parking improvements. Included in the agreement was a plan to increase season ticket sales from 1,925 to a targeted goal of 4,500. Indians general manager and part owner Gabe Paul said that from "the beginning it has been our earnest desire to stay in Cleveland" but in light of their poor financial experience, it would "not have been fair to our stockholders to ignore proposals made by other cities." Among their targeted cities, besides Atlanta, were Seattle and Dallas–Fort Worth. Lamar Hunt, owner of the American Football League's Kansas City Chiefs, and his business partner, Tommy Mercer, owned two minor league baseball teams in Texas. Mercer said that they were disappointed not to have convinced the Indians franchise to move to the Dallas area. He added that he and Hunt had invited team officials from Cleveland and Milwaukee back in June but never heard a response from the Braves because it was apparent that "Milwaukee is going to Atlanta."[47]

"The darkest day for Milwaukee since Prohibition"

The race for the Braves to leave Milwaukee had been moving at an accelerated pace for local fans and glacial speed for the ownership. Months of rumors, some later confirmed to be true and others completely false, finally were coming to an end. In an eleventh-hour attempt to purchase the team before the Braves' board of directors meeting, Cutler again informed the owners that the local group he represented was still interested in purchasing the team. There was nearly a universal feeling among locals, he said, that the Braves owners had been misleading "Milwaukee citizens, the fans, and the county government." The resulting corrosion of fan patronage could be reversed through local owner-ship of the Braves. At minimum it could recover Bartholomay and La Salle Corporation's investment in the team or even bring a greater profit from their two-year ownership of the franchise. If Bartholomay and Reynolds would meet with him, most likely Cutler's group would make a formal offer to purchase the Braves once they understood the specifics of the capital structure of the team and its current financial situation.[48] The owners rejected the invitation to meet as well as the group's prospective offer of $6 million. Besides, the Braves were not for sale.

Days before the board of directors met in Chicago to finally and formally vote on relocation, Bartholomay informed its Wisconsin members that he ex-pected the board to approve the move to Atlanta and offered the Wisconsin delegation a chance to resign their positions to avoid embarrassment.[49] In an anticlimactic move, on October 21, the board voted 12–6 to move the Braves to Atlanta. Of the five members who were absent, the only one from Wisconsin was Vince Lombardi.[50] Bartholomay claimed later that Lombardi had respected the position of the principal owners of the Braves.[51] What Lombardi really thought about the Braves leaving, or himself being removed from the board, is not known. He made no public statement, and reporters were more focused on the Packers' season than Lombardi's attitude toward the Braves.

After the board concluded its business, Braves publicity director Ernie Johnson read a prepared statement that the "Board of Directors of the Milwaukee Braves, Inc., voted today to request permission of the National League to transfer their franchise to Atlanta, Ga., for 1965" and at "the request of Warren Giles, President of the National League, no further information will be released until after the league meeting in New York Thursday."[52] With that, the fate of the Milwaukee Braves was official. Barring a rejection by the National League owners, the franchise was headed for its third city and henceforth would be known as the Atlanta Braves.

The next day the six Wisconsin members issued a formal statement that they remained steadfastly opposed to the transfer of the Braves. Milwaukee had proven itself to be one of the best baseball markets, they said; almost 17 percent of the total paid attendance in the National League was in Milwaukee. Wisconsin fans had led the league six out of the previous twelve seasons in total attendance.[53] The move would harm the franchise and all of baseball in general because it violated the public trust.[54] On the contrary, said Mayor Allen, the move would finally make baseball a national game because the twenty-four million people in the southeastern states would now have major league baseball. Despite all of the denials from the team over the last several years, Allen believed the move was handled in an above-board fashion and was necessitated by a lack of interest in the Braves in Milwaukee.[55]

It was now evident that the Braves ownership had decided to move months before the October announcement. After a disappointing campaign to sell season tickets saw sales rise only about 22 percent, or a mere 750 more than 1963, the owners were committed to leave Milwaukee. They even hired experts to study available cities and determined that Atlanta was the ideal place for the Braves. An annual broadcasting deal in Atlanta promised to be worth as much as $1.5 million, as opposed to the current $525,000 deal with Schlitz Brewing Company.[56] Unlike their deal in Milwaukee, in Atlanta the Braves would have rent-free furnished offices and control over concessions prices and sales. There were also no restrictions on brands of beer, unlike the requirement to sell only local brands in Milwaukee.[57]

On top of the shocking news that the team was leaving Wisconsin came the realization of the devastating economic impact on Milwaukee. Among the losses were stadium rental, parking, and concession fees that accounted for 75 percent of the income generated from County Stadium; tax revenues from merchandise sold at the ballpark that were split among the City and County of

Milwaukee and the State of Wisconsin; and tax revenues from local businesses that fans patronized on game days. According to the Braves themselves, out-of-town fans brought more than $50 million into the region from 1953 to 1963. Braves players and employees spent money too, about $17.6 million in payroll, and more than $5.4 million in perishable goods had been locally sourced for sale at the stadium. In addition to a loss of the investment in a mostly empty ballpark, the interstate highway system that was designed and built to provide maximum access to County Stadium could now be considered inefficient for the entire county and at substantial cost.[58]

The First of Many Legal Obstacles

Within hours of the Braves' announcement, Milwaukee County supervisors sought and obtained a temporary injunction from circuit court judge Ronald Dreschler to keep the team from leaving immediately.[59] This was the first of many legal actions that agencies of Wisconsin state, county, and local governments were expected to take against the team. The provisional ruling prohibited the Braves from scheduling any home games away from Milwaukee County Stadium for the 1965 season. It also prohibited the transfer of the team or the removal of any of its assets from Wisconsin and any move to dissolve the Milwaukee Braves Inc. Nor could the team apply to the league for permission to move or "render impossible the performance required of the Milwaukee Braves, Inc., under the terms of the agreement between the Braves and the county."[60] The county argued that the transfer was unconscionable and violated the terms of the contract that the Braves had previously signed to play at County Stadium.

In response to Judge Dreschler's ruling, the Braves notified Ford Frick that the team intended to draft the Atlanta territory, which would make the transfer easier. They also said they would not ask to move until they were legally free of all obligations, though they remained determined to move to Georgia as soon as possible. Giles publicly supported the Braves and their move, saying that the owners did not feel they were depriving an area of major league baseball because two teams remained in Chicago and another in Minnesota only 285 miles away.[61] The National League was fully expected to grant the request once it was formally received. Only six votes were required, including one from the Braves, to make the transfer official. The Pittsburgh Pirates agreed with the move, but the Philadelphia Phillies were rumored to be against it. Allegedly the remainder of the league was open minded but not likely to vote against a fellow owner, so the vote would be a mere formality.[62]

Blame It on the Fans, Public Officials, and Even the Press

At the National League meeting in New York, only two days after the transfer announcement, no move was made by the Braves owners for approval to be in Atlanta in time for the 1965 season. The league owners agreed to waive the normal ten-day notice requirement and hold the vote if legal matters were resolved in Wisconsin. Several members of Milwaukee's civic and political leadership, among them county board chair Eugene Grobschmidt, had opportunities to address the National League owners in an effort to keep baseball in Wisconsin.[63] The local mission returned home after the meeting with a hint of optimism.

In typical gruff and belligerent style, Grobschmidt made it clear to the owners that Milwaukee County and his constituents would not tolerate the move. "Every effort, be it legal, legislative, psychological, and even moral persuasion will be exercised to prevent this contemplated tragic and unconscionable change from ever occurring," he said. The history of the Braves in Wisconsin was "built around a bonanza of paid attendance"; never had any city "welcomed a sport as Milwaukee did the Braves and Professional Baseball in 1953." Since 1953, only two teams in all of Major League Baseball had eclipsed the two million attendance mark, the Braves for four years and the Brooklyn/Los Angeles Dodgers for five, as well as the million mark, the Braves for nine years and the Dodgers for twelve. Despite unparalleled success, the team was now being stolen from Wisconsin by a group from Chicago who spoke of a "public trust" at the same time they were prepared to violate that trust. The team's continued denials of relocation eventually became the truth and this, more than anything, negatively impacted attendance at County Stadium. He reminded the owners of the existing lease that obliged the Braves to play out the 1965 season in Milwaukee, and he highlighted the community efforts to assist the team.[64]

Grobschmidt expressed frustration that during the time the Braves were flirting with Atlanta they never came to the county board to ask for adjustments in their contract. Instead, the board came to the Braves and still, "even as of today," had never "received a dignified reply from them." It had been evident since June 1963 that the team was leaving, and Milwaukee fans deserved better treatment and loyalty from the inexperienced ownership group. Only eight months after purchasing the Braves, the new owners "resolved internally to move the Franchise, and by some coincidence Atlanta suddenly undertook a crash program to erect a stadium." Furthermore, according to Grobschmidt, the lure of fast money in Atlanta made the Braves leave Milwaukee, but they

blamed it on the fans, public officials, and even the local media. He then listed
solutions to the problem, such as sale of the team to a local group of civic and
business leaders, legal action, and/or antitrust action on behalf of Wisconsin.[65]
If the Braves were to stay in Milwaukee, they would have the full support of newspapers and the public, although there were fences to mend for many fans. He
was willing to bury everything and "willing to forget about the things I've said."[66]

Lloyd Larson of the *Milwaukee Sentinel* also addressed the league and argued
that Wisconsin and Milwaukee were not in decline. Rather, they matched up
well to all other major league cities, including Atlanta. He noted the substantial
differences between the Braves' exodus from Boston and the proposed move
from Milwaukee. Boston had two teams at the time and the Braves owned their
own stadium; if the team were allowed to leave Wisconsin, it would be the first
time that baseball had completely abandoned a major league city and be far
more economically damaging to Milwaukee than it had been to Boston. This
meant that "the Braves and baseball have a tremendous moral as well as legal
responsibility" to do the right thing. Larson felt that several issues combined to
create the attendance decline over the previous few seasons, but they were not
unique to Milwaukee. He believed it could be reversed and attendance might
rebound to somewhere between 1.2 and 1.5 million. The very "institution of
baseball would suffer great harm if Milwaukee is abandoned. Baseball already
has enough enemies making capital of its every wrong move." Moreover, baseball could not "afford to feed its enemies and develop new ones by a move so
inexcusable as another switch for the Braves."[67]

We Hope to Keep the Braves Here

Many in Wisconsin mourned the pending loss of the Braves, but most realized
there was not really much they could do unless the team attempted to leave before the end of the stadium lease. Milwaukee mayor Henry Maier told reporters
that the Braves had shown that baseball was not a sport but just a business.
Furthermore, the circumstances of the transfer gave "big league baseball a
black eye" and as the "story is told—and it will be told and retold around the
country—that baseball generally will not feel the joy will have been worth the
pain of it." Baseball "has now adopted the pattern of threatening moves, as was
done in four major league cities—Philadelphia, Cleveland, Kansas City, and
Milwaukee—in an effort to stimulate the gate, or actually moving" in an effort
to gain "a temporary windfall." Doyne said he was not surprised by the developments and it was unfortunate that the county had "to do business with this kind
of organization." Governor John Reynolds asked attorney general George

Thompson and his staff to assist Milwaukee County officials in their legal efforts to keep the team. This was "a sad day for baseball," said Reynolds. "The owners of the Braves are showing a callous lack of faith in the people of Milwaukee and Wisconsin."[68]

Wally Rank of Rank & Sons, a prominent Milwaukee automobile dealership that had had a great working relationship with Braves players since 1953, said it was "a black day for Milwaukee" and the unwarranted move would make Milwaukee appear to be "awfully small townish" to the rest of the nation. Bud Selig, the future owner of the Milwaukee Brewers and later the commissioner of baseball, said that it "certainly is not unexpected and there's nothing more I can say. We tried to negotiate with them."[69] Rank and Selig were part of the local syndicate that had previously offered to purchase the Braves. When asked if they would pursue another team, Cutler said the group was solely "united for the purpose of retaining the Braves in Milwaukee." If Bartholomay did not sell and the Braves left, however, they would be interested in getting a different team for Milwaukee.[70]

On October 22, WTMJ-TV aired an editorial by station manager Robert Heiss that condemned the Braves announcement. "It seems incongruous," said Heiss, that Milwaukee County would have to go to court to prove it has been hospitable to the Braves. As much as the team was embraced when Perini owned the team, now "Bartholomay's Braves were just as welcome" and Milwaukee County "did everything just short of turning the stadium over to the club to prove how welcome they were." Unfortunately, the new group did not embrace the "old-fashioned kind of red carpet treatment" and instead preferred "a carpet made of gold." To the Braves, welcome was now "spelled M-O-N-E-Y," and because Atlanta offered more of it, the team "considered themselves more welcome there than here." Apparently baseball should be viewed as a big business that continues to operate outside of antitrust regulations while getting "free publicity the likes of which few other businesses can ever dream of receiving." Milwaukee needed baseball, and Heiss encouraged the community to "bolster our efforts to bring another team. Milwaukee can't afford to drop from the ranks of other Big League cities."[71] Noteworthy in this editorial is the emphasis on securing another team rather than engaging in a prolonged legal battle to force the Braves to stay against the will of its board of directors and owners.

"The County Board is as much to blame as anybody"

Milwaukee County officials were deluged with mail that expressed antagonism, hope, gloating, and melancholy in the days leading up to and the months

following the devastating news. Grobschmidt received letters from across the
nation, including a few from Atlanta. Many of the notes, handwritten and
typed, showed that fans felt truly hurt and simply asked that someone fight for
their community identity, for their team. One fan suggested that the county
needed to take legal action against the Braves and the National League because
"greed and contempt for the fans must be stopped or baseball will be destroyed." The writer encouraged a law that would make the Braves "belong to
the community, home owned, and owners must be forced to sell to local interests who promise to keep it in the city." In addition, because "the present owner
of the Braves acted in bad faith" he "should be forced into bankruptcy." A
seven-page letter from E. A. Howard, director of public works for Milwaukee
County, took exception to the comparison between the Braves' move from Boston and the proposed move to Atlanta. Howard argued that in 1953 Lou Perini
asked to come to Milwaukee and induced the county to spend more than $2 mil-
lion to accommodate them in the new stadium, just the opposite of the situation
now. Howard wondered if the "new management of the Braves" would "return
any of this money to Milwaukee County," or perhaps "Atlanta will reimburse
the County."[72]

A letter writer from Vermont was glad the Braves were moving because
"you people don't deserve a good club" in Milwaukee, and he hoped "you
don't get a franchise again, you don't need it." He deplored the Milwaukee fans
and would laugh when the National League voted against putting another team
in Wisconsin. Signing the note an "Atlanta Braves fan now and before," he
asked to "hear your complements [*sic*] so do write back." Joseph Konz of Green-
dale said it was best to let them go "to the land of their dreams." Forcing them
to remain against their will would only gain Milwaukee "a reputation for small-
ness, acridity and vengefulness." If they were released from the stadium contract,
said Konz, Milwaukee would "gain more respect from the sports world than we
already have." Ultimately, it would be "painfully evident" to all baseball owners
"how financially foolish it is NOT to have a club in Milwaukee."[73]

Milwaukee attorney Arthur Gazinski wrote that despite encouragements
from the local media to go to Braves games in 1965 to show the major leagues
that the region was still great for baseball, he did not intend to support the team
in 1965. Going to games would only put money into the pockets of owners who
did not know the meaning of the word *integrity*. Gazinski perceived that it was
problematic to disregard the previous twelve years of attendance in Milwaukee
and focus on attendance only for the year ahead as a measure of the region's
interest in baseball. He regretted his personal boycotts of Braves games, but
"the officials of the Club certainly took into consideration the empty Stadium
for 1965 and will be reimbursed by the City of Atlanta."[74]

While other writers blamed Bartholomay and his fellow owners, they were not solely responsible for the nightmare unfolding in Milwaukee. E. M. Heslin of Milwaukee noted that the county board had antagonized the Braves by being "*too* petty, *too* argumentative and *too* un-cooperative" and if the Braves left "the County Board is as much to blame as anybody." County Stadium did not belong to the board but to the taxpayers who financed its construction. Moreover, he asked, how many county officials had personally purchased stock when it was offered, besides Doyne, who had been pictured in the local newspapers purchasing one share.[75] Even one of its own, Lawrence W. Timmerman, criticized the county board for its dealings with the Braves. He accused his fellow supervisors of "penny pinching" and failing to implement and enforce a ban on scalpers and beer carry-ins.

Long-Range Best Interest of Baseball

The Braves initially believed that leaving Milwaukee in 1964 would be as easy as it had been when the franchise left Boston in 1953. But unlike the Boston club, the Milwaukee Braves played in a municipal stadium and had a contract binding them for a fixed period of time. The owners appeared to believe that the contract could be breached, and they fully intended to be in Atlanta for opening day 1965. Reynolds said the team was willing to make a fair financial settlement to Milwaukee County that would cover "rental, concessions, parking, the works." He confirmed that the Braves believed breaking the contract was "the same as firing a manager who still has a year to run on his contract" and that is what they "were prepared to do in this case."[76] On November 2, the Braves claimed that Milwaukee County itself had broken the lease and had displayed "malicious disregard" of the implied agreement that the governing agency would not "interfere with, obstruct, or frustrate the Braves enjoyment of the lease." In particular, the Braves claimed that Grobschmidt accused the team of "deliberately trying to have the Braves not win games" in an effort to anger the local population and give the team a reason to leave.[77]

On November 6, U.S. district court judge Robert E. Tehan refused to move the legal challenges to the Braves' relocation attempt to federal court. The Braves action was premised on the grounds that the franchise was a Delaware corporation and its principal office was in Chicago. Tehan's ruling sent the case back to Milwaukee circuit court where the Braves remained under a temporary restraining order that prevented them from even asking the National League to approve such a transfer.[78] Despite Tehan's ruling, Bartholomay and McHale planned to attend the special owners meeting in Phoenix, Arizona, called by Commissioner Frick to consider the Braves relocation.

At the owners' meetings on November 8, Frick announced that it was impossible for either the Braves to relocate to Atlanta in time for 1965 or another team to materialize in Georgia. He expected the Braves to retract their formal intention to play the 1965 season in Atlanta. This was a formality within the rules of baseball that prohibited teams from moving in 1965 because the deadline for drafting new territories had passed; therefore, this was now a dead issue. National League owners did, however, give the Braves formal permission to start playing in Atlanta in the 1966 season.[79] Milwaukee representatives were asked to leave the room before the vote was taken, and it was unanimous. Giles believed it was in the best interest of baseball to have the club in Atlanta by 1966.[80] A disappointed John Doyne responded that these owners "certainly must feel that Milwaukee isn't a good baseball town for the National League and we'll concentrate our efforts on getting an American League ball club."[81] Most likely, the Kansas City Athletics, whose owner clearly wanted to be in a new city.

As in Milwaukee a generation earlier, the Braves began formal claims to the Atlanta territory by purchasing the local minor league team. On November 29 McHale announced the purchase of the Atlanta Crackers for $285,000, clearing Atlanta for Milwaukee's team.[82] McHale added that he did not want to go through a significant amount of litigation and have the coming baseball season "clouded" by it. Worse for Milwaukee fans, when asked if there was any team that might come to Wisconsin in 1966, Frick responded, "I couldn't think of any right now." He also reiterated that Major League Baseball felt that Atlanta was a "great area that deserves baseball."[83]

After the owners' meetings and despite the one-year delay, Atlanta officially welcomed the Braves franchise to Georgia. Mayor Allen announced on November 10 that the Atlanta–Fulton County Recreation Authority and the Milwaukee Braves had signed a twenty-five-year lease that ensured the franchise would be in Georgia by at least 1966.[84] Tom Reynolds promised that there would be some exhibition games and possibly regular National League games in Atlanta in 1965. He hoped the Braves would not be legally challenged or forced to play out their lease at Milwaukee County Stadium. Reynolds felt that the National League would reconsider an immediate move if all legal obstructions were eliminated. Moreover, the team had offered to "pay off Milwaukee in full for releasing us from our 1965 contract. As I see it, that contract constitutes a right rather than an obligation to play in Milwaukee." It would be "in the best interests of Milwaukee to release the Braves. I can't see how having a 'lame duck' team can do either Milwaukee or the ball club any good." Even if they played out the contract in Wisconsin, "you can be sure our hearts will be in Atlanta."[85]

"The unmentionables in Chicago"

By late 1964, the Braves owners were personae non gratae in Wisconsin. Tom Reynolds admitted that if he and the others were "running an election against Adolf Hitler we would lose up there." In a rare moment of agreement, Grobschmidt said, "I agree 100 percent. I could think of some worse guys than Hitler who could beat them." The Braves remained optimistic that they could get Milwaukee officials to let them out of Wisconsin immediately, certainly by December 15, claiming it would be in the best interests of Milwaukee, Atlanta, and baseball in general for the team to move in time for the next season. Grobschmidt retorted that the Braves would remain in Milwaukee for 1965. When asked about fans coming out to support the team, Grobschmidt said he was encouraging Milwaukee to support baseball, but the fans "don't want any part of the Braves." Worse, he said many felt the Braves should "play to an empty stadium."[86]

On November 12, at a strategy luncheon organized by the Greater Milwaukee Committee, business and government officials charted a course of action. They understood that the Braves ownership was committed to play in Atlanta as soon as possible, and the National League owners would most likely support the transfer after all legal restrictions were removed. It was assumed that Milwaukee County was likely to get an injunction to prevent the move, but the Braves could probably defeat it. Many felt baseball's future in Milwaukee beyond 1964 depended on the transfer of another team or an expansion, and the latter would require at least two more teams per league. The cities thought most likely to get a team were Milwaukee, Seattle, Oakland, and Dallas.[87] Legal action could trigger the possibility of immediate expansion, as well as the threat of a congressional investigation. Any legal action had to be followed with support of the team in 1965.[88]

The strategy session led some to believe that the best course of action to keep baseball in Milwaukee, either the Braves or another franchise, would be great attendance in 1965. If this happened and a local group landed an existing team or gained a coveted expansion team, Milwaukee would have baseball after the Braves. Local government officials would have to work with at least three other cities to pressure baseball into a four-team expansion plan. There was no consensus on the best course of action in regard to a financial settlement. Many felt that because the team owners had defied morality, contract obligations, and public support, they should be compelled to live up to their contractual obligations regardless of the consequences. Some went so far as to suggest that nothing should be done to help the Braves "so long as the unmentionables in

Chicago would receive a nickel of the proceeds." A small minority understood the war was already lost and even the best leadership could not prevent negative public incidents and low attendance that would hurt the chances of obtaining another franchise for Milwaukee.[89]

Four days later, fans of the Milwaukee Braves received a reprieve, albeit a temporary one. The team owners informed the circuit court that they would not fight a permanent injunction. Now, outside of a financial settlement, the Braves would play out their contract in Milwaukee for the 1965 season. In a letter to Frick, Bartholomay reiterated the Braves' "definite intention and desire to acquire and include in the National League the City of Atlanta" and to operate the Braves in Georgia starting in 1966.[90] The Braves seemed to be abiding by the National League's order to remain in Milwaukee for 1965 and then move to Atlanta to begin their twenty-five-year lease in the Peach State.[91]

Meanwhile, some Braves front office personnel were sent to Atlanta to begin the transition into the new market, although McHale denied this was being done immediately because "we've got a job to do" in Milwaukee and the most important concern for the owners was the welfare of the club. He said the Braves had a fairly substantial operation in Atlanta with the Crackers, and key people associated with the farm club and the pending relocation were now in Georgia. The first ones scheduled to go after the Braves completed the purchase of the Crackers were John Mullen, the farm director; Richard Cecil, assistant farm director; and Ray Hayworth, director of player personnel. More Braves officials would be sent as needed, but several would have to remain in Milwaukee for the 1965 season. Traveling secretary Donald Davidson would accompany the team; Ernie Johnson would remain in Milwaukee. McHale also made it clear that since the Braves would be in Wisconsin for the following year, "There has been no further consideration of permanency in Atlanta for any employee." McHale would not have a central office but would operate out of Milwaukee, Chicago, and Atlanta. However, once the Crackers were purchased, he said, "Most of my time will be spent in that city."[92] In late December the Braves hired Patsy Knight, the first Atlanta-based resident, as Cecil's secretary. In early January, Bartholomay moved into an Atlanta apartment to oversee operations as the Braves hired more local personnel.[93]

In a move to streamline operations as the Braves entered a lame duck year in Milwaukee, the stockholders reduced the number on the board of directors from twenty-two to fifteen. Six of the seven directors who were removed had strong Wisconsin roots and had voted against the franchise shift. The seventh was reportedly Vince Lombardi, who was not formally informed he'd been removed. The stockholders returned the remaining directors, including

Bartholomay and Reynolds, to their positions of authority. When again asked if the team would be sold to local interests, Bartholomay stated that he and his associates owned 86 percent of the team and had "no intention of selling to Milwaukee people or anyone else." Despite the likelihood of a potential boycott of Braves games in Milwaukee, Bartholomay said the team was committed to putting the best club on the field and thereby offset any negative factors.[94]

Edmund Fitzgerald, one of those removed from the board, said that he and his fellow Wisconsinites were not at the meeting. He took issue with statements that the Braves had made earlier that there was no solid offer to purchase the Braves. However, he added, if "they had no intention of selling, then it was not a firm offer." He was not "going to chew over weasel words with them. I'm devoting all of my efforts to bringing in another major league club here and let's face it—they've won the battle."[95]

"Why prolong the issue?"

At this point, there really were no good options left for the club or its Wisconsin fans. Even new local ownership was unlikely to get out of the contract between the team and Atlanta. Doing so would create more litigation and impel Atlanta officials to enforce the agreement that had just been signed. Therefore, the future of baseball in Milwaukee after 1965 depended on a legal decision requiring the Braves to stay permanently, a new expansion franchise, or another team relocating to Wisconsin in hopes of recapturing the Milwaukee Miracle. Some in local government wanted to pursue litigation to enforce the existing lease and thereby keep the team for at least the next season. In contrast, many in the business community were willing to let them go and instead actively pursue another baseball franchise. Regardless of which direction the community went, it appeared inevitable that Milwaukee would be the first city completely abandoned by major league baseball and County Stadium would sit empty, at least for a while.

Former Braves general manager John Quinn, now with the Philadelphia Phillies, offered a plan to help Milwaukee transition to another team. He said Milwaukee had nothing to accomplish by forcing the Braves to stay for 1965 now that they were committed to Atlanta by 1966. But freeing the Braves immediately would enhance Milwaukee's national image—"all of baseball would also have to admit there are real big people there"—and improve "Milwaukee's chances of getting another major league team, either by transfer or by expansion." The county had nothing to gain by holding the Braves against their will, so "why prolong the issue?" Plans to expand the National League to twelve teams in a few years might put Milwaukee in a good position. Quinn urged Milwaukee County to get a AAA team for 1966 if a major league team was not available. Once the Braves were gone, Milwaukee would be an open city and any team, major or minor, could potentially move in. In a tongue-in-cheek suggestion, maybe the Atlanta Crackers, now looking for a new home, could become the Milwaukee Crackers in 1965.[96]

Lloyd Larson wrote that the community was really in a tough position, as "no city or group of people ever faced a more perplexing problem." It was apparent to all that the Braves wanted out as soon as possible and the "shifting of key personnel to Atlanta and setting up official headquarters in Chicago" indicated their desire for an expeditious transfer. It made financial sense for the team to offer a large buyout to Milwaukee County because it was looking at "a big loss in revenue because of the year's delay and the Braves appear to be a cinch to operate at a big loss here next season."[97] On December 30, the Braves denied having offered the county $1 million to get out of the lease a year early. Reynolds said the "report is not true" and "I will not say anything more about it." Doyne said he had not been informed of any settlement offer.[98] Bartholomay said the Braves recognized that they had a financial obligation to Milwaukee and were willing to reach an equitable settlement but there currently was no specific proposal from either side. He added that the Braves had paid the county around $200,000 in tickets and concessions and would most likely pay less in 1965 since only twenty-eight season tickets had been purchased.[99] Furthermore, sponsorship of radio and television broadcasts had been canceled, forcing the Braves to sell radio and television rights in Georgia.

Some felt that the less interest and business the Braves generated in Milwaukee, the greater the likelihood they might be allowed to leave in time for 1965 in Atlanta. According to Grobschmidt, three conditions could release the Braves from their Milwaukee contract: (1) a letter of intent from Major League Baseball giving Milwaukee first consideration when expansion became reality; (2) a guarantee of some form of baseball at County Stadium through 1966; (3) an acceptable financial settlement from the Braves to the county for all damages sustained by their transfer to Atlanta.[100] None of these conditions would be met.

As for a relatively minor matter, the county board deferred a vote on a measure that would prohibit the resale of tickets on the grounds of County Stadium. While some believed this would be a good step to show that the board was not petty and prepared for another team, other supervisors were against doing any favors for the Braves. Grobschmidt had allowed the vote only because he had previously promised the team to do so and did not "want the Braves saying we're damned liars" over scalped tickets. Supervisor Pohl suggested that season ticket holders were opposed because it would prevent them from offloading tickets they no longer wanted. Grobschmidt replied, "I don't think we'll have to worry about season tickets." William O'Donnell argued this was not the right time to help the team as the "general public is mad at 'em."[101] The uncertainty about dealing with the team for 1965 would lead the board into the very pettiness some had tried to avoid. Obviously they were in an uncomfortable spot in hosting the Braves for the lame duck season, and there were no good options to pursue.

In a scathing editorial, Arthur Daley wrote that baseball owners were "people so blinded by their greed" that they were going to move a team that was still legally obligated to be in Milwaukee for at least another year. The owners, Daley insisted, "persist in destroying the once lofty image the game enjoyed and then can't understand why fans become cynical and apathetic." He warned that the Braves' lame duck status might be comparable to Bill Veeck's experience when he first tried to move the St. Louis Browns to Milwaukee and then Baltimore in 1953. Attendance was miserable, Veeck was forced out of baseball, and the Browns then left. The Braves owners, Daley added, would get the sympathy of other baseball owners, but certainly not the fans. Worse, for Bartholomay and his group, the Braves mostly likely would "not get much of their patronage either." Daley was perplexed that "supposedly smart men could paint themselves into a corner the way these fellows did." He closed by saying that as "some sage once wrote: Baseball must be a great game to survive the people who run it." Fans of baseball in Milwaukee most certainly agreed with that sentiment.[102]

It is too simple to argue that the Braves owners hoped that a new market with fresh fans would flood their modern stadium and all would be rectified. Daley later argued that the "allure of Georgia" was not so "old fashioned" as it appeared. In contrast, the move was "geared entirely to the marvels" of the new "electronic age" as Atlanta would give the club "a thumping whack at richer television markets." Because baseball did not share television revenues, teams like Milwaukee were at a clear disadvantage compared with their NFL and AFL counterparts who did split television money. The Green Bay Packers were, and remain, the smallest city in both football leagues. As evidenced by their success in the 1960s, however, they were able to compete with much larger media markets. The revenue sharing in professional football created "sounder and stronger" leagues from top to bottom. Television was now "baseball's unmistakable sugar daddy. The Braves have already indicated that their heart belongs to daddy—but only in Atlanta."[103]

The Braves' departure was, and remains, too often seen as a purely emotional loss. This certainly cannot be discounted, as only fans can understand the feelings of abandonment as the team that they loved made clear it did not love them in return. Others saw it in purely economic terms to the city, county, and state. Additional problems were apparent almost immediately. Milwaukee County had been preparing promotional materials, including a $10,000 film called *Home of the Braves*, that featured the Braves as a principal asset of the city. If the team moved to Atlanta, no longer could Milwaukee make that claim.[104] Philip Wrigley said he was willing to bring the Cubs to Wisconsin for a few games in 1965 "for the good of baseball and if I can get the consent of both leagues." He said that if all teams played at County Stadium, former Braves fans would have "more varied baseball than any other city in the country." Though he was not willing to sell the team or move it permanently to Wisconsin, he was apparently willing to work out this arrangement because baseball owed it to Milwaukee. Grobschmidt immediately endorsed the plan and said that if forty-five or fifty games were scheduled in Milwaukee in 1965, the Braves could expect to be released from their stadium contract. It was hoped that this type of arrangement could carry Milwaukee until expansion was an option.[105] Larson wrote that this could be the future of baseball at County Stadium, but he could not "imagine fans storming the gates for a neutral look at outside teams."[106] Unfortunately, the stalemate between the county, the team, and Major League Baseball would continue into 1965.

7

Lame Ducks

1965

Not since the days of William Tecumseh Sherman has there been such a wild scramble to get to Atlanta in a hurry.

Arthur Daley,
June 10, 1965

"We've got a job to do in Milwaukee"

The Braves ownership group remained convinced that they would ultimately prevail, despite the roadblocks put in place by the Wisconsin courts. In November 1964 they began to transfer key personnel to Atlanta. Corporate headquarters were still in Chicago and offices were maintained at County Stadium. In order to establish an official presence in Atlanta, thirty full-time employees were offered the choice to relocate to Georgia or face termination. Those who chose to stay with the Braves would be relocated as soon as possible. Braves president John McHale publicly denied this move was ongoing because "We've got a job to do in Milwaukee," as the Braves had "agreed to play here in 1965 and the most important concern is the welfare of our baseball club. Our goal is to turn out a first-class baseball show here."[1] But by March 1965 Earl Yerxa, the Braves' concessions manager, was in Atlanta helping to get the new ballpark set up and would divide his time between Georgia and Wisconsin for the 1965 season. In April the Braves opened a ticket office at Atlanta Stadium and began to sell tickets for Crackers games for the upcoming season. The team's accounting office also moved to the new ballpark, and the team formally trademarked the Atlanta Braves name.[2]

In more bad news in Wisconsin, the county board passed a measure in mid-December that once again banned beer carry-ins at County Stadium, forcing fans to patronize concession stands for the beer they drank to drown their sorrow over the Braves' departure. While other teams had bans on carry-ins, many saw this one as just another swipe at the pockets of the dwindling numbers of fans expected to grace County Stadium with their presence. Arguably, the real aim of this move was to hurt the Braves owners, who would feel the economic pinch of smaller crowds at the ballpark.

In December, McHale made it clear that the team was willing to settle for $400,000 for broadcast rights for the 1965 season and approached the Schlitz Brewing Company to continue sponsoring radio and television broadcasts of Braves games in Wisconsin. The deal offered $125,000 less than in 1964.[3] Schlitz rejected the offer on December 9, explaining that when the original three-year deal at $525,000 per year was negotiated, the team had denied that it was attempting to move. Schlitz's "sole interest in making this offer, which we considered generous from any standpoint," was to "help keep the major league franchise in Milwaukee and Wisconsin." As a result of the "events of the past weeks, culminating in the announcement that the Braves will move in 1966," the company felt that "under the present circumstances it can no longer justify participation in sponsorship of the Braves broadcasts." If plans to relocate changed, Schlitz would "certainly take a look at the matter."[4] The Schlitz statement pointed out that when president Robert Uihlein Jr. and others in the community tried to purchase the Braves from its current ownership group, they were informed the team was not for sale. When asked to comment, Tom Reynolds offered nothing while Bill Bartholomay said it was "self-explanatory" and that at the present time, no sponsor had yet come forward to sponsor the Braves broadcasts in Milwaukee.[5] Bartholomay later testified that radio rights were ultimately sold to Teams Inc. for a "minimum price of $60,000 which was to scale upward if they in turn could acquire strong commercial sponsors for the show." This did not happen and he stated that as of early January 1966, the team had not "received any more than $60,000."[6]

Meanwhile, the Braves were making moves behind the scenes to phase out their Milwaukee identity even before the 1965 season began. When the annual team yearbook and press guide was published, the cover showcased photos of manager Bobby Bragan and a sliding play at the plate, along with the logo featuring Chief Noc-A-Homa that the team used for brand identification. The word *Braves* appeared on the cover but not the word *Milwaukee*. The omission might have been either an intentional slight for forcing the Braves to return for a lame duck season or a hedge in case the team was allowed to leave before the end of the year. At the top of the table of contents on page two was the team name *Milwaukee Braves, Inc.* with address and phone number at Milwaukee County Stadium, as well as the phone number in Atlanta.[7] The team sent speakers out across the state of Georgia to begin the process of building a fan base and pump up season ticket sales. Throughout 1965, the Braves would make more than two hundred stops across the South to promote the club. The team also entered into an agreement with Delta and Southern airlines to sell Atlanta Braves tickets in all the cities they served.[8]

At the same time, Arthur Allyn, co-owner of the Chicago White Sox, said there was no justification for the Braves' relocation and the commissioner of baseball could prevent the move. He appealed directly to Ford Frick, saying he had "asked the American League to discuss the Braves' question at our meeting in New York on February 1 with the hope of requesting the commissioner to cancel the move." He had "fought for it each time and tried to get the commissioner to squash the move but he wasn't about to do anything about it." He personally felt that the Braves' ownership group most likely "signed their contract with Atlanta before looking at their obligations in Milwaukee. Now I wonder if they can get off the hook in Atlanta." He also said, arguably correctly, that he suspected the owners "spent so much money in the purchase of the club that they couldn't get enough of a return to support their investment. But that is not the fault of the fans." It was instead the owners' "tough luck," and the "near nineteen million people who have turned out for the Braves' games in the past twelve seasons have proved Milwaukee is a major league city."[9]

In the first days of January 1965, U.S. Representative Clement Zablocki introduced legislation to end the antitrust exemption that baseball still enjoys. The Milwaukeean argued that recent developments in regard to the Braves' pending relocation "dispelled any doubt that baseball is first a business and only secondarily a sport." Without the antitrust exemption, existing leagues could expand or a third major league be created. The Braves situation "demands new legislation to bring sanity back to our national sport."[10] The bill was unlikely to be signed into law, and it never was.

Teams Inc. in Action

In late January Teams Inc. president Edmund Fitzgerald sent a report to county executive John Doyne that outlined the current baseball situation in Milwaukee. Teams was a nonprofit association organized by nine Wisconsin business leaders, spearheaded by Fitzgerald. He acknowledged that it was not an official agency or voice for Milwaukee fans, but its recommendations were in "the best judgment" of those who had been studying the situation for the previous two months. According to surveys by Teams, interest in baseball across the state was going down and antibaseball sentiment was on the rise. Many outside the region believed that local fans had "failed to support the Braves" over the last few years. These negative attitudes were "exaggerated all out of proportion and the positive aspects have been severely minimized or neglected completely." This effort by Teams was beginning too late, as they should have been meeting with National League officials "a year or more ago and maintained on a regular basis so that the real Milwaukee situation could be kept before these men." Unfortunately, many baseball officials believed Atlanta was now a better town. Despite the Braves' great success in the 1950s, their fans were now solely judged on "the performance of the last four years in which our average annual attendance" eclipsed only the Chicago Cubs and the Houston Colt .45s.[11]

Teams Inc. did not offer advice for keeping baseball in Milwaukee but it was, in their opinion, best for all parties for the Braves to play through their lease at County Stadium in 1965. All fans of Milwaukee baseball should support the team and achieve "national recognition" that will "enhance throughout the nation the overall image of our city and of our state." The decision to allow the Braves to relocate in time for the 1966 season was "for all practical purposes irreversible," and the Atlanta lease already signed "precludes the possibility of the Braves playing baseball in Milwaukee after the 1965 season."[12] A few months later, however, Teams said the "best remedy under state law would be an action by the Attorney General of Wisconsin in the Wisconsin courts to enjoin the Braves from moving from Milwaukee until the Braves, the other National League clubs and the League provide an 'expansion' franchise and a supply of players to be operated by a competent Milwaukee group." The team and the National League had violated federal and state antitrust laws, and there was a "reasonable chance of success" through legal action. In fact, even if the federal courts ruled that there was no antitrust violation, they might "enjoin the Braves from moving unless and until" another franchise was located in Milwaukee.[13]

There seemed to be nothing that could derail the Braves from moving to Atlanta by 1966 at the latest. Frick said he could not veto the move because that "would be a breach of contract." Frick and National League president Warren Giles had met with members of Teams and warned them that the deal between the Braves and Atlanta was a long-term contract and he could not break it any more than he could terminate the lease the club had in Milwaukee through 1965. The delegation from Teams included Fitzgerald; Irwin Maier, president of Journal Communications; and Ben Barkin, a public relations executive and organizer of Milwaukee's Great Circus Parade. Fitzgerald said that they had "been meeting with National League owners and today's meeting was to further explore the situation" as "Milwaukee fans are extremely interested in getting a major league club." Giles said that the Wisconsin group asked about "possible expansion and I would think that's what their meetings with our owners have been about. We told them we don't know when there will be expansion." Frick stated, "Milwaukee should be given prime consideration in the event of expansion. But there's no telling now how or when it will come."[14] Teams Inc. did not have a specific proposal, but it was apparent that their long-term concern had more to do with baseball in Milwaukee than it did with the Braves. Teams also spent "more than $30,000" on 1965 radio rights in Wisconsin but was unsuccessful in selling advertising rights in Milwaukee or at the national level. The "broadcasts were the only solid medium of advertising the Braves had."[15]

In late February 1965, Milwaukee-based Pabst Brewing joined Schlitz in avoiding the Braves and instead signed a deal to sponsor Detroit Tigers telecasts. Schlitz did the same for the Houston Astros (the Colt .45s changed their name in December 1964, preceding their move into the Astrodome). Although local breweries still sold their products at County Stadium, it was evident that local money was moving away from the Braves. At the same time, it was announced that the Braves had sold a broadcast package in the South with sponsorship from Coca-Cola and Anheuser-Busch. The deal included fifty-five radio broadcasts of the Milwaukee Braves, mostly weekend and holiday games, into the Atlanta market. There were also plans to telecast eighteen games into Georgia and beyond. Games of the Atlanta Crackers, the Braves farm club that spent 1965 in the future home of the Braves, would also be broadcast as part of the agreement. In early March the Braves hired former New York Yankees broadcaster Mel Allen to be the voice of the team in Atlanta for 1965. Braves publicity director Ernie Johnson and Hank Morgan, sports director of an Atlanta radio station, would join Allen in the booth. Morgan later said the potential audience for the televised games was more than 622,000 homes in the new market of Georgia and the rest of the Southeast. The first game the new Atlanta crew called was an exhibition game in Atlanta between the Milwaukee Braves and the Detroit Tigers on April 9, 1965. The Braves received only $150,000 from the southern stations. McHale announced the Atlanta crew at the same time he said that there were no arrangements yet for Milwaukee broadcasts but an announcement was expected soon. He added that the Milwaukee broadcasters would be distinct from the Atlanta crew, presumably Merle Harmon and Tom Collins on WEMP and Blaine Walsh from WTMJ, who had called Braves games on radio and television for years.[16]

The Diamond Dinner

The twelfth annual Diamond Dinner, sponsored by the Milwaukee chapter of the Baseball Writers Association of America, featured current and former players and regional media. About seven hundred people attended, but the team's owners were conspicuously absent. Lloyd Larson wrote that there was still plenty of life left in the "corpse" of baseball in Milwaukee and the "huge throng that turned out proves conclusively that Milwaukee is not a baseball disaster area." Several leading government officials attended, including governor Warren Knowles, John Doyne, Eugene Grobschmidt, and mayor Henry Maier. Together they hit on a recurring theme of keeping the Braves for the duration of the 1965 season. Knowles encouraged the remaining Braves fans across the state to back the team "to the hilt and cheer them on to another world championship." In response to the Braves vice president Tom Reynolds saying that the team's heart belonged in Atlanta, Maier jokingly answered with an "old German proverb, which translated means: 'His heart is where his money is.'" Maier remembered giving the owners a key to the city of Milwaukee that turned out to be a skeleton key "which worked in Atlanta as well as here." The mayor added that no matter what happened to the Braves or "what names of other cities are put on their uniforms, the best wishes of the people of Milwaukee go with them. Nothing that happened is going to break the relationship between the Braves' players and the people here who have taken them to their hearts."[17] Representatives from Teams recommended that Milwaukee County require the Braves to play out their stadium contract and announced that they had an agreement from Giles that he would "promptly establish a three-man committee of league officials to work with a committee from Milwaukee for exploring methods by which major league baseball can be returned" at the earliest date. Unlike elected officials, Teams believed that the decision by the National League to transfer the Braves to Atlanta in 1966 was irreversible.[18]

A Good Baseball City

After the Teams meeting, Commissioner Frick wrote a letter to Fitzgerald in which he described Milwaukee as "a good baseball" city but cautioned that it would be hard to get a new team after the Braves left. Frick had responded to a report from Teams that called for ongoing support for the departing Braves to confirm Milwaukee's status as a major league city worthy of another permanent franchise. Frick considered the report to be "100 percent factual, 100 percent sensible, and 100 percent co-operative" and the program it outlined to "do more to re-establish the image of Milwaukee as a city of great baseball interest." It would not be easy but it was not impossible "and certainly your committee deserves the deep gratitude of the Milwaukee people and of baseball for the job you are attempting to do." Fitzgerald was encouraged by the commissioner's response and said the goal was still "to acquire a permanent franchise for Milwaukee at the earliest possible date." To accomplish this there was a need for the "co-operation of organized baseball and this letter from Mr. Frick indicates that we will receive that co-operation."[19]

"Our partners in this final season here"

The Braves owners realized that as long as they were locked into playing in Milwaukee in 1965, they could not afford to have an almost empty stadium for their entire slate of home games. In their attempts to get the very angry people, who normally would have supported the Braves, out to games, they sold tickets at Milwaukee- and Waukesha-based Sears stores, in twelve cities across the state, and at the Humphrey Cadillac and Oldsmobile dealership in Rockford, Illinois, as well as at the stadium and by mail order. Ticket prices ranged from $1.55 for general admission in the grandstands to $4.10 for a seat in the mezzanine. On Ladies Day, women got into County Stadium for fifty cents, the same price that was charged every day for children.[20]

On February 12, 1965, Teams Inc. met to discuss an offer by the Braves to contribute money to Teams for every ticket sold at County Stadium in 1965. McHale said that the Braves would contribute to any promotional fund designated by Teams to get another team to Milwaukee. Doing so would invite "Milwaukee to become our partners in this final season here." The Braves proposed to give a nickel for every ticket sold to a maximum of 766,927, the lowest attendance at County Stadium to date. The number would rise to twenty-five cents for every ticket sold from that point to one million tickets. Every ticket sold above the million mark would garner Teams a dollar. The payments would be made on the basis of paid attendance as defined by the rules of the National League. Such an arrangement was a first, to his knowledge, and it was "an offer we make freely and in the friendliest spirit, for the good of Milwaukee and the Braves." He also said that the club lacked a sponsor for broadcasts, so none were yet scheduled for the 1965 season. Fitzgerald said the money could be designated for three purposes: obtaining a new team, promoting that team, and possibly improving the stadium. He viewed the proposal as an "incentive for fans to help get a new team for Milwaukee as well as support for the Braves in their final season here." Highlighting a growing divide between civic leadership and governmental agencies, Grobschmidt criticized the offer because he felt that the Braves should contribute to Milwaukee County rather than a promotional fund through Teams Inc.[21]

In mid-February, Teams began a major effort to retain baseball's presence and Milwaukee's big league status and welcomed the Braves' participation, saying that the "gate sharing plan will be incorporated into this effort, and should provide significant additional incentive to purchase tickets for this year's games." The funds that Teams received from the Braves in 1965 would go in a separate account at First Wisconsin Trust Company, where they would be managed, invested, and disbursed accordingly. None of the funds would be used to purchase, on their own behalf, "equity in a new baseball franchise." Teams was also "barred by intent and by charter from participation in the operation of a baseball franchise." Fitzgerald's group could "receive as much as $675,641" in their effort to gain another team for Milwaukee if the club's twelve-year "average of 1,563,027 fans is achieved in 1965."[22]

Teams Inc. announced its intention to sell one million tickets for 1965 Braves games and that Bud Selig would chair the ticket drive. Selig said he hoped to have the help of prominent Milwaukee citizens and organizations and together "concentrate our efforts on people who have purchased season tickets in the past" and "encourage as much new business" as possible. Fitzgerald added this was in "line with our determination to get a major league baseball club here to replace the Braves" and to showcase that "Milwaukee is still enthusiastic about good baseball and will continue to be."[23] The goal was to sell at least 1,800 season ticket packages by Opening Day on April 15, 1965. Fitzgerald noted that he and other civic leaders believed that "Milwaukee isn't on trial as a baseball town" but rather "baseball was on trial."[24] Unfortunately, he was wrong.

The local media was mixed in their response to this proposal. In late February WITI Channel 6, at that time the ABC affiliate in Milwaukee, editorialized over the folly of pursuing the deal. They argued that local fans did not "want to sell their pride to those who have chosen to desert our city for reasons" justifiable only to the Braves owners. This would allow Bartholomay's group to "pat us on the head as they go out the door with the nickel-a-ticket offer to soften our feelings." While the print media endorsed the plan with full-page ads, WITI believed that this "sales gimmick" was an insult to Milwaukee. Any attempt to use this ticket sale to protect the "good name" of the fans of the city was misguided, as they had averaged more than a million and a half for over twelve years. Therefore, the Milwaukee fans should "not start groveling in the dirt before those who have demonstrated most clearly no loyalty to us as a city" regardless of "how much loyalty and support" Wisconsin had already displayed to their team. WITI encouraged fans to go out to County Stadium to support the players and enjoy baseball and not to "salvage a pittance." If baseball wanted to offer something substantive, let them "offer us a team in 1966 if we hit a million in attendance this year. Or better, let them order the Braves to sell to local interests."[25]

In February, the Journal Company, publisher of the *Milwaukee Journal* and the *Milwaukee Sentinel*, produced a forty-six-page booklet in cooperation with Teams entitled *Milwaukee . . . Major League City*, highlighting the value of southeastern Wisconsin to baseball.[26] It was designed for and distributed to "owners of major league baseball clubs and to others closely connected with baseball and other major league sports. It will not be available to the general public."[27] Charts within showed that over the previous twelve years, the Milwaukee Braves had trailed only the Dodgers in attendance. In fact, while the Dodgers averaged 2.2 million fans in America's two largest cities, the Braves averaged almost 1.6 million in a much smaller market. At the same time, the Braves were third in the number of season tickets sold in 1964 despite rumors the team was leaving. Over its history, the Braves averaged 9,260 season tickets, again behind only the Dodgers. County Stadium also had one of the larger seating capacities of any club in the National League, and it could be expanded from the current 44,613 seats to 70,000. Because of its location, near the brand new interstate system, and its hub of four major bus routes, fans would not have any problems getting to the ballpark. There was also information about Wisconsin fans' interest in all sports, and the financial earning prospects of potential fans, growth prospects of the region, and the Milwaukee area in general. In sum, Milwaukee was a city of progress, and the future of baseball would be bright for any team that decided to relocate, or even for an expansion franchise.[28]

Blair Scanlon, the district sales manager for Ford Motor Company's Milwaukee district, said he was "impressed by Teams' efforts and realized that what the group is doing is the only way for Milwaukee to retain its major league status. I feel the same way—That only by continued support here in 1965 can we stay major league." Scanlon's group promised at least 150 tickets for Opening Day and that number could grow to as many as 300 by game time. Selig remained optimistic that their message was spreading, and now "the temper seems to have changed and we are greatly encouraged by favorable response." Still, not all fans were receptive. Bragan said most preferred to wait and see what was going to happen, but it was evident "that Teams Inc. has changed the attitudes of a lot of people."[29]

Bragan had joined Selig's effort to sell tickets. Never popular with Wisconsin fans, especially after making some very disparaging remarks about Milwaukee, Bragan later wrote he stayed in the city to help "hustle season tickets sales" during the winter of 1964–65. He noted that there was an "extra obstacle to my goodwill efforts in the community; the ownership tried to break its lease" and leave for 1965. He said anger remained, as stores and banks across the city "removed Braves' schedules from their counters. Because Atlanta was the home of Coca-Cola Company, Milwaukee bars and restaurants stopped selling Coke." At the beginning of spring training, McHale warned his players and coaches that it was "going to be an unusual year for all of us, but I'm sure you realize that the only thing for everybody is to do his best. And don't get involved in the controversy."[30]

"Milwaukee is interested in baseball, not money"

Although some success in ticket sales was noted in March, it was not enough. The community remained divided about whether to fight to keep the Braves or simply let them go. WISN Channel 12 reported a movement that might allow the team to leave for Atlanta before the start of the season. Despite the number of season tickets being sold, more than 840 at this point, some members of the county and Braves management were willing to negotiate a settlement that would allow the team to leave in time for Opening Day. One item being discussed was approximately $250,000 in "concession and other equipment" at County Stadium that the Braves might donate if allowed to leave. Furthermore, said Channel 12, they and other National League teams could still play several games in Milwaukee and thereby preserve major league baseball at County Stadium for the upcoming year. Regardless of these concepts, or the $500,000 local officials had already rejected, it is clear that Milwaukee officials and fans did not trust the Braves management. Channel 12 editorialized that if the Braves made a firm offer to buy out its final year at County Stadium, it should be considered and the "County Board of Supervisors should not be swayed by emotions but, from a good, solid business standpoint" and "if possible, accept it."[31]

Selig remained optimistic about the sales drive and noted that his group of sixteen volunteers had already sold 934 season tickets and were likely to get to 1,700. William Eberly, the Braves sales director, said that just over half of 1964's season ticket holders had been notified and reaching the remainder was essential to hitting the targeted goal. Selig said there had definitely been a "thawing out in the attitude of the fans toward the season ahead." Teams Inc. reminded all that they wanted not to assist the Braves owners but rather to show that Milwaukee was still truly deserving of the big leagues. Ben Barkin said, "Milwaukee has nothing to prove and Teams Inc. has no brief for the Braves. We are interested only in enhancing our chances of getting a major league baseball club. This represents a challenge to Milwaukee and an opportunity for Wisconsin fans."[32] Local officials came under a bit of fire when it was pointed out they were encouraging people to purchase tickets at the same time they were "first in line for free tickets." Many asked why should there be any attempt to make McHale and his group "rich before they leave."[33]

At the same time, despite Selig's optimism, the Braves and Teams struggled to sell tickets. Meanwhile, the Packers announced that their upcoming season in Green Bay and three games in Milwaukee were sold out. It was interesting to note that the sellout included an eight-thousand-seat expansion at City Stadium (Lambeau Field).[34] It could be argued that by this time football had surpassed baseball as America's favorite sport, and clearly the Packers were now more important than the Braves in Wisconsin.

"The happiest occasion for Atlanta"

Before returning to Milwaukee after spring training, the team spent three days in Georgia breaking in their new home for the fans in Atlanta. Mayor Allen called the Braves' arrival the "happiest occasion for Atlanta since General Sherman decided to head south for Savannah in 1864." The reception was similar to the one the team had received in Milwaukee twelve years earlier. More than sixty thousand fans greeted the team's motorcade as it paraded through the city. More impressively, an estimated 194,000 turned out for six exhibition games.[35] The games were well received, and the team felt welcomed by the community.

The new Atlanta Braves Booster Club was racially integrated, as was seating at the new stadium, unlike at Ponce de Leon Park, the home of the Atlanta Crackers. The ushers and other employees at the new park were also integrated, as were the areas around the stadium where white and black customers spent money at restaurants and other establishments. Bragan said Atlanta had made significant strides over the last decade, and while it seemed inevitable that the team would be in Atlanta permanently in the near future, there was still hope for Milwaukee. He stated that the ten-team league structure was not well liked and there would most likely be expansion in the future. With its past success, Milwaukee needed to "apologize to no one" because it was a "good baseball town" and the city had "too much to offer baseball to be bypassed in the future."[36]

Meanwhile, in a small act of protest against the Braves organization, county executive John Doyne returned his season pass for all 1965 home games. He thanked McHale for the pass but returned it "for reasons that should be quite obvious."[37] Like many civic leaders across the region, Doyne had come to the frightening and inevitable conclusion that Milwaukee's status as a major league city would be greatly reduced once the Braves were gone. Beyond the economic and entertainment value of major league baseball was the idea of a city losing its heart and community identity. Atlanta would gain this status at the expense of Wisconsin fans of the Braves.

Opening Day

Teams Inc. announced that it had purchased the remaining tickets for the 1965 home opener at County Stadium and said it would be a "stand up for Milwaukee day." It hoped that it would give "every citizen a chance to stand up and be counted for Milwaukee's future, in baseball and in many other ways. Industry and business will be watching, too, and our spirit and performance will be noted." Edmund Fitzgerald said if "we are to show others that Milwaukee is truly major league, we must fill the stadium to capacity and more. We must make our points while we have games to attend. We know there is resentment about the Braves' move after this season. But this is now a Milwaukee promotion, not a Braves' promotion."[38] The gate was expected to be significantly down from all previous Opening Days in Milwaukee.

On the eve of the game, the Braves were reported to be significantly in debt, at least $4.9 million since Perini had sold the club for more than six million only three years earlier. One creditor stated that the new owners "paid too much for the ball club" and ultimately owed too much to stay in Milwaukee. The players did not expect fans to take out their anger on them personally. Henry Aaron said the players were professionals and had a job to do. Furthermore, the Milwaukee fans were not like those "in Philadelphia or places like that. In eleven years I've never heard them boo and I've made some boo-boos here. We all have." According to Bragan, it makes no difference where they play although "players like to perform before full houses. They respond. But what is most important to them is the first and sixteenth of every month—payday."[39]

On April 15 County Stadium was pristine and vibrant with red, white, and blue bunting as fans filtered into the ballpark. There was a mixture of nostalgia, anger, and sadness over the pending loss of the Braves as Blaine Walsh introduced members of the original 1953 team before the game. Excitement peaked when Walsh introduced the last of the originals, Eddie Mathews. Laurie Van Dyke wrote in the *Milwaukee Sentinel* that it was cold and overcast at the park, and the "chill felt by the crowd was deepened, perhaps by thoughts that Milwaukee might have no baseball season in 1966." She noted "no sign of a grudge against the players. Cheering was frequent and enthusiastic" and "the Braves' owners, mindful of their roles as the villains of the piece, were among those absent."[40] Unlike previous years, the 1965 Opening Day brought out politicians and civic leaders not to praise the team but to look past it and into the future. Instead of team owners, Teams was in the management box. Mayor Maier and his wife refused to sit in the owners' box because he wanted to "stand up for Milwaukee, but we don't have to honor the moneychangers." Governor Knowles threw out the first pitch and the season was under way. Fitzgerald did not care at all if the owners' decided to "show up or not. No one from our organization talked to them about not coming." Carlton P. Wilson of Robert W. Baird & Company said the cold at the ballpark reminded him of the previous December when he and others were unceremoniously dumped from the Braves board of directors.[41]

Tom Reynolds, who listened to the game on the radio instead of attending, said that the Braves were "determined to find a way of demonstrating our cooperation with Teams, Inc. Staying away from the game was a concrete example of co-operation, although an unpleasant one." He contended that approach to showcasing Milwaukee as a great baseball town would improve the chances of getting another franchise because the packed stadium effectively was "proving we're wrong." Moreover, the approach by Fitzgerald's group was a "much more reasonable one than that of Mr. Grobschmidt and his cannonading and courtroom approach." Reynolds said he and his fellow owners would return to County Stadium as soon as they received an "all-clear signal."[42]

Not until the last day of April did Bartholomay receive that "signal" and return to the owners' box at County Stadium. According to Lou Chapman, the owner "shut himself off from the press in the Braves' mezzanine box. An attendant stationed outside the doors prevented writers from entering." When Chapman asked to enter the president's box he was refused, and the guard said that he would use force to keep the reporter out. "Nobody can get in without authorization" and everyone "has to be screened first and get special permission to enter." Bartholomay left about fifteen minutes before the final pitch and made himself unavailable to reporters afterward. It was noted that when the team was rooted in Wisconsin, the owner always made himself available to the press. Now that their heart was in Atlanta, he made himself scarce.[43]

"People will have to fight for baseball"

Despite the best efforts of Fitzgerald and Selig, many fans took out their frustration on the organization and stopped going to games. Barkin of Teams suggested that it was "just wrong. People will have to fight for baseball if they want it. I know we're going to have to do something to help boost Braves attendance." Early in the season, the average crowd at County Stadium was only around twenty-five hundred, as opposed to the almost thirty-four thousand that greeted the Braves on Opening Day. Barkin called it a fight and said "the people of Milwaukee must realize the Braves must be supported if there's going to be major league baseball in Milwaukee after this year." The unofficial boycott of the team appeared to be growing, as more wanted to prevent putting money in the accounts of the very men who they believed were stealing their team. Barkin and Teams were in a tough position, and time was running out to salvage Milwaukee's image as a great baseball town.[44] The campaign to save baseball was failing, but Selig later said Teams desperately "needed to get the door open. Here was a chance to do something very positive. This was a vehicle to try to develop a positive relationship" with baseball and Milwaukee.[45]

As the season got underway, cold weather and ambivalence combined to keep fans away in record numbers. The largest crowd at County Stadium since Opening Day came on May 20, when more than seventeen thousand fans turned out to see their old hero Warren Spahn, now pitching for the New York Mets, hit the mound one last time in Milwaukee. He did not last into the sixth inning and even surrendered a home run to his old teammate Eddie Mathews, who "trotted around the bases expressionless." It was perhaps an ironic summation at this moment in time of the Braves in Milwaukee. Apart from this minor bump on May 20, the Braves were averaging less than three thousand in attendance.[46] In the first twelve home games of 1965, 64,957 fans went through the turnstiles at County Stadium, including the 33,874 on Opening Day, or less than half of the 1964 total of 137,409.[47]

Anger and fan disinterest continued to plague the team. Two nights in April saw County Stadium host 1,677 and 1,324 in total attendance, as Milwaukee appeared to be giving a "death warrant" for its baseball future. While these numbers were minuscule in comparison to the heady days of the past, other ball clubs also had poor numbers in early 1965. Detroit had two crowds under five thousand, Yankee Stadium had one of 3,001, Baltimore's Memorial Stadium hosted 3,571, and Cleveland's cavernous Municipal Stadium had a game where 3,827 fans sat among almost seventy thousand empty seats.[48] The anger of the team leaving plus apathy over a declining team added up to a dismal future.

One unhappy Braves fan commented, "Atlanta can have 'em." For eight years he had bought tickets and "then they want me to buy beer—at their prices. They have got to have all the money." Another said that the poor turnout is "just this town. They don't stay interested in anything very long. Nothing will ever go here except bowling—and beer drinking."[49]

It was evident by mid-June that the volunteers were wasting their time trying to save the Milwaukee Braves. Lloyd Larson acknowledged that "county officials have absolutely no intention of going for any offer" that would let the Braves leave early. Baseball officials said that they would make no guarantees on returning the Braves or another franchise. Larson noted the importance of baseball at County Stadium, and regardless of what the future held, if you were a fan of baseball, you needed to go see the Braves while you still could. The players had done nothing to deserve anything less than "all possible encouragement and support." There was even some increase in ticket sales, both individual and group, and ticket manager Austin Brown said they were "very hopeful and certainly will try our best to be ready to accommodate the fans at all times." Even with the unofficial boycott underway, attendance in 1965 to this point was well ahead of the Braves' last year in Boston, 125,606 to 101,446.[50]

In June the legendary Hall of Famer and retired Brooklyn Dodger Jackie Robinson appeared on WTMJ-TV with a panel of Milwaukee sports reporters to discuss the deteriorating situation with the Braves. Robinson said that baseball "is big business and if things are not going well, as obviously they aren't in Milwaukee, the owners look to greener pastures." If he were the commissioner of baseball, he would let the Braves go immediately. The situation in Milwaukee was not good for baseball, but franchises that simply moved "to make more money" also hurt the sport. Addressing concerns expressed by Henry Aaron and Lee Maye about playing in Georgia, Robinson contended that they "will be treated well, if not better, in Atlanta than in some northern cities because it is an enlightened city with firm leadership in race relations."[51]

"To hell with 'em"

In early June, Bartholomay offered Milwaukee County $400,000 and Teams an additional $100,000 to let the Braves out of their contract in July, allowing them to play full time in Atlanta. The Braves' proposal went to Doyne, Grobschmidt, and Fitzgerald. Doyne did not immediately comment, but Grobschmidt did: "To hell with 'em." He said that the county had a restraining order in place that obligated the team to play out the season at County Stadium. If the county approved anything less, it "would be going back on the public. We fought to make them play here in 1965. Now, why should we turn around and accept this offer?" To accept the offer would weaken the county's position in their suits against the Braves, and the public would be "99 to 1 against it." Some board members might have been willing to accept a financial settlement, but this offer from Bartholomay struck them as too low.[52]

The county board and Teams accused the Braves of sabotaging attendance at County Stadium in mid-June by not promoting games, printing schedules, or adequately staffing ticket offices. Team representatives continued to make statements that "had the effect of continually fanning the flames of antagonism among Milwaukee citizens." They also had prevented Teams from buying out tickets at County Stadium for three community-wide promotional games, as Teams had done for Opening Day. Grobschmidt accused Bartholomay of "destructive efforts which you and your associates have had on 1965 fan enthusiasm and attendance." Consequently the county was "not interested in the least in your effort to buy your way out of a situation of your own making. I believe it would be well if you and your associates would finally come to the realization that Milwaukee is interested in baseball, not money." Fitzgerald, who issued a statement on behalf of Teams, said that up until this time, "Despite repeated later requests that Milwaukee permit the Braves to leave before the end of 1965, no one in organized baseball has given the city any assurance of a solution to the basic problem which baseball has created for Milwaukee by giving the Braves permission to move their franchise in 1966." Asked if the team planned on having any promotions for the remainder of the season, Bartholomay said that the "best promotion is our second-place ball club."[53]

On June 20 the Braves made the extraordinary move of banning *Sentinel* sportswriter Lou Chapman from the clubhouse because of his negative columns about the ball club, despite having covered the team since they arrived in 1953. The Braves later backed down and banned Chapman for only twenty-four hours, but they limited him to the office of assistant general manager James Fanning. It was only here that Chapman was allowed to meet with Braves' players, although he was not banned from the visiting clubhouse, the field, or even the dugouts before the next game. He was told that he had to meet with Fanning, who was running the club in Milwaukee, as McHale was "already based in Atlanta setting the stage for the club's move in 1966." Fanning accused Chapman of having a "disquieting effect on the players in the clubhouse, the employees in the ticket office and throughout the Stadium." He further contended the Braves staff in Milwaukee would "tingle" when Chapman was around because they were afraid of what he would ask and "if they're going to say anything wrong." He wanted the "Milwaukee operation to go—to be successful. We're trying the best we can. However, it's discouraging not to see crowds at the games." The local chapter of the Baseball Writers Association denounced the team's action as "unwarranted and an infringement of the freedom of the press."[54] The ban was lifted, although Chapman made it clear he would not change his style of reporting the facts as he saw them.

While the Braves were looking for an expeditious departure from Wisconsin, Milwaukee County weighed its options. An internal memo laid out the problem of retaining the Braves or attracting a new team. The Braves were going to Atlanta primarily because the multistate radio and television package was more lucrative than in Wisconsin. The Braves in Atlanta would be the only major league city in the South. The city was more than three hundred miles from the next closest team, and it was the epicenter of a seven-state television network, in contrast to Wisconsin, which was isolated by Lake Superior to the north, Lake Michigan to the east, the Cubs and White Sox to the south, and the Twins to the west. In Atlanta the Braves were expected to earn between $5.5 million and $7 million in broadcast revenues over the first five years, excluding income generated from Major League Baseball's telecast of the *Game of the Week*. In Milwaukee, in 1964, the Braves made approximately $400,000 from broadcasts with an additional $75,000 to $100,000 in network money. This made "the Atlanta pasture" about "$500,000 to $600,000 a year richer in radio and television revenue" than Milwaukee's—"a considerable sum to a major league club owner and . . . often . . . the difference between profit and loss for any one year."[55]

The county board understood that if it was going to be successful in coaxing a franchise to Wisconsin "rather than Buffalo, Seattle, New Orleans or some other comparable area," Milwaukee had to offer "a financial package that will far outweigh any package one of the other communities can offer." Consequently, Milwaukee officials first had "to decide whether we really want a major league franchise in Milwaukee County." If so, then there must be a way "to pay such a franchise; or to put it in another way, the County will have to subsidize the franchise to some extent." Only three teams at this time made less in broadcast revenue than the Milwaukee Braves, but this discrepancy could be offset by "a highly favorable rental and concession agreement" that could include free rental and no concession percentages paid to the county until reaching the million mark in attendance. After that, the amount owed would be on a sliding scale that would pay the county more as attendance grew but less than the current lease required. Milwaukee would also have to install concession apparatus at the ballpark because the Braves owned the current equipment at County Stadium and would take it to Atlanta unless someone purchased it. It was also recommended, most likely owing to recent experience, that if a new team came, the minimum lease deal should be ten years.[56] Unfortunately for Milwaukee Braves fans, such an approach was too little and far too late. Perhaps if these terms had been offered in 1957 or 1962, Milwaukee would have remained the home of the Braves.

The news for baseball fans in Wisconsin continued to get worse as the summer wore on and tempers flared. In early July, Grobschmidt again accused the Braves of underperforming in games. At a Kiwanis Club meeting in Wauwatosa, he asked a crowd how it would look if the Milwaukee Braves went to the World Series but then departed for Atlanta? Bragan responded by calling Grobschmidt a "dim-witted politician" who, "if a baseball hit him on that bald head of his" would not know "if it was a baseball or a softball." Bragan argued that players' livelihoods depended upon their personal performance, and therefore they were giving everything they had. Even more, playing in the World Series was an honor, whether the Braves played it in Newark, Hoboken, Oklahoma, or Sheboygan. Bragan thought that Grobschmidt's comments were potentially libelous, and he was surprised that "the players don't sue him," especially after he had made the same claims a year earlier. Several players, including Henry Aaron and Eddie Mathews, commented on Grobschmidt's statements, but none of them seemed to take Grobschmidt too seriously. In response, Grobschmidt contended, "Coming from a dim-witted manager, I'd expect something like that." When informed that Bragan was coaching in the 1965 All-Star Game, Grobschmidt said that baseball must "really be scraping the bottom of the barrel."[57]

Hopes of landing another franchise weren't encouraging. Commissioner Frick felt that the greater Milwaukee area could support major league baseball, but when asked why he did not tell the Braves to stay, his response was cold and to the point. He did not feel he had a right to "tell a man to sell or not sell. After all, this is America. I can use my influence. I can try to persuade him, but if someone tried to prevent it, that would be dictatorship." Furthermore, he felt that he "could be sued for $10 million and so could anyone connected with the act. I could be in lawsuits up to my neck if I try to stop them." Two owners, Gabe Paul of the Cleveland Indians and Bill DeWitt of the Cincinnati Reds, further dampened Milwaukee's hopes when they said there was unquestionably no chance another team would arrive in Milwaukee for the 1966 season, including any existing franchise or expansion club. The Indians, who had been rumored to move, had made a new deal to stay at Cleveland's Municipal Stadium, and Paul said, "I know we are staying where we are." DeWitt said no National League clubs would be moving and "I know I wouldn't move there."

Lou Chapman added that other "baseball people avoided comment on the Milwaukee situation—and its reporters—as if they were afraid of contracting a contagious disease." Most of them seemed to "be embarrassed at the shabby way in which the city was treated." Comments from Bartholomay and Reynolds were hard to come by as they were "off and running" whenever they saw a Milwaukee reporter. Interviews were done on the move and Chapman "could have used track shoes to keep up with sprinting owners" who wanted to be in Atlanta sooner rather than later.[58]

As the 1965 season wore on, the Braves were in contention until September. Reporters asked Bartholomay what would happen if the team won the pennant and went to the World Series. He replied that the team's "primary obligation is to the season ticket-holders right here in Atlanta—uh, Milwaukee."[59] He added that if the Braves played in the World Series, the revenues generated still would not offset the estimated $1.5 million the Braves lost. He believed the Milwaukee fans had engaged in a boycott, and he hated "to think what we'd be drawing if we weren't a half game out of first place." He now believed that Milwaukee was no longer a major league city because the team had been near the bottom in attendance for the last four years. He added that only the Cubs drew fewer during that time. He did not doubt they could sell out County Stadium if the Braves played in the World Series, as they "could fill the park in San Diego" if the Braves "played the series there." The team was "not going to sell series tickets in Atlanta," but the fans from their new hometown would be allowed to buy tickets. The Braves did not have plans to invite Atlanta officials to any World Series games played at County Stadium.[60]

In Retrospect and into the Courts

Bill Veeck weighed in on the Milwaukee situation in early August when he appeared on WTMJ-TV and elaborated afterward. The former minor and major league owner said the antitrust suit might compel the Braves to remain in Milwaukee or expedite an expansion franchise that "might force baseball to realign" and include expansion in other cities. He added that if you assume "that after a series of lawsuits the Braves would have to remain in Milwaukee," they would be "under new management, of course." If that happened, "the National league could give Atlanta one new expansion club and Seattle another. The American league then could put expansion clubs in Oakland and Buffalo." When Veeck was asked what he would do if he were the general manager under a new Braves ownership, he joked that the first thing he would do would be to "put up a sign at County Stadium two hundred feet long and twenty feet wide with the words: 'Open Under New Management.'" He added that he would "be polite, which would be a change in itself. Also, I would operate the club on the premise that the fans were doing me a favor when they come to the park instead of vice versa." The owners might be nervous about the lawsuits, and he had a feeling that "the Braves' carpetbaggers aren't blithe and cheery as they were when they first thought of flying off to Atlanta in their chase of the depreciated dollar." He also noted that the Milwaukee fans were "determined not to give these guys their traveling money." Prophetically, Veeck predicted the team would not draw as well in Georgia as in Milwaukee for the first three years. "Milwaukee will continue its eminence in baseball," and he remained hopeful that baseball would remain in some manner, "whether it'll be the Braves—or as I prefer it, the Brewers of sainted memory—or an expansion club."[61]

In a surprise move, on July 26, the Braves ownership asked the U.S. district court in Milwaukee to approve the move to Atlanta for the 1966 baseball season and to forbid Milwaukee County from suing to require the team to be in Milwaukee beyond 1965 or force the establishment of an expansion franchise in Wisconsin. Bartholomay said the Braves had acted to "give everyone an opportunity to secure a final, binding, adjudication as to our status." Milwaukee County's corporate counsel, Robert P. Russell, responded by stating that the county would file its expected antitrust suit in early August. The owners claimed that the Milwaukee fans' unofficial boycott in 1965 had already cost the team at least a million dollars and they would "face financial ruin" if the team remained in Milwaukee in 1966. They believed the team had the lawful right to play home games in Atlanta next year and beyond. Additionally, in what would become a recurring theme, the Braves accused county officials of conducting a campaign of harassment designed to prevent the move or guarantee a replacement team for Milwaukee.[62]

On July 29, the future of baseball in Milwaukee was officially incorporated by a group of local business leaders. Although it included some of the same influential men from Teams Inc., the new group was created to actually purchase a franchise. Among the main investors of the new Milwaukee Brewers Baseball Club Inc. were Schlitz president Robert Uihlein Jr., Bud Selig, clothing manufacturer Jack Winter, and the resolute Edmund Fitzgerald. Reaching into the recent past with its name, the Brewers would apply for a franchise in the National League. It was not clear if they would apply to the American League, but they did acknowledge that Milwaukee County had already done so with both leagues.[63]

"The creepy feeling that this could be the end"

September 22, 1965, felt decidedly different from April 14, 1953, the day of the first Milwaukee home opener for the Braves. Back in 1953, when the future was bright for baseball, coverage of the Braves' opener was on the front page as well as the sports pages, which were filled with stories about the team, the players, and the overall excitement of finally being in the major leagues. On this rainy early autumn day in 1965, however, the remaining Braves fans in Milwaukee were disconsolate. At County Stadium, the field was made ready for the final home game in Milwaukee, barring a miraculous change of heart by the owners or a court-ordered mandate. The morning paper's front page had extensive coverage of First Lady Claudia "Lady Bird" Johnson's visit to Wisconsin and the ongoing conflict between Pakistan and India. Outside of a despondent cartoon Indian, one that had graced the paper for thirteen years, there was no mention of the final Braves game. In a somber column that addressed the finality of the situation, Lloyd Larson wrote that the joyous spirit of 1953 was missing and "instead the gloom is thick because of the creepy feeling that this could be the end." There was still a chance that baseball could be played at County Stadium beyond this season, and even by the Braves, he said, but in the interim it might be practical to face the likelihood the worst would happen and baseball would be gone.[64]

The final home crowd of only 12,577 watched the Braves lose to the Los Angeles Dodgers 7–6. As the fans said farewell to the 1965 season, to summer, and to the Braves, there remained a "mixture of enthusiasm and sadness." Some clung to the belief that the Braves, or some other team, would be at County Stadium in 1966. One fan, Dick Emmons, said that many "people are really hurt. I'm hurt like everybody else, it's hard to realize that they're leaving." It was reported that people were purchasing souvenirs at a brisker pace than normal, especially "anything that had Milwaukee on it."[65]

As the game began, the original Milwaukee Braves broadcasters, Earl Gillespie and Blaine Walsh, were in the booth one last time and called the first few innings of the game. As the game went on, the scoreboard lit up with a simple message: "Braves Say Thank You Fans." Bartholomay said he was present because when "the greatest left hander, Sandy Koufax, is pitching against us, I've got to see the game." When asked if he would help Milwaukee secure another franchise, Bartholomay was noncommittal. He did say Milwaukee had every reason to be encouraged about "its future in baseball" because the Brewers and Teams represented responsible groups that were "willing to undertake the job and the financial risk that goes on year after year of owning a major league team." He did not answer questions about his responsibility for the Braves leaving; however, he added that the team owed it to the National League and the American Southeast to bring baseball to that new market.[66]

Former Braves shortstop Johnny Logan wrote that it was "unbelievable" to him that "Milwaukee is going to be without baseball." Milwaukee was "the backbone" of the National League and it was "still big league." He acknowledged that attendance was down now, but understood that "these things run in cycles," and it was tremendous that the Braves reached half a million fans in spite of "all the bad publicity." Logan contended that what was needed was a team that was locally owned so "the Braves are a city team and a state of Wisconsin team. Baseball ought to stay in Milwaukee."[67]

Meanwhile, the sixty full-time and two hundred part-time employees of County Stadium faced job reductions. The state would lose the income of taxes collected from stadium operations, including salaries and concession sales. Others affected were concessioners, vendors, and suppliers, as well as the taxpayers who had built and maintained County Stadium at a cost of $8.6 million since it opened in 1953. Most businesses that depended upon major league baseball in Wisconsin faced a critical loss: "gasoline stations, restaurants, nightclubs, hotels, motels, utilities, retail stores, newspapers, and television and radio stations" in addition to the bus and taxi service to the stadium and stadium suppliers of food, soft drinks, and beer. The Braves estimated "$50 million in out of town revenue, $2.8 million in stadium rent, $1.6 million in parking fees, taxes on Braves payroll, and $5.4 million in products purchased locally for sale at County Stadium."[68] And now, with the exception of a handful of Packers games every year, County Stadium would lie mostly empty, a memorial to days gone by.

Two days after the Braves' last game in Wisconsin, a stunning report by Jim Enright appeared in the *Chicago American* and was picked up by the Milwaukee papers. Stadium manager Bill Anderson had announced that if the Braves made the World Series, a fading possibility at this point of the season, there would be no general sale of tickets in Wisconsin except to the thirteen hundred season ticket holders. This meant that only about two thousand Milwaukee fans would be in County Stadium if all ticket holders bought their full allotment. Anderson said that he had been informed, as had Teams Inc., of this decision. Someone, most likely McHale in the Braves front office, had said that the Milwaukee fans could not "cold shoulder us all season" and then "be first in line to purchase World Series tickets. I don't know where they would be sold but it won't be in Milwaukee—and you can wager the family jewels on that." It was not clear if

Frick would support this planned boycott of local ticket sales or if the commissioner could intervene and order local sales.[69] Regardless, it was evident that the Braves could not wait to get out of Milwaukee and were prepared to slap the faces of those who had supported them since 1953, especially those who remained fans throughout 1965.

Later that afternoon, James Fanning denied the *Chicago American* report. He claimed it was "ridiculous, the idea of freezing out a state" from purchasing World Series tickets. He affirmed that he never informed Bill Anderson or "any members from Teams, Inc., or anybody else that they wouldn't be able to buy tickets. The idea is to sell out the stadium." Furthermore, the Braves had authorized tickets to be printed after Frick gave them permission back on September 8. However, according to Fanning, the team "ordered the printing company to discontinue" producing tickets once it was apparent that the Braves were not going to win the 1965 National League pennant. The club canceled ads promoting the tickets and closed the World Series ticket headquarters. Fanning said the ticket office had "intended to handle applications almost the same as they were handled in 1957 and 1958." Season ticket holders were the first priority and then after the team "had fulfilled our obligations to the baseball commissioner and to other major league clubs, the sale would have been open to the public." With team obligations included, Fanning believed that between thirty-six thousand and thirty-eight thousand tickets would be offered for public sale, and if there were "any intention of freezing out fans in Milwaukee or Wisconsin, I don't know about it—and we had enough meetings to work out arrangements in detail." Anderson denied that he had any knowledge of the Braves' plans for World Series tickets and he said Teams had not been told they could not purchase tickets. He said that he "was told by a friend connected with the club not to plan on series tickets—and that's all I know about it."[70]

Whether the story is true, it was certainly plausible. Fanning was a close friend of McHale and followed him to the Montreal Expos in 1968 when McHale was named president of that expansion franchise. Therefore, the ticket story resonated with the local Milwaukee media as a further example of the hostility of the Braves toward the fans who would be abandoned once the season was over. And from the Braves' perspective, why should they reward the very people who were threatening to drag them through the courts in an effort to force them to linger in a city where they were no longer wanted?

In Los Angeles on October 3, the Milwaukee Braves lost their final game ever 3–0. They finished the lame duck year in fifth place, eleven games behind the pennant-winning Dodgers. Both Milwaukee newspapers noted the passing of the era but said little more. Instead, the sports pages of the *Journal* and the

Sentinel were filled with photos and stories of the most recent game between the Chicago Bears and the victorious Packers. Braves coverage was minimal and, frankly, easy to miss unless one were looking for it. After thirteen seasons in Milwaukee, the Braves had finished in the upper half of the National League twelve times; won two pennants and one World Series; and finished second five times, third once, fourth once, fifth three times, and sixth once (1963).[71] And with that, the Milwaukee Braves era was over, and the future of professional baseball at County Stadium was extremely bleak.

According to the terms of the 1962 Milwaukee County Stadium lease, the Braves were still responsible for the lucrative concession sales and stadium operations in Milwaukee, which included all games played by the Packers in Milwaukee. November 14, 1965, marked the last Packers game played at County Stadium under the Braves lease, and at the conclusion, the baseball team was free and clear of its Milwaukee obligations. While the lease officially ran out on December 31, there was nothing more for the team to do after the Packers played their final Milwaukee game of the NFL season.[72] On November 15, the Braves removed most of their remaining assets from County Stadium, including some of the equipment that had come from Boston back in 1953. They removed concessions files, equipment, bases, the backstop, the pitching rubber, and other miscellaneous property and sent it to the new ballpark in Atlanta.[73] The following day, the Braves closed out their accounts at Marshall & Ilsley Bank, First Wisconsin Bank, and the City Bank of Milwaukee and effectively removed all assets of the team from Wisconsin with the exception of a $10,000 cash bond the county owed the team at the end of the year. In early December the team filed a formal notice of withdrawal of business from Wisconsin. They were joined by the other National League teams that were no longer doing business in the state because games would now be played in Atlanta. The team estimated its financial losses from the 1965 season to be in excess of $700,000, substantially higher than the $45,000 from 1964, but offset by more than $750,000 in 1966 season tickets already sold in Georgia. All that remained for the people of Milwaukee, said Veeck, was an empty stadium and "a few tired memories and a bitter void."[74]

Valid Expectations of Securing Favorable Judgments

On August 3, Milwaukee County filed the long-awaited suit in U.S. district court that alleged the Braves front office, the National League, and its members had violated federal antitrust laws and Wisconsin state statutes. Milwaukee County sought either the sale of the Braves to local interests or an expansion franchise.

This legal action was a response to the Braves motion in federal court in July to forestall the antitrust suit and simply allow the team to play in Georgia in 1966. Milwaukee County asked to restrict the Braves from playing any home games outside of County Stadium until either a new ownership group was in place or a new franchise arrived. It also demanded triple damages for any and all costs associated with the Braves' attempt to relocate. The manager of every visiting team that came to County Stadium in August and September was issued a subpoena, although it is not clear what this would accomplish.[75]

Grobschmidt was deposed by Braves attorney Ray McCann in late September and asked several questions. Had the Braves ever attempted to secure a long-term lease with Milwaukee County? Grobschmidt said no: "As I recall it, the Braves wanted a short term lease. I sat in on the meetings." Had the Braves asked for a ten-year lease before the 1957 season was over? He acknowledged they had but added there "was a dispute about television rights" because the team wanted the long lease "without television provisions." Did Milwaukee County refuse to agree to a five-year deal in 1962, one that would have kept the Braves through the 1967 season? Grobschmidt responded that he did not recall but he did know they eventually signed a three-year deal. He also clarified that County Stadium was run by the Milwaukee County Park Commission, with members appointed by the county executive, but operated under the supervision of the county board.[76]

It was hoped that the threat by Wisconsin and Milwaukee County would force Major League Baseball to do something to help maintain baseball in Wisconsin or face the possibility of the destruction of the game if it lost an antitrust case because of the Braves. In November 1964, federal judge Robert E. Tehan had ruled that the antitrust case filed by the state attorney general's office against the Braves would go to Milwaukee County circuit court before it could go to a federal court. This meant that the State of Wisconsin could seek an injunction in its courts, before December 31, 1965, that would prevent the Milwaukee Braves from relocating in 1966. Once Tehan made his ruling, the state began to work to accomplish this goal. Braves attorney Earl Jinkinson stated that he feared that if Wisconsin prevailed, "Then all the other states too can claim that they are being prevented from having teams. We might end up with sixty teams."[77]

Ford Frick clearly described the owners' position: The situation in Wisconsin was different than in Washington, DC, where baseball immediately voted to put in a new franchise right after Calvin Griffith took his team to Minnesota because the American League expanded to ten teams "and there was a franchise available." He still thought Milwaukee was "a good baseball town" and for the "first few years attendance was very good. I have no reason now to think that Milwaukee does not qualify as a major league city." However, Frick believed that owners had the right to move if they incurred financial losses by remaining in an unfavorable situation. He said an "owner has a responsibility to himself, his partners, and his stockholders" and therefore he "has no responsibility to lose money or to stay where he can't get by or where it appears the city is not going to support big league baseball." He also believed that the Braves' attempt to move to Atlanta and Charles Finley's effort to relocate the Athletics to Louisville were different because Finley's was considered "detrimental to baseball" and he faced "penalties imposed by the commissioner."[78]

Despite his public compliments about Milwaukee, Frick was said to be critical of actions taken by elected officials to keep the Braves. In a deposition given by C. Hayden Jamison, an executive director of the Wisconsin Investment Board, Frick's thoughts about Wisconsin were a bit more revealing. Jamison testified that Frick had told him the team would be in Atlanta for the 1966 season and if there had not been an antitrust suit, Milwaukee would have obtained a franchise. This was a certainty especially if Grobschmidt "would just shut up." In the *Journal*, Kuechle tackled this issue directly by asking if Frick had believed what he was alleged to have said. If so, why had he not said it "before the state's and county's separate suits were instituted?" He further outright dismissed Frick's statement about Grobschmidt because it was "ridiculous to think that a major league club would pull up stakes because an official once or twice said unkind things about the ball club's play on the field."[79]

As Milwaukee was passed over in the years that followed, resentment about baseball in Wisconsin endured. Milwaukee County Stadium was no longer home of the Braves, and an eerie silence resonated in the shadows of the empty ballpark.

8

Milwaukee v. The Braves

1966

The first batch of carpetbaggers from the North to be accorded the warmest welcomes in Dixie.

Arthur Daley,
March 8, 1966

"Meant the most to us since we lost the Civil War"

Realistically, it was far too late in the process to save major league baseball in Milwaukee for 1966, and it would perhaps be even bleaker in the future. As the legal challenges worked their way through the courts, hopes for a decision that meant the Braves' returning or the immediate granting of an expansion team slowly died. A season ticket campaign for a team that wanted to leave or a new one that would probably not be competitive would be futile. The fate of the Braves would ultimately be resolved by the United States Supreme Court. There was no room for sentiment in any legal decision, and the fans had no effective voice in these proceedings. There was no way to involve them because they were not the landlords, owners, or holders of any particular asset of the team—except for a place in their hearts where the Braves once resided. Even worse, the very fans responsible for the Miracle of Milwaukee are still blamed for abandoning the team, which made the departure from Wisconsin particularly stinging.

Just three weeks after the Milwaukee Braves played their last game in Los Angeles, the Atlanta Braves debuted in Georgia, on October 27, 1965. Many players, including Milwaukee stalwarts Eddie Mathews and Henry Aaron, participated in the promotions for season tickets for Atlanta's 1966 season.

187

Assistant general manager James Fanning said more than two thousand season tickets had already been sold in Georgia and the Braves expected that number to climb once their campaign gathered momentum. More than a dozen players were scheduled to travel throughout the Southeast to make personal appearances and give speeches to support the ticket drive. Most of the team's employees had already come to Atlanta; only the head groundskeeper and one ticket office assistant were left in Milwaukee. Moving their financial assets to their new home, the Braves opened a payroll account at the Citizens and Southern National Bank. They also sold the venerable Ponce de Leon Park, once the home of the Crackers, for $1.25 million and demolished it to make room for a shopping center, leaving the new stadium the only home for baseball in Atlanta.[1]

When the team reported for spring training in early 1966, it was the first time since 1952 that Milwaukee fans did not anxiously await Braves baseball and the upcoming season. Both major Milwaukee newspapers still followed the team with articles, editorials, and box scores. But throughout 1966 the team was simply referred to as *the Braves* until it was determined they were not going to be forced to return. When players were in the news, the papers often used older file photos of them, with the prominent *M* on their caps. One sign above the main entrance to the stadium prominently carried the old Milwaukee Braves name, until its photograph was published, at which point the Braves painted over the word *Milwaukee* and eventually removed the sign.[2]

Indecision was rife among the players, and many were reluctant to purchase houses in Georgia because there was no guarantee the team would not return to Wisconsin. In fact, only two players were reported to have bought homes in the Atlanta area by early 1966. Many new fans in Atlanta remained tentative about the future of the team, and countless people had tired of the legal wrangling. Still, the Braves front office remained optimistic that they would prevail in the courts and continued to push for more ticket sales in Georgia. Earle Yerxa, the former concession manager in Milwaukee and now director of advertising and mail orders in Atlanta, was optimistic. A remarkable backlog of orders had not yet been processed, season ticket sales were close to five thousand, and more than thirty thousand tickets were sold for Opening Day. Yerxa noted strong interest in the Braves from new fans across the South, including the Carolinas, Alabama, and Tennessee, but group sales were disappointing, as most orders were for only two to eight tickets per game.[3] Fortunately for the Braves, the multistate broadcast deal would help offset the potential of less-than-capacity crowds at Atlanta Stadium. It may be noteworthy that, despite the appearances of success, season ticket sales were still between five and six thousand lower than their thirteen-year average in Milwaukee.[4]

Especially excited about the relocation was the Atlanta Braves manager Bobby Bragan. He had been the target of fan anger in Milwaukee for much of the last two seasons, and he now believed that a positive and excited fan base could be the difference between winning and losing. He added that the last year in Milwaukee "was the happiest in my managerial career. No one wanted me for personal appearances and I therefore was able to spend more time with my family than ever before." Bragan acknowledged that he did not like being booed and noted the fans only wanted to cheer for their favorite players. He was also bothered by the lack of fans and believed that "the entire ball club can't wait for the different reception we're bound to get in Atlanta."[5]

At the mayor's welcoming party for the Atlanta Braves, attended by local officials, dignitaries including Warren Giles, and team officials, several speakers made light of the current situation between Milwaukee and the Braves. Mayor Ivan Allen Jr. targeted Eugene Grobschmidt for his past remarks and credited him with doing more "to bring major league baseball to Atlanta than any other man." William Bartholomay joked that he felt a little nervous because "in the last three or four years, nobody from the Braves had a chance to speak to a sellout crowd." He further said he had "learned a little law on the job in the last few years" because of the legal entanglements with his franchise. Georgia senator Richard Russell told the crowd that it would be great to now "be able to support a team with a chance to win." Governor Carl Sanders added that the arrival of the Atlanta Braves meant "the most to us since we lost the Civil War."[6]

"They made this bed. Let them lie in it."

Among the supporters of the Braves remaining in Milwaukee was Chicago White Sox co-owner Arthur Allyn, who was not a fan of the new Braves owner-ship group. Having previously dealt with them when they were minority owners of the White Sox, Allyn remarked sarcastically that if Bartholomay's group were forced to sell the Braves to local Milwaukee interests, it could not happen to a nicer group of fine fellows. He believed that the Braves might, after several legal obstacles, be returned to Milwaukee and that expansion was not a practi-cal option. As for another team moving to Wisconsin, Allyn noted that none was looking to move but if one did it would trigger the same legal problems the Braves had because the franchise's owners would face local lawsuits to prevent any move to Milwaukee. The National League owners had in fact encouraged their American League counterparts to allow Charlie Finley and the Kansas City Athletics to move to Milwaukee County Stadium, which would allow the Braves to get to Atlanta without a problem. However, continued Allyn, his fellow

American League owners "had the good sense to keep Finley from doing this very same thing when he wanted to get out of Kansas City and go to Louisville." As for the Braves owners, "They made this bed. Let them lie in it."[7]

Among all of the personalities in the saga of the Braves in Milwaukee, arguably none had a more lasting impact than the man who was not even part of the organization. Bill Veeck was instrumental in the transfer of the team to Milwaukee in 1953 and had actively supported baseball in Wisconsin from the days he owned the minor league Brewers. Veeck was also a significant thorn in the side of major league owners and remained a strong critic of how the business of the sport was conducted. In particular, he was outspoken in his criticism of what had transpired in Milwaukee between the new owners of the team and a state that in the recent past had supported the Braves in record numbers. In the autumn of 1965 Veeck and Ed Linn released a book entitled *The Hustler's Handbook* that excoriated many of the business practices of baseball, including franchise relocations. In many ways their arguments about the Milwaukee Braves have become a major part of the legend of their fall in Wisconsin. Once the team was sold to "the Milwaukee Carpetbaggers," the pattern of leaving a city for greater riches elsewhere became a common practice and baseball teams were now "a piece of merchandise that passed from hand to hand." Owners were far too focused on profitability and attendance rather than fan loyalty and previous patterns of patronage at the old ballpark. Veeck said the relocation of the Dodgers from a great Brooklyn market with a fervent and loyal fan base to an unproven Los Angeles displayed owners' disdain for their own fans. By 1964 owners were, according to Veeck, willing to abandon cities that had been loyal and had a single team. This had never been done before, and it marked a complete change in the business model for baseball.[8] In many ways, baseball owners were not concerned about the fan bases in the old cities because new fans would be generated in fresh markets.

The Beginning of the End

On January 25, 1966, circuit court judge Elmer W. Roller ordered Major League Baseball to face the first serious challenge to its antitrust exemption in more than four decades. He rejected the attempt by the National League to have the case dismissed, and he said his action did not touch upon Wisconsin attorney general Bronson La Follette's request for an injunction against Braves relocation unless a new franchise was offered to Milwaukee. Roller ruled that Atlanta–Fulton County Recreation Authority had no direct legal interest in the State of Wisconsin's antitrust suit and it was not an indispensable party in the proceedings. He also contended that previous cases involving antitrust and baseball had dealt with the internal dealings of baseball and "held that local aspects were subject to state antitrust laws."[9] Many felt that the State of Wisconsin might have a chance to win this case.

Roller's initial decisions were seen as a major impediment to an immediate relocation for the Braves and possibly at least a temporary return of the team to Wisconsin, especially after he issued three orders. The first restrained the Braves from entering into any contract or any other obligation in Atlanta for the 1966 baseball season. He then ordered the Braves to make all necessary and preliminary arrangements to begin the season in Milwaukee "during the 1966 baseball season and thereafter" if so ordered by the court at a later date. Finally, Roller directed the National League to "make plans for expansion of the defendant league so as to permit major league baseball to be played in Milwaukee in time for the 1966 season." Bartholomay responded to Roller's ruling quickly and stated that the team was "currently before the Superior Court of Fulton County, Georgia and that an order had been issued by that court preventing the Braves from taking any action that would have the effect of breaching the agreement with the Atlanta Stadium Authority." Furthermore, the team planned on playing in the new ballpark. He understood, however, that "until the Milwaukee order is reversed, the Braves may be faced with the regrettable decision of choosing which court to obey." The Milwaukee faithful were hopeful that the decision by Roller would be upheld, and La Follette believed that any order issued by a Wisconsin court would be recognized by all other states under the "full faith and credit" clause of the Constitution.[10] One wonders if La Follette felt the same about any court decision made in Georgia.

The National League's response was quick and predictable. After meeting with their attorneys, the league reiterated its commitment to Atlanta. A press release from the league said the superior court in Fulton County had already ordered the team to fulfill their lease in Georgia and the league was thereby restrained from "taking any action which would impair the Braves' performance under the Atlanta lease." The National League also stated that "expansion in 1966 is clearly not feasible and operation in 1966 or at any time of an eleven-club league would be a disaster for everyone." The owners remained confident that they would prevail because they believed they were legally permitted "in the exercise of their experienced judgment to authorize transfer of the Braves to Atlanta and that the Milwaukee County court has no power to grant the very extraordinary and unprecedented injunctions" obligating major league baseball to remain in Wisconsin. Furthermore, they intended to vigorously fight the lawsuits and were completely confident they would eventually prevail.[11] This was a consistent position for baseball. Warren Giles stated in 1962 that no team should be forced to remain in a city unless it received a needed and compensating benefit. He added that the league regards the transfer of a team as a serious matter and it would not to be undertaken without good reasons. In his experience as a baseball executive over four decades, no team could continue a struggling operation to the point of bankruptcy for its owners.[12] There is no doubt that this was a real possibility if the current Braves ownership remained in Milwaukee by choice or court order.

Something for the Legal Geniuses to Work Out

One of the most important aspects of Roller's decision was, outside of further orders from the court, an order for the Braves to make at least some arrangements for the use of County Stadium to conduct their 1966 baseball operations. Milwaukee officials indicated that a new stadium lease could be worked out quickly because the previous contract could simply be renewed or new terms drafted. If there were any conflicts with the lease, the court could settle the terms. Roller's initial rulings were warmly greeted across Wisconsin, but it was clear that the battle for the Braves was not over. Atlanta Stadium Authority head Arthur Montgomery expressed anger over Roller's decision. He said the team was in Atlanta now—offices, staff, and physical assets. Atlanta had a new twenty-five-year lease with the Braves and their old contract with Milwaukee was expired. He fully expected the Braves to fulfill the new terms of their contractual agreement in Atlanta.[13]

As a possible solution to the dueling court decisions, Cubs owner Phillip Wrigley, vice president of the National League, suggested that the Braves split their season between Milwaukee and Atlanta. He also believed that expansion in general, and in Wisconsin in particular, was not likely, and he saw no team that would be willing to relocate to Milwaukee because of the legal entanglements now facing the Braves. Immediate expansion was not beneficial, in Wrigley's mind, as it took several years to develop the New York Mets and they had just completed the worst season in major league history. He believed that "these young fellows who own the Braves brought some of the trouble on themselves when they tried to move before their contract was up." But the obligations of the stadium lease were now completed, and, Wrigley argued, the Braves knew their financial problems better than anybody. For that reason he had originally voted to allow the Boston Braves to move to Milwaukee and now he voted with the Braves to move to Atlanta.[14]

As Roller's initial decision was being interpreted, there were reports that contact had been made between the Braves and the Milwaukee Brewers Inc. The effort to reach an out-of-court settlement might settle the Braves' move to Atlanta. Sources told the Associated Press that an offer was made that included an expansion franchise in three to five years and the possibility of Milwaukee hosting twenty major league games per season in the meantime. If the reports were true and Milwaukee officials accepted the deal, Milwaukee would have a new team sometime between 1969 and 1971. Ben Barkin, on behalf of the Brewers, denied there was a formal proposal although he said his group would be ready to move on one if it were offered. It was also reported that the Brewers had rejected the proposal because there was no firm commitment on a specific timeframe for the new franchise and no permission was granted for the Brewers to begin a farm system and immediately develop players.[15]

"A continuing campaign of harassment and intimidation"

While the legal battles of the Braves and Major League Baseball were unfolding in Wisconsin, Sam Phillips McKenzie, a superior court judge in Atlanta, issued a temporary injunction that required the Braves to play their 1966 home schedule in Georgia. Atlanta and Fulton County officials had sought the injunction to protect their financial stake in the team and gave the National League until February 16 to state why the injunction should not be made permanent. Montgomery said the injunction was filed "to fully protect [the Stadium Authority's] contractual agreement with the Atlanta Braves, Inc." He said it seemed appropriate that "such a ruling be made in a Georgia court which has jurisdiction of all parties to the agreement."[16] On February 8, McKenzie made the injunction permanent, and two weeks later the Atlanta Stadium Authority filed suit in federal court in Houston, Texas, to prevent the National League owners from playing a schedule in 1966 that did not include the Braves in Atlanta. Responding to a petition from the Atlanta–Fulton County Recreation Authority, federal judge James Noel in Houston supported the position of the Braves and the National League in signing a temporary injunction that required the National League to play the Braves 1966 home schedule in Atlanta. He cited the difficulties of a schedule change, which would cause harm to Atlanta and all of the National League: the teams had already scheduled transportation, broadcasting, and housing for games in Georgia, and it was too late to make the necessary changes if the Braves returned to Milwaukee. He also noted inconsistencies in the attempts of Milwaukee officials and civic leaders to keep the Braves or major league baseball in Wisconsin.[17] His ruling would not be made permanent until the Wisconsin case was adjudicated.

The National League gave permission to the Braves to ignore Roller's initial decision and honor the agreements the team had already reached with Atlanta. During a closed-door meeting that lasted more than three hours, league officials also agreed to ignore the directive to prepare for an expansion plan. They believed that the Georgia court's order for the Braves to execute their twenty-five-year lease with the Atlanta Stadium Authority was valid, expansion in 1966 was not feasible, and an eleven-club league would be a disaster. The Braves had been granted permission to move to Atlanta after they fulfilled the terms of their contract with Milwaukee County, and the league remained confident it would ultimately prevail in court.[18] Giles said the league was not defying the Wisconsin court but rather they were honoring the Georgia court. He did not believe Roller had the authority to require the Braves to return to Milwaukee and hold the team hostage in Wisconsin until expansion under a plan dictated by the courts.[19] Bartholomay echoed the league's statements, vowed that the Braves would be in Atlanta for the 1966 season, and argued that only the Georgia court had jurisdiction. The Braves had left Milwaukee because of "a continuing campaign of harassment and intimidation carried on against the Braves by certain persons in Milwaukee," had met all contractual commitments to Milwaukee, and now fully intended to fulfill their contract and "larger obligations to the citizens of Atlanta."[20]

The Monopolistic Control of Major League Baseball

The antitrust case against the Braves franchise and Major League Baseball began in Judge Roller's courtroom on February 28. Projected to last between three and six weeks, the case would ideally be decided before the Braves were scheduled to play their first game in either Georgia or at County Stadium. For Wisconsin and Milwaukee County, the arguments were simple: The move to Atlanta violated Wisconsin's antitrust laws because the monopoly that is Major League Baseball was depriving Milwaukee of its product. The club owners were substantially in debt and needed to increase revenues immediately, and Milwaukee did not offer this solution. The team and its owners had made millions during their thirteen-year run in Milwaukee, and the loss of the Braves would have a dire impact on the regional economy.

The Braves countered that the reasons to move to Georgia were substantial, legal, and authorized by the National League: Poor fan support in Milwaukee led to financial losses that were incurred since the team was purchased in 1962. The local media remained hostile to the Braves, as did the antagonistic Milwaukee County Board. Milwaukee interests wanted to secure an expansion franchise. Broadcast revenues were insufficient in Wisconsin, especially compared with those in the Southeast. The Braves had a long-term lease with the Atlanta Stadium Authority, something that Milwaukee County officials refused to consider. The county board had negatively impacted attendance by banning beer carry-ins in 1961, failed to agree to a beer-price increase, refused to ban ticket scalpers at games, and made derogatory statements, especially by Eugene Grobschmidt. If forced to remain in Milwaukee, the Braves would lose more than a million dollars by 1970. Finally, since 1922, baseball has been protected from antitrust legislation because the Supreme Court had determined that baseball is engaged in sport, not commerce.

With both sides having made their statements, the trial began in earnest. The first few days focused on the state's economic case against the Braves. Most of the witnesses were local officials or former members of the Braves organization, including Ralph Delforge, the former assistant secretary-treasurer. He testified that the team had indeed had cash profits in its first two years in Milwaukee, in contrast to the Braves' claim that they had lost $3.5 million during the same time frame. He noted that the Braves requested to move to Atlanta in October 1964 because the team believed that Milwaukee was no longer of major league caliber and the team could not continue in Wisconsin.[21] The Braves felt they were no longer wanted in Milwaukee but did not feel it was abandoning the region because the Chicago market was nearby, as were the Minnesota Twins for those fans outside of southeastern Wisconsin. Bill Eberly, the former Braves business manager and ticket director at Milwaukee, testified that attendance declined primarily because of the team's performance on the field. The 1959 departure of John Quinn, the architect of the 1950s Braves teams, and the refusal by former owner Lou Perini to televise games in Milwaukee also were detrimental. Ticket price increases in 1961 and 1962 had hurt gate receipts by asking fans to pay more for a less competitive team. The impact of the Minnesota Twins on Milwaukee attendance, however, was negligible, according to Eberly.[22]

Perhaps the most compelling testimony on behalf of Wisconsin came from an internationally recognized economist, Robert R. Nathan, the president of a consulting firm that bore his name. Nathan said that his firm had been hired to study the state, in particular Milwaukee's market area, in comparison with other current or prospective major league regions, and found that many fans who attended Braves games at County Stadium came from a market range of up to one hundred miles from the ballpark. The loss of the Braves would create an annual loss to the state of $18 million in income and hundreds of thousands of dollars in tax revenues. There would be an additional loss of more than $260,000 in revenues for Milwaukee County and a further forfeiture of roughly twenty-six hundred jobs. The economic impact did not include money spent by local fans at County Stadium on game days. He concluded that Milwaukee was indeed a good baseball city with more support than any other major league city. During the team's time in Milwaukee it averaged 94.4 out of 100 people attending games from the metropolitan area compared with only 22 out of 100 for the National League and 21 for the American League cities. This meant that the attendance at County Stadium was four times more concentrated in relation to the population "than for all of the National league and American league teams put together."[23] In 1961 only the Cincinnati Reds, who won the pennant, finished with a higher attendance per capita. The following year, as the Braves slipped to fifth in the standings, the Reds again were the only National League club to outdraw the Braves on a per capita basis and only two teams finished ahead of the sixth place Braves in 1963, the Reds and the St. Louis Cardinals.[24] Even in 1965, when it was apparent the team was leaving, Nathan testified, "Attendance was still remarkable in relation to population as compared to other cities," and all teams experience "fluctuations and low years" that are not unique in baseball. Yet, the decline in attendance was the crux of the team's reason to move and the hardest to ignore.

After two weeks of testimony, multiple witnesses, and several days of deliberations over the introduction of 250 exhibits, the State rested its case. The Braves' attorneys immediately attempted to dismiss the lawsuit, arguing that the State's case was without merit. Earl Jinkinson, the primary attorney for the Braves, contended the State had not proven any violation of antitrust laws and furthermore, only Congress could regulate organized baseball. This lawsuit, he said, was brought on behalf of not the State of Wisconsin but the Brewers organization, which was trying to force major league baseball to stay in Milwaukee. The lawsuit, however, would harm rather than help in this effort and the best way to rebuild Milwaukee's reputation as a sports town "is to end this suit now—this suit and Grobschmidt, Kuechle and Barkin already have slathered slime on this town's reputation" that would remain in the future. He accused the plaintiffs of a double standard that considered the rules, agreements, and regulations of baseball to become illegal only when Milwaukee does not have a piece of the action. Jinkinson argued it was reasonable for the league to simply let the Braves go to Atlanta and deny Milwaukee's attempt to force expansion. The Braves did not fare well in the recent past and "it is beyond belief that this court would ever entertain the thought that they can be compelled to return to this continuing hostile atmosphere," which would force the team into bankruptcy.[25]

The main protagonists in the drama, the Braves' owners, would not be given the opportunity to testify in front of Roller. Jinkinson said the fear of additional lawsuits was real if they appeared in person, and their testimony would be read into the record from their depositions. Although "these suits wouldn't have any standing in court," said Jinkinson, he could not stop them from being filed, and it was very "expensive to fight suits like that, so why take the chance?"[26]

The first witness for the defense was Eugene Grobschmidt, the polarizing chairman of the Milwaukee County Board of Supervisors. He was declared a hostile witness, and the exchange between him and the Braves lawyers was arguably a microcosm of the complex problems between the county and the team.

For three hours, Grobschmidt was asked about derogatory statements he had made about the team, its owners and management, and whether he encouraged harassment of the Braves. Grobschmidt denied the charges, despite newspaper reports that recorded many inflammatory statements he had made in the recent past. He did not believe he had encouraged a boycott, and he had even appeared on television with members of Teams Inc. to encourage attendance at County Stadium. When asked if he had called the ownership group liars, in particular Bartholomay and McHale, Grobschmidt responded he had, about as many times as they had lied and said the Braves were staying in Milwaukee.[27] Ray McCann, a Milwaukee-based defense attorney, asked Grobschmidt if he ever said, "To hell with the Braves." He responded, "I think I did several times" but not necessarily in public. He denied promoting legislation that would shore up the State's case against the Braves and the National League. In the end, he was cordial but combative, and clearly still angry with the Braves.

A federal bank examiner, John Finnegan, was brought in by the Braves on March 24 to corroborate that the team was indeed losing money in Milwaukee. Finnegan testified that the $3 million in financing that the team received from First Wisconsin National Bank was considered to be a substandard loan, which carried more risk because of the condition of the borrower. Owing to "insufficient revenues, the Milwaukee Braves, Inc., would be unable to retire their loan in the normal course," said Finnegan, because their "revenues had dropped off rather drastically and were not adequate to service the debt." Although attendance was up in 1964, it would continue to decline as the team descended to the bottom of the National League standings.[28] While this was not the primary defense for the Braves, it is perhaps closest to the truth. It would be impossible for the Braves to continue in Milwaukee under the current conditions of declining baseball interest and increased financial demands. Perhaps local ownership would have made a difference, but we will never know for certain.

More Testimony

The same day, the court heard depositions from Bartholomay and McHale. The former testified that the ownership group had been committed to Milwaukee in the very beginning and even wanted to bring in local investors and eventually did so, including several Wisconsin members who joined the board of directors. However, the total local investment in the team was never close to the money that Bartholomay and his partners had at stake in the Braves. As for the 1963 stock sale, Bartholomay indicated that its purpose "was to provide a portion of the ownership to represent local ownership, by that I mean Milwaukee and Wisconsin residents," not to recoup or raise money to pay down their debt, and it was promoted in several Wisconsin cities. The group lost money on the stock sale, he said, as they were obligated to purchase unsold stock, and after legal fees were included, it cost more than ten dollars per share.[29]

Bartholomay testified that the team lost money immediately in 1963, a situation that created concern among the board of directors, especially the local members. Several meetings were held in Milwaukee to address the growing financial concerns and relocation rumors, including a particularly long one on September 22, 1963, that included "the power structure of the city, of the county" and the people they represented. Bartholomay told of problems, including broadcast money totaling $325,000 still owed to the team by WEMP, and attendance issues, that exacerbated the Braves' finances. Bartholomay said he even asked *Milwaukee Sentinel* publisher Irwin Maier to restore the Indian cartoon that had appeared on the front page every day to indicate whether the Braves lost or were rained out, something that Bartholomay considered to be highly effective publicity in the past. He also asked for reporters to cover all road games and neutralize reporting that "we felt had been negatively directed at the Braves and all of baseball." When he asked for a commitment to sell a total of at least 7,500 season tickets for 1964, county executive John Doyne said that the figure might get as high ten thousand.[30]

Bartholomay said there was also concern over reported losses of approximately $50,000 to WTMJ television because they had not been able to sell all of their advertising. He was assured that the Braves would nevertheless get the same amount in broadcasting for the 1964 season and some help in "making up any differential relief on our rent." Another problem addressed at the September

22 meeting was ticket scalpers. Sales of previously purchased tickets competed with the box office at the ballpark, and "they were competing with very excellent tickets." With assurances gathered at this meeting, Bartholomay made the commitment to local officials to remain in Milwaukee for the 1964 season. In his mind, however, these commitments were not completely fulfilled, especially the vexing problem of scalping, nor were the other issues adequately addressed. In fact, by early April 1964, only 4,391 season tickets were sold (the Braves themselves had sold all but 482 of the total), far fewer than the team was promised, even after the massive "Go-to-Bat for the Braves" campaign that involved several high-profile players and manager Bobby Bragan. When asked if the commitment to sell tickets was finally met, Bartholomay simply answered no.[31]

When asked why he wanted to take the team to Atlanta, Bartholomay detailed the failure of commitments, problems with local officials, and his own conclusion that the Midwest market was already saturated with baseball. Four teams "represented 20 percent of the total Major League teams with far less than 10 percent" of the American population. It did not seem feasible to him that the area could support that disproportion of the teams while at the same time the Southeast had none. He felt that there was an overall decline in sports in Milwaukee, with the move of the NBA's Milwaukee Hawks to St. Louis in 1955, as well as the recent loss of a major golf tournament and the elimination of college football at Marquette University. He was also concerned with the team's inability to generate the same dollars that other baseball teams did because the Braves' "per capita income from home tickets was substantially less than virtually all of the teams in our league." The board was not likely to approve an increase in ticket prices. The expanded use of broadcasting also hurt the Braves because, according to Bartholomay, more televised baseball was coming from Chicago to the Milwaukee market.[32]

Bartholomay noted that the sports editors of both local newspapers were not present at spring training and or even at the recent World Series because, he believed, they disliked the Braves owners or were disinterested in baseball. He claimed that there was "no bona fide offer" on the table and no "specific dollar amount offered by a resident of Wisconsin or the County of Milwaukee" to purchase the Braves, despite the documented attempts by Richard Cutler's group to purchase the Braves in 1965. Bartholomay also said the Braves had already invested in the Georgia market with the printing of tickets and construction of team offices, and had signed a twenty-year agreement with the Automatic Retailers of America to provide concessions at the new stadium. When asked about his interest in the Southeast, Bartholomay said he heard about Atlanta at the 1963 All-Star Game. He was fascinated by any city that was a prospect for major league baseball, including San Diego, Dallas, Seattle, and several other cities.[33] In the end, it is clear to see that they might have been interested in keeping the Milwaukee market in early 1963, but Bartholomay and his fellow owners soured on it fairly quickly. By mid-July, nothing was going to derail the move of the franchise out of Milwaukee other than a sale of the team, and this was not going to happen any time soon.

John McHale testified that the problems with Milwaukee County ran deep and items that seemed small on the surface had created financial hardships for the club. He was among the last to know that the team was considering moving to Atlanta. Despite countless stories since 1963, and all of his own denials since then, he said he was not made aware of the move until the National League meeting in August 1964. He said he had never questioned others in the ownership group about the report, and there were "just so many rumors that there were not enough hours in the day to deny them." McHale also said that he had never visited Atlanta in regard to the current relocation and had previously been there on behalf of former Braves owner Louis Perini and the possibility of expansion. This statement was in stark contrast to claims made by the sports editor of the *Atlanta Journal*, Furman Bisher. McHale testified that he spoke to Bisher only about Atlanta's possibilities as a major league city and had had no knowledge of a meeting between the Braves and representatives from Atlanta at the 1963 All-Star game. He claimed that he had not conferred with anyone "to learn about such a meeting, if there was one" and did not remember making statements to the newspapers after an April 1964 meeting between the Braves and Atlanta officials, nor did he recall attending it. McHale contended he was truthful when he said that the Braves would stay in Milwaukee "today, tomorrow, next year" and as long they were welcomed. However, that "was before Milwaukee civic leaders disappointed us by failing to live up to their commitments," and he believed he was often quoted out of context.[34]

McHale denied any effort by the team or its fellow National League owners to deprive Milwaukee of baseball after the Braves were gone, although he did not believe a team could be put in place for the 1966 season. It was on the record that Milwaukee was not excluded from getting an expansion team in the future, but it could not possibly be forthcoming. McHale did not believe that, despite the negative publicity Milwaukee had garnered from this lawsuit, the city should be the last one in the nation to get a new team. The past season had been difficult for McHale, with personnel in both Milwaukee and Atlanta and heavy travel between the two cities. In fact, he estimated that he spent less than two weeks in Milwaukee in all of 1965. During cross-examination, McHale acknowledged that half of the Braves' moving costs as well as the legal fees from the current litigation were to be paid for by the city of Atlanta and Fulton County. This meant the team would be reimbursed, up to a total of $500,000, through a rent reduction of $50,000 per year for the first ten years of the lease in Atlanta.[35]

McHale thought they had stopped the rumors of relocation after the meeting with civic leaders in Milwaukee. When asked if the talk of the move to Atlanta hurt attendance, he responded that he could not answer the question without a greater context of the "background of what makes up attendance." When asked about specific programs conducted to promote ticket sales for 1964, McHale had an interesting response: The Braves had a program of selling season tickets that included sending brochures "to prospective season ticket holders, follow up by phone calls, plus the employment of a full time speaker's bureau" that traveled all over the Midwest. They carried pictures from the World Series, made speeches, and often included many of the Braves staff at various civic functions. When asked if these were similar to the promotions currently being conducted in Georgia, McHale responded, "No, not that big." He later added that he still felt that the Braves' 1964 effort in Wisconsin was greater than the one currently being conducted in Atlanta. He also commented on concerns about the restrictions on home game telecasts in Milwaukee, although it should be noted that the Braves didn't telecast the maximum number of games allowed under the contract because they lacked sponsors for some broadcasts.[36]

McHale spoke of conflicts over money. The team was not allowed to raise concession prices without first going before the county, and that opened it up to growing negative publicity. The only thing the Braves had formally sought to increase was the price of beer, and the county turned them down. The county also declined a request to forgo a $10,000 deposit on the stadium lease because the team had already been there for years. (Milwaukee County had not returned the deposit at the time of the court case.) McHale said the team was dissatisfied with the parking fees, which again were controlled by the county. County Stadium's parking prices were the lowest in the country and were not raised during the three-year agreement, but the Braves were concerned the team would become an "island in the middle of a parking lot" if the prices were raised. In contrast, the Atlanta Braves now had more control over the pricing and were able to double the parking price per game over what was charged in Milwaukee.[37]

To McHale, it was apparent that the Braves had done well in Milwaukee. They were the only team besides the Dodgers to draw more than two million fans in any given season between 1953 and 1965. The Dodgers did it six times and the Braves did it four, while other teams considered to be good baseball cities did not break the mark, including both Chicago franchises. McHale attributed this to normal highs and lows associated with baseball. He also believed that the Braves would draw between $3.75 and $2.50 per seat in Atlanta versus the $1.60 they made recently in Milwaukee, and the new season ticket prices were almost double what they had been at County Stadium.[38] On March 25, Ronald Wipperman, a Milwaukee-based accountant, echoed the financial disparity. Contrary to Delforge's testimony, he argued that the Braves had indeed lost significant money in Milwaukee. Declining attendance under the current ownership had caused a loss of more than $775,000, a dramatic increase over the $45,270 lost in 1964 and $43,378 in 1963. The difference in numbers between Delforge and Wipperman was attributed to depreciation and amortization of player contracts for tax purposes.[39] He also testified that when the Perini Corporation sold the Milwaukee Braves, it registered a profit of more than $5 million in addition to the estimated profits of $7.7 million from team operations in Milwaukee since 1953. Again, this was significantly different from the $13 million the State claimed. However, "as an accountant, he would not classify all this as profit."[40] For the average Braves fan in Milwaukee, it was not clear if the team had indeed made or lost real money before the 1965 lame-duck season. Regardless, many of the fruits of their love of the Braves, money spent at games and concessions, were now ensconced in Massachusetts or Chicago.

After several days of testimony from a number of individuals, including Bud Selig, the defense turned to their own financial expert, John Clark Jr. The situation in Milwaukee was, according to Clark, not nearly as stable as it would be in Atlanta, where the Braves could count on greater broadcast revenues, higher ticket prices, and a greater population within two hundred miles of the ballpark. Contradicting the consultant Robert Nathan, he said the Braves had a negligible economic impact on the region. Furthermore, more money left the state when the Braves were in Milwaukee than came in, and he questioned whether 30 percent of their total attendance came from beyond fifty miles of County Stadium. It was noted that Clark did not base his testimony on surveys of local businesses or attendance in Milwaukee.[41]

With that, the defense rested its case, after two weeks of testimony that culminated in the Braves accusing Teams Inc. and the Milwaukee Brewers Baseball Club of harassment. Furthermore, they tried to link these two groups with the antitrust lawsuit that was now in Roller's courtroom. According to the Braves' lawyers, the main villain in this drama was Edmund Fitzgerald. As an officer for Teams and the Brewers, who were involved "in everything that is attempted to harass the Braves," he had been front and center at meetings, demanding the expansion of baseball to include Milwaukee.[42] Perhaps from the perspective of the National League and the Braves organization, this would seem to be true. Most likely Fitzgerald would take pride in obstructing the removal of major league baseball from Milwaukee in general or the Braves in particular. But he was not the sole reason for this legal battle, and in many ways he represented all the Braves fans who had no means of keeping the club in Milwaukee and simply wanted their beloved team back.

"The excitement has worn off"

Meanwhile, as the drama of the trial was coming to an end, Milwaukee County Stadium was ready for baseball in 1966 in case the Braves returned or a brand new expansion franchise arrived. Stadium manager William Anderson was confident that it could be up and going within twenty-four hours, as the playing field and the stands were in good shape and the scoreboard was operational. Milwaukee County had a grounds crew ready to work and it could get extra help if necessary. The largest hurdle to overcome would be the printing of tickets, which Anderson argued would be a problem for the Braves to solve and not for Milwaukee County. Nothing was scheduled at the ballpark that would interfere with baseball until the fall, when the Green Bay Packers were to play three games, including one against the upstart Atlanta Falcons on October 23. The NFL games might create a problem but it had been worked out in past seasons and could be again without too much trouble. With no baseball at County Stadium, it was far easier to paint and make repairs, without having to schedule maintenance around games. Whether or not the Braves returned, the facility would be ready, and there would still be "plenty of time to consider possible sports and other events to be booked into the Stadium."[43]

Atlanta also prepared for baseball and the traditional celebration of Opening Day. Many schools and businesses were closed for the official welcoming ceremonies, yet it was apparent to some that much of the excitement had already run its course. Part of the reduced interest in baseball was the drawn-out court case in Milwaukee, as well as the lame duck season in 1965. Third baseman Eddie Mathews contended his teammates were not as excited about the move as they had been when the Braves left Boston and went to Milwaukee back in 1953. Then, moving a franchise was a novelty, but this time it "has been talked about for so long that most of the excitement has worn off." In fact, Atlanta Stadium had already hosted a two-game exhibition series between the Braves and the Dodgers that drew a total of twenty-five thousand fans, about half of what the owners expected. It appeared that the arrival of the Atlanta Falcons generated more interest than the Braves, as did stock car racing, at least in Georgia.[44] The Braves still hoped that drawing well from surrounding states would economically justify their move the South.

In final arguments in early April, lawyers for the State of Wisconsin insisted that the Braves needed to be returned to Milwaukee by the scheduled Opening Day in 1966 or an agreement had to be reached to expand into Milwaukee by 1967, a year later than originally demanded. The State also requested that Roller maintain jurisdiction in this case until a new competitive team was granted and stocked with players obtained at fair prices and that the Braves and their fellow National League owners each be found guilty and fined $5,000 for violating Wisconsin's antitrust laws. Moreover, said the State, the money lost by the new owners did not substantiate the move to Atlanta, which would deprive Milwaukee of recreation, trade, and commerce.[45]

Substantially Restrained Trade and Commerce

Roller issued his judgment on April 13, 1966. The 176-page decision ruled, for the first time in history, against organized baseball in an antitrust case. Roller ordered Major League Baseball to either commit to putting an expansion franchise in Milwaukee in time for the 1967 season or return the Braves to Milwaukee by May 16 for the 1966 season. The Braves and the National League had conspired to monopolize the business of Major League Baseball in Wisconsin, and the decision to move the team to Atlanta had violated the state's antitrust laws. The National League and all of its franchises were held financially liable for the damages to Wisconsin and were each fined $5,000. This part of the ruling would be revoked upon compliance of the decision and a return of the National League to Milwaukee in 1967.

Roller listed more than forty findings of fact in his decision. For one, the new ownership group became fascinated with the idea of moving the Braves to Atlanta as early as July 1963, and their interest continued to grow over the next year. The relocation rumors negatively impacted attendance at County Stadium as stories circulated in the press. For another, Major League Baseball, and in particular the National League, had unlimited power and discretion to determine the location of a team, and there were no rules that allowed a "city, county, or state from which any such proposed transfer would be made" an opportunity to plead their case.[46]

Roller also determined that the Braves had a total income of $836,900 on a cash basis during the five-year period 1960–64 but reported net losses to their shareholders in those years. The total income of the team was "reduced by interest expense on the funds" borrowed to buy the team, and in 1964 the team had additional expenses of $48,800 in connection with relocating that were charged against income. Moreover, if the team had capitalized its scouting expenses as it did with "player acquisition and development costs as sound accounting methods would require, the Braves would have shown a net income of approximately $170,000 in 1963 and $151,000 in 1964." He noted that the broadcasting revenues generated in Wisconsin compared "favorably with the net receipts of the defendant clubs that submitted figures to this court." Roller believed that the team was financially successful during its thirteen years in Wisconsin, and Milwaukee had "the demographic, economic, and population characteristics" necessary to support major league baseball.[47]

While Wisconsin responded favorably to Roller's decision, many still expected the Braves to remain in Atlanta and there was no certainty when or if major league baseball would indeed return to County Stadium. In fact, Roller's decision was stayed pending an appeal to the Wisconsin Supreme Court. Grobschmidt proudly said, "I told you so" and the case "turned out the way I expected it to turn out." Doyne credited Roller with making a correct, albeit difficult decision that was "well thought out with a plan and an alternative, not just a simple judgment." Barkin said this was "wonderful news for all who believe in fair play and common decency," and it reaffirmed Milwaukee was a "top flight major league city." Anderson added that "our position was morally right" and now baseball had the opportunity "to work out an orderly" program for expansion and the ballpark was "groomed and ready" for baseball.[48] Attorney General La Follette noted the decision should eliminate the abuse of monopoly powers that baseball has had in recent years. He fully expected Wisconsin to enforce the ruling despite all the contrary rulings in Georgia courts and the federal court in Houston. "Wisconsin will have the benefit of a major league franchise operating in full compliance with the laws of this state," he said, and the State was prepared "to first go to a state court in another state where a league team is headquartered and force them to obey the injunction." Moreover, if the teams did not respect Roller's verdict, "then they would be in contempt of that state court." La Follette said that either an appeal of the federal ruling that required the Braves to honor their Atlanta lease or an appeal of a ruling in another state court could end up before the U.S. Supreme Court, which would ultimately rule on Wisconsin law and not on baseball's antitrust protection.[49]

The Braves were already in Atlanta and had played two games at their new ballpark when Roller's decision was released. Their response was swift and pointed. The Braves would fulfill their obligations to Atlanta, Bartholomay said. The Wisconsin court had exceeded its jurisdiction and had "no rightful power to make us breach our lease in Georgia." The team no longer had leases, contracts, or another connection with Wisconsin and would win an appeal of Roller's decision. There was, according to Bartholomay, "as much chance of the Braves playing in Milwaukee this summer as there is of the New York Yankees."[50] McHale said that Roller's decision became "a rallying cry for the Atlantans. It's a matter of civic pride. They know we've gone through hell with this thing." Regardless of Roller's verdict, the team's equipment now had *Atlanta Braves* painted on it, and the team was referred to as such across the National League.[51] Giles said the league also expected to win the appeal and this battle would continue because baseball was "carrying the torch for all team sports— pro football, pro basketball and pro hockey" in the fight to control their own games and franchise locations.[52] Meanwhile, the federal court in Houston had prohibited the other National League teams from scheduling road games against the Braves in any state outside of Georgia.[53] The Milwaukee Braves would be relegated to history books and the memories of the abandoned fans in Wisconsin.

People Abandoned by Baseball

In late July 1966, the Wisconsin Supreme Court reversed Roller's decision and cleared the way for the Braves to make permanent their new home in Georgia. On a 4–3 vote, the court determined that because Major League Baseball was protected by existing federal antitrust laws, the enforcement of Wisconsin's laws would create a conflict and only Congress could bring baseball under antitrust action. If the Braves were obligated to return to Milwaukee or an expansion team was forced upon baseball, it would be inconsistent with the very policy of an antitrust law for Wisconsin to insist that Milwaukee have baseball "at the expense of Atlanta or communities elsewhere which may seek to have a team." In other words, Roller's decision was inconsistent in saying that the Braves, or Major League Baseball, could retain their monopoly power as long as they remained in Wisconsin. The court noted that baseball had a tremendous economic impact on Milwaukee, but the organization now operated completely out of Wisconsin. The agreement among the National League clubs to move the Braves "terminated very substantial business activity in Wisconsin" and "totally and effectively" prevented its resumption in 1966. Interestingly, both the majority and minority positions acknowledged the negative ramifications of the protected monopoly status of baseball and Congress's insufficiency in regulating the sport.[54]

At this critical juncture in the battle for the future of the Braves, there was really nothing left for the Wisconsin faithful to do but appeal the decision to the

U.S. Supreme Court. The Braves were free to play the remainder of the 1966 season in Atlanta, and the National League would not be forced to grant Milwaukee a franchise. The fines that were levied against the teams were vacated, and the antitrust protection of baseball remained, unless the Supreme Court reversed the ruling. La Follette announced that he would, to avoid further delay, bypass a rehearing in the state and instead make a petition directly to the Supreme Court. At the federal level, Congressman Clement Zablocki declared he would seek special hearings and legislation in an effort to regulate the American Pastime. He said he hoped "that congress will now give immediate consideration to the various bills which are now pending before it to remove baseball's antitrust exemption."[55] But, like other times before and since, there would be no substantive action that could make it out of the House and Senate and ultimately to a president's desk.

"A lousy decision but who cares?"

Local officials were surprised and disillusioned with the reversal of Roller's decision and what it meant for the future of baseball in Milwaukee. County executive John Doyne said they would have to weigh their options, including pursuing their own antitrust legal action or just "forget the whole thing." It seemed that the legal deck was stacked against Milwaukee and maybe "we should devote more time and emphasis now on planning a program for bringing a ball club to Milwaukee. This is a selling market, and competition for major league baseball is keen from such cities as Oakland and Seattle." Mayor Henry Maier said that regardless of what "the current legal situation is, what happened to Milwaukee is morally wrong." One alderman, future Wisconsin governor Martin Schreiber, noted that the city's main role in pursuing the legal action was "to prevent the wholesale move of clubs to other cities, building new or bigger stadiums, and creating hardships on the people abandoned by baseball." He said it "cost a lot of money to bring this matter to the attention of the courts" but it was money well spent. It might save other municipalities "from the anguish we went through in losing a team." Finally, Schreiber argued, "We should continue to press for a team here" because the fighting spirit of the city was noted and "I hope the city will be considered in any expansion plans." Perhaps the one local official that most people wanted to hear from, Eugene Grobschmidt, was unavailable for comment because he was away on vacation.[56]

Many of the locals in Milwaukee were now ambivalent about the Braves. There was nothing they could do to bring the team back, and some would not pay money to see them again even if they returned. One local declared simply it was "a lousy decision but who cares?" Another said he would prefer to see an American League team come to Milwaukee. Others felt that there was nothing to lose, but "it's just a waste of time, money and effort to appeal this and try to get a ball club back here." There was also a general apathy about baseball, and some said they did not care about the outcome of the case because they were "just not interested and I've been a baseball fan my whole life." Finally and succinctly, one fan noted that a "change of scenery and southern exposure didn't improve Braves baseball."[57] At County Stadium, weeds slowly took over the parking lot and routine maintenance continued to cost the taxpayers money as only a few events were scheduled at the ballpark. When asked about this latest development, only one worker submitted any regrets. He said that baseball generated millions "that would come back into this city, this county, this state" and "money is what counts in baseball."[58] Perhaps the one advantage of no baseball at County Stadium was the turf had "thrived and the playing surface was largely a lush green carpet" when the Packers hosted the New York Giants for a game on September 3.[59]

The setback did not end the attempts to get baseball back to Wisconsin. Bud Selig said his group was "going to be as active in the future as we've been in the past" and would continue to pursue a major league franchise with the same vigor as in the recent past. He added that the Brewers organization had "never been parties to the litigation, so this action today doesn't affect us in any way." And there was hope for the future of Milwaukee baseball outside of Selig's group. Noted sportswriter Leonard Koppett of the *New York Times* opined there was a chance that the ruling against Milwaukee may "have the effect of hastening the return of major league baseball" to Milwaukee with "most likely an American League franchise in expansion before 1970." He argued that had Milwaukee won, any new team granted to Wisconsin would be "bound by its restrictions and therefore reluctant to operate there. By losing the case, therefore, Milwaukee may have won more favorable conditions for a new club." Perhaps Warren Spahn, the former ace of the Milwaukee Braves, said it best: "Milwaukee is a good baseball town and I'm sure it could support major league baseball. But, unfortunately, the club moved out of there and I don't believe throwing stones at the game is going to help."[60]

"No hard feelings against Milwaukee and Wisconsin"

The news in Georgia was much different from the somber reality that encompassed Milwaukee. McHale said that they were of course happy their decision to move the franchise to Atlanta had been justified, but he did not know what other legal hurdles were still in the future. Despite his previous assurances to Milwaukee that the Braves would stay as long as they were wanted, he now felt that the team had given fair warning to Wisconsin about what would happen if the team left. He argued that the Braves were "certainly aware of the damage the move would cause" in the region, and they "kept pointing out to them what losing the team would mean and appealing for them to support the team so that it wouldn't have to move." In McHale's mind, the people of Milwaukee "were the ones who weren't aware of the damage that would result—not us. Apparently they just never would believe that we might move, not until we actually did, despite all our warnings." He added that if "Milwaukee had shown half as much fight and effort while we were still there and needed support as they have shown in trying to get us back, we'd still be playing our games in Milwaukee."[61]

Mayor Allen noted that this was indeed great news and the Wisconsin Supreme Court had now "confirmed our feelings that the Braves' move to Atlanta was just and fair." He said that there were "no hard feelings against Milwaukee and Wisconsin. We are proud of the Atlanta Braves" and they could now make Georgia "truly the land of the free and the home of the Braves." Mills Lane, an Atlanta banker who was instrumental in the construction of Atlanta Stadium, noted that anything that cleared "the air is good for the people in Atlanta and Milwaukee and the people as a whole." Bobby Bragan said that the news was "the best awakening I've had. I think it's wonderful."[62]

Unfortunately for the new fans of the Atlanta Braves, the news on the field was not as good, as the team struggled to be competitive for much of 1966. Because the people of Atlanta had been promised a contending team, and it appeared the 1965 Milwaukee Braves were close to winning a pennant before a late season collapse, expectations were high. The reality was the team was on the decline, as its win-loss record reflected.

Bragan was fired as the Braves' manager on August 9, despite signing a contract extension the year before. Lloyd Larson of the *Milwaukee Journal* noted that it had not taken long for the Braves fans in Atlanta to realize the team was not as good as promised and that "they had been sold a bill of goods" and therefore gave Bragan "the full boo treatment." Larson wrote that most people do not like to see someone lose their job, but "in Bragan's case, they are willing to make an exception." Bragan had called Milwaukee a "two bit town," said he would not "manage there again for three times my salary," and contended he would "rather be in eighth place in Atlanta than in first place in Milwaukee." Oliver Kuechle argued that the firing of Bragan was a continuation of the turmoil in the Braves front office "almost from the day the club came here from

Boston." Previous managers had been given support within the organization and then unceremoniously removed from their positions. Moreover, the upheaval was noted even in the manner that Lou Perini had sold the club without a word to local interests. Kuechle also noted that the relationship between Bartholomay and McHale was very strained and he would not be surprised if "McHale himself could be next."[63] This turned out to be the case in early September when McHale was restricted to administrative duties and Paul Richards took over player acquisition and development. In early January 1967, McHale left the team to become the administrator for baseball commissioner William Eckert.

Despite the turbulence in the front office, by the end of the 1966 season, the Atlanta Braves had drawn more than 1.5 million fans, the highest for the club since 1959 and in a year that attendance was marginally up in both leagues. By the middle of June, in just twenty-nine home games, they had surpassed the entire 1965 attendance in Milwaukee. A net profit of more than $991,000 for the 1966 season was the most recorded to date for the new ownership group and helped the team move past the $1.5 million lost in 1965.[64] Compared with the Braves' first season in Milwaukee, however, the numbers were not as impressive. More than 1.8 million came to see the team play in 1953, with an average attendance of 23,719 per game, compared with 1.5 million and an average game attendance of 19,010 in Atlanta. The most telling statistic was the comparison with the rest of the National League: in 1953 Milwaukee attendance had doubled the league average of 927,465, while in Georgia it was just over the league average of 1,501,547.[65]

Lloyd Larson addressed the ongoing decline in attendance across all of baseball in 1966. He wrote that the average of 12,478 fans per game at County Stadium in 1964 had outpaced six teams in 1966 that were not under threat of leaving. Teams under the mark set by the 1964 Braves included the Cincinnati Reds, Pittsburgh Pirates, Chicago Cubs, Washington Senators, Kansas City Athletics, and the Boston Red Sox (though the Senators and Athletics would both relocate in the years ahead). A year later, Larson brought attention to the obvious problem that had developed in Georgia: attendance was not as expected and in only the second year in Dixie some were already comparing it to the decline in Milwaukee. The Braves had dropped almost 10 percent of the previous year's gate. Larson pointed out that in September alone, the Braves had seven games that averaged 5,572. In fact, four games drew fewer than five thousand, one drew only 2,963, and a Saturday night crowd of more than ten thousand brought the total to 39,003. By comparison, during the first eight years at Milwaukee County Stadium, the crowd was under ten thousand only twelve times.

The lowest crowd total from 1953 to 1961 was 6,090 for an afternoon game in April 1956. It was obvious to many that the Braves' owners had oversold the team to Atlanta, promised them a pennant contender, and delivered a mediocre ball club.[66] But the Braves were now safely ensconced in Atlanta, and nothing short of the Supreme Court or a congressional order could return them to Milwaukee.

"So who lost? Everybody lost."

In December, as a final setback to Milwaukee's attempt to get the Braves or major league baseball back to County Stadium in the near future, the U.S. Supreme Court refused to review the reversal of Roller's decision. Three of the justices were willing to hear the case, but that was not enough to bring it before the highest court in the land. La Follette told reporters that he would meet with special counsel to consider a petition for a rehearing, in light of the close margin on the court. Some still believed that Congress would help, but congressmen's intentions to act at the federal level went nowhere. With nothing ahead but a protracted legal battle that was draining on the taxpayers, on January 31, 1967, the Milwaukee County Board voted overwhelmingly, 21–1, to drop the anti-trust suit against the Braves and the National League. Grobschmidt told local press this decision would save "the county a lot of money by dropping it." He said that one of the options for Milwaukee to pursue was the possibility of the establishment of a third major league, something that never developed.

While the Braves enjoyed their new stadium in Atlanta, the situation in Wisconsin remained bleak after the first season without organized baseball in Milwaukee since the nineteenth century. Lou Perini, the former owner of the Boston and Milwaukee Braves, addressed the situation in 1968. Speaking from his position as the former chairman of the executive committee, Perini said that had Milwaukee County simply let the Braves go play in Atlanta in 1965, the team might still have played a few games at County Stadium. Perini "suggested we go into Milwaukee and play one series against each club." Moreover, the team "would have done it until such time as Milwaukee got an expansion club" be-cause we "owed Milwaukee something. But the people of Milwaukee wouldn't go for it." Even worse, they "thought they could jam something down the own-ers' throats. So who lost? Everybody lost."[67]

Oliver Kuechle remained dubious of Perini's statement. The sportswriter commented that if indeed Perini had said this, "He must have done it to him-self locked in his hotel room with all shades drawn and stuffing under the door." No one could recall any such statement or offer, "not the county board, not the newspapers, not any wealthy individual vitally interested in keeping baseball here." No such testimony was presented in court or in any of the depositions. There was no indication that a plan like this was mentioned as sort of "compensation" to Milwaukee for letting the team immediately move. Despite Perini's apparently hollow words about playing in Milwaukee in 1965, he did say that the "thing right now is to get another club in Milwaukee. There is no animosity toward Milwaukee."[68] Perini also said that the long court battle was "politically inspired" and that the "Braves felt inclined to admit some of the blame, but at least we did it a year ahead of time. We could have waited until the contract ran out and done it by surprise."[69]

Having been an absentee owner since 1953, Perini apparently did not understand how deeply this decision had wounded the hearts of Braves fans in Wisconsin. They had been far more loyal to his team than fans in Boston had been, and even in a lame duck year had almost doubled the attendance compared with Boston in 1952. Springing it as a surprise might have made it a bit easier, but with so many rumors there was no way to keep the move a secret. The reality was that as of early 1967, the battle for the Braves was finally over. They now truly belonged solely to Atlanta, and the hopes of a return of the Milwaukee Braves faded like twilight on a late summer evening at County Stadium. Milwaukee would have to find a new team to call their own.

So the question remains, Why did the Braves fail in Milwaukee? The court case and the appeals laid bare the problems that the team had in Milwaukee since they first arrived. Fan excitement and the performance of the team did not allow for a leveling off of attendance for almost eight years. This was far longer than it took for other teams that moved, and therefore Milwaukee attendance was expected always to be near the top of the National League, regardless of the team's performance. This was unrealistic. The lack of televised broadcasts of Braves games into Wisconsin homes failed to generate interest in the next generation, which grew up with football. The success of the Green Bay Packers under Vince Lombardi displaced fan interest in baseball, and the Packers became, arguably, the most beloved team in the state at the expense of the Braves. Media coverage led and reflected the strong interest in the Packers.

Milwaukee County government shares much of the blame for the departure of the Braves. The county board had viewed the team as a revenue stream to benefit Milwaukee County, and clearly they did not grasp the financial problems faced by the Braves. The stadium leases obligated the team to pay more for the ballpark than any other team in baseball. Furthermore, the county had too much control over the other revenue streams that the team counted on, including concessions and souvenir sales in County Stadium. The team was also obligated to expend resources to light and maintain the vast parking lots without receiving any of the revenues generated from thousands of vehicles at games; therefore, the Braves began to look south.

Lack of local ownership also hurt the team from the time that it came in 1953. While Perini was initially beloved in Milwaukee, he remained a Boston man at heart and, over the years he owned the team, he spent less time in Milwaukee and the front office remained distant from the fans. The loss of general manager John Quinn hurt the quality of the team at a time when the Braves really needed to sustain success on the field. The hiring of John McHale did not solve the problems for the team, and he almost immediately became the target of fan animosity. This certainly became evident when the team was sold to Bartholomay's group in 1962. The new owners were never any closer to the community than Perini had been. Despite team efforts to encourage local ownership groups to join through the sale of stock, the Braves ownership remained outsiders to the Wisconsin fan base.

It appears the new owners overpaid for the team at a time when its revenues were in decline. Because they purchased it primarily through loans, they needed sufficient revenues to pay down the debt and interest, which required an attendance base similar to the 1950s. When that was no longer the case and performance on the field was in decline, fan interest waned further. The economic resources of the area were also limited, as were the broadcast revenues. Therefore, when it became possible to have a long-term lease in a brand new stadium, with more control over revenues sources, including parking and generous broadcast revenues, it is obvious that Atlanta made better fiscal sense for the ownership group. Because they did not want to sell the Braves and their options were limited in Wisconsin, it was only a matter of time before the team left.

Epilogue

We felt we owed Milwaukee something.

Lou Perini, former owner
of the Milwaukee Braves,
March 21, 1968

For the five decades before the Braves moved to Milwaukee, major league baseball was incredibly dormant as no teams transferred to new cities. Therefore, it is stunning to realize that since 1953 a total of nine major league baseball teams have relocated. The Brooklyn Dodgers and the New York Giants introduced big league baseball to the West Coast in 1958 after abandoning New York City. The St. Louis Browns, the Seattle Pilots, and the Montreal Expos moved back east and changed their names to the Baltimore Orioles, the Milwaukee Brewers, and the Washington Nationals, respectively. Two teams actually moved twice, with the Braves going first to Milwaukee and then to Atlanta in 1966 and the Athletics leaving Philadelphia for Kansas City in 1955 before eventually landing in Oakland in 1968. The Washington Senators had two incarnations: The first put down in Minneapolis in 1961 and became the Minnesota Twins, a move that would have ramifications on Milwaukee as it boxed in the Braves. The second Senators club, an expansion team created in 1961, ended up in the Dallas–Fort Worth area and became the Texas Rangers in 1972. In addition, eleven other teams entered the league as expansion teams. Baseball now goes coast to coast, into Canada, and down to Arizona and Florida.

This movement of more than half of the existing franchises along with expansion teams in new cities dramatically increased big league attendance across the nation. Before the Braves relocated to Milwaukee, total attendance in the big leagues was more than 14.6 million. By 1969 that number had increased to more than 27.2 million fans.[1] In 2015 just over 73.1 million fans attended games, the eleventh highest total in Major League Baseball history.[2] In fact, the lowest attendance for any team in the majors in 2016 was 1.3 million for the Tampa Bay Rays.[3] Fifty years earlier, that number would have been a dream season for almost any club in baseball. It is especially staggering when you consider that in 1952, the Boston Braves drew a total of 281,278 paying customers to Braves Field.[4] By comparison, in 2016 the Milwaukee Brewers drew 2,314,614 and the Atlanta Braves 2,020,914. This averaged out per game to 28,575 in Milwaukee and 25,138 in Atlanta, compared with about 3,600 for the 1952 Braves.[5] Clearly, baseball has thrived in the era of television and franchise mobility, and both Milwaukee and Atlanta benefited from the relocation of the Braves to their cities.

"With the Braves, it came too fast"

After the Braves left, the Milwaukee Brewers organization hosted exhibition and regular season games for the Chicago White Sox from 1967 through 1969 at County Stadium. One game between the White Sox and the Minnesota Twins during the summer of 1967 drew more than fifty-one thousand. So impressed were officials from both leagues that baseball commissioner William Eckert mentioned the possibility of Milwaukee as a location for expansion. Calvin Griffith, the owner of the Twins, noted that "The way some clubs in our league are drawing, they would be better off to move to Milwaukee." Moreover, when considering expansion locations, how "can you not consider a great town like Milwaukee?" Fred Haney, the pennant-winning former manager of the Braves, said Milwaukee had proven "what a great baseball town it is." Even former Braves president John McHale said he had "always been in favor of major league baseball in Milwaukee, with one stipulation—that it be locally owned. Milwaukee's baseball future with local ownership is much brighter than any other way."[6]

When baseball finally did expand in 1969, Milwaukee was passed over for a variety of reasons, including being located too close to existing franchises in Chicago. Finally, five years after the Braves' last season in Milwaukee, major league baseball returned full-time to Milwaukee when the expansion Seattle Pilots of the American League were purchased out of bankruptcy court by Selig's group and relocated to Milwaukee as the Brewers. Much like Milwaukee in 1965, Seattle officials sued baseball but, unlike the Wisconsin case, they were able to get the American League to put an expansion franchise back in Seattle after agreeing to drop the lawsuit. The Milwaukee County Board had learned the value of a long-term lease and tied the Brewers into County Stadium for twenty-five years at a cost of one dollar per year up to one million customers and a percentage of the gate thereafter. The team maintained concession rights at all baseball games, paid for maintenance at the stadium, and, like the Braves, got none of the parking revenue. Eugene Grobschmidt defended the lease because Milwaukee County made significant income from parking during baseball games. Since the Brewers paid for maintenance, the revenues generated offset any costs to the county for the ballpark, including expansion of the facility to fifty-five thousand. Moreover, the return of baseball to the region generated millions of dollars. Grobschmidt warned that what "started out as a beautiful civic story has shown signs of deterioration because some have forgotten that a strong moral and legal commitment exists." He added that the Brewers and baseball were "good for Milwaukee" and the county's role has "been good for the Brewers. It is incumbent upon all of us to continue this relationship honestly and with foresight."[7] While the association between Milwaukee County and the Brewers continued, it did so without Grobschmidt, who retired in 1972 and passed away the following year. While he was often an obstacle to a resolution with the Braves, no one could doubt his belief in baseball in Milwaukee.

In May 1970 the Milwaukee Brewers and the Atlanta Braves played an exhibition game at County Stadium before a crowd of more than twenty-five thousand fans. Bill Bartholomay said he hoped that this could become a regular opportunity for the Braves to return to Milwaukee to play the American League Brewers. Only three Milwaukee Braves were still on Atlanta's roster just five years after they left for Georgia. Most prominent was Henry Aaron, who was well on his way to becoming the all-time home run king. He received a standing ovation from the Milwaukee crowd that still considered him to be one of their own. Aaron later said this was one of the highlights of his career and it rivaled the crowd reaction when he hit the pennant-winning home run on September 23, 1957. The crowd that showed up for an exhibition game showed that Milwaukee fans "don't have to take a back seat to any in the country. I still remember the free milk and gasoline and the cars we got to drive for free." Aaron met with reporters after the 1–0 loss to Milwaukee and reflected on the Braves teams that played in Wisconsin during their championship runs of the late 1950s. He said that the 1957 World Series–winning club was good, but the best was the 1959 team that lost in the playoffs to the Dodgers. For the Brewers, in their first month in a new city, having come from Seattle just a few weeks earlier, the game was also special. Brewers infielder Mike Hegan said afterward that although it was an exhibition game, it "was special because it was the Braves." Some fans even asked Bartholomay for his autograph, perhaps the first step in recovering from the public estrangement between the city and its beloved Braves.[8]

But the Milwaukee fans of the early 1970s did not embrace the Brewers as quickly and completely as they did the Braves. One writer noted that the new team "must defrost a city hardened" by the Braves' move to Atlanta, and many in Milwaukee still resented baseball "for allowing the team to be spirited south by Chicago interests." No longer would County Stadium be "an insane asylum with bases" as it had been in the fifties, but baseball was back.[9] Former Milwaukee Braves owner Lou Perini, the man who made Milwaukee baseball famous, had an opportunity to see the Brewers play at Fenway Park in his hometown of Boston. It was the first time he had seen them in action, and he relayed some of his thoughts about it to Lou Chapman of the *Milwaukee Sentinel*. It "could be a good thing in disguise having an expansion club in Milwaukee," Perini said, because then "the enthusiasm in the city could be built gradually. With the Braves, it came too fast." He said that he always believed that Milwaukee was "a major league city, but the fans left us. They were spoiled by our early success." He "had a great team when we moved to Milwaukee. The fans will have to be patient with the Brewers for a couple of years." Asked again if any significant Milwaukee "money people" had attempted to purchase the team from him before he sold it to the Chicago group, Perini responded, "Definitely not."[10]

Meanwhile, the Atlanta Braves drew over one million fans for each of their first six years in Atlanta, but attendance fell off every year except 1969, when the Braves made the playoffs for the first time in Atlanta. In October 1968, Lloyd Larson noted that thirteen of twenty major league teams had decreases in attendance in 1967, and nine of them failed to get to one million. For some teams, decaying stadiums contributed, but "supposedly solid baseball cities never should drop that low, regardless of the quality and location of the playing facilities." Larson correctly pointed out that this type of decline had "caused Milwaukee's goose to be cooked despite the fact the gate count—honest count, too—jumped to 910,911" in 1964.[11] The struggle for customers haunted all of baseball in the sixties and early seventies, even in Georgia. In 1972 the Braves hosted 752,973 fans at Atlanta Stadium, which was twenty thousand less than the worst season in Milwaukee, excluding the lame duck season of 1965. But the story was not over, and the bottom fell out in 1975, when the Braves played in front of only 534,672, their worst crowds since the dreadful 1952 season in Boston.

After the 1975 season, Bartholomay agreed to sell the Braves to Ted Turner, and the Braves had local ownership for the first time since 1952 in Boston. Bartholomay remained chair of the board of directors and as of 2018 he remains the chair emeritus of the club. In April 2015 Bartholomay said he was proud of being the first professional franchise owner to move a club to the Southeast and was particularly pleased with the success the Braves had, especially since 1990.

As for the decision to leave Milwaukee, he said it "was the right choice for baseball and the right choice for America. Americans needed some good news in 1966, with Vietnam and all the other things that were going on. Baseball being played in the Southeast one hundred years after Reconstruction was a pretty good thing."[12]

Bartholomay always maintained that his group did not purchase the Braves to move the team and has never wavered in his statements that "there never was any serious effort" in Milwaukee to buy the Braves. Furthermore, if "there had been, it might have been difficult to get unanimous approval of our league to move the franchise." It should be noted, however, in 1965 he did not need "unanimous approval" to relocate the Braves. He remarked that it was not clear why no one stepped up for the Braves because "a few years later, they went out and paid an awful lot of money for the Seattle Pilots, which wasn't exactly a strong franchise." Bowie Kuhn, one of the National League's attorneys during the 1966 court case and later commissioner of baseball, concurred with Bartholomay. He said that even as it was rumored the team was going to leave, "There was no realistic effort made to come forward and try to buy the club for Milwaukee." Even more, the "same fine people who might have made a move earlier" for the Braves later "got the Seattle Pilots franchise and have done a terrific job with it." But, said Kuhn, the Milwaukee people did not take "seriously the threat that the club might go." Both men believed that had Milwaukee fought for the Braves with their checkbooks rather than with lawyers, they "might have won and kept the Braves."[13] Bartholomay later added that the Atlanta Braves had indeed been "a disappointment overall. Artistically, it has been a difficult twenty-five years." Even more, in Bartholomay's opinion, Atlanta was a good and affluent city, but from a fan support perspective, it was "not a season ticket city. You have to win to draw."[14]

My Ghosts of the Milwaukee Braves

In 2016 I was able to take my family, including my granddaughter, to see the Braves play the Brewers in Atlanta during their final season at Turner Field. As we walked around the stadium, I could not help but wonder what would have happened if they had stayed in Milwaukee. Despite some information posted throughout the ballpark about the Braves' tenure in Milwaukee, most fans evidently were unaware of the team's history before it came to Atlanta. We took our picture by perhaps the most ironic item at Turner Field, a statue of Hall of Famer Warren Spahn, in a Milwaukee Braves cap, immortalized in bronze, in a city where he never pitched. Meanwhile, there is no statue of him in Milwaukee where he won the majority of the games that made him baseball's all-time leader in wins for a left-handed pitcher.

Unfortunately, there was nothing the Milwaukee fans of the Braves could have done to save their team. Maybe, in the end, it is better for our collective memories that the team did leave. Their brief window of time allows us to still see them with an appropriate level of nostalgia that would not be possible had the team remained in Milwaukee. We now have this golden era of Milwaukee baseball to remember. Some fans want to remember only those great days at County Stadium rather than the sparsely attended games in the early sixties. They can focus on memories of the 1957 World Series rather than the strike-shortened seasons of the eighties and nineties. Images of the classic flannel uniforms of the Milwaukee Braves are etched in their minds and have never been replaced with the brightly colored polyester uniforms that the Atlanta Braves embraced over the next two decades. We can close our eyes and still see the excitement of our predecessors at County Stadium during the glory days of baseball in America. It is there that the ghosts of the Milwaukee Braves, stolen from the fans who loved them, will live on as people continue to embrace their story.

Appendix: Seasonal Attendance Following Relocation

The Atlanta Braves drew fewer total fans than the Milwaukee Braves and the Milwaukee Brewers during the first thirteen years of their existence (chart 1). While this does not demonstrate profitability of the Braves or the Brewers, it does show that Milwaukee was not the bad baseball town that the Braves ownership claimed when the team left Wisconsin. The dramatic spike downward in attendance for the Brewers in the eleventh year was a result of the Major League Baseball strike in 1981.

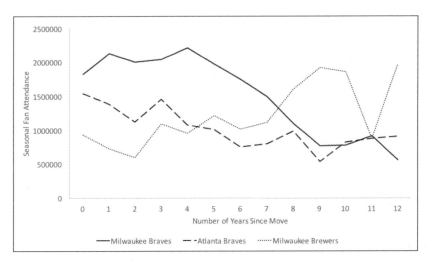

Chart 1. A comparative graph of three franchises for the first thirteen years of their existence in a new market.

Notes

Prologue

The chapter-opening epigraph is from "Braves Will Ask League Today for Permission to Shift to Atlanta," *New York Times*, October 22, 1964.

1. Tom Flaherty, "Home of the Braves," *Milwaukee Journal Sentinel*, June 2, 1998.

2. Jack Wilkinson, "Jilted City Sees Old Flame Return," *Atlanta Constitution*, June 2, 1998.

3. Terrence Moore, "A Soft Spot for Aaron, Not the Braves," *Atlanta Constitution*, July 20, 1999.

4. Lou Chapman, "Perini Says Fans Must Be Patient," *Milwaukee Sentinel*, July 20, 1970.

Chapter 1. "You Keep the Brewers, We'll Keep the Braves"

The chapter-opening epigraph is from "Schedule Tells Rickey Why Perini Quit Boston," *New York Times*, March 19, 1953.

1. To learn more about Borchert Field, see Bob Buege's *Borchert Field: Stories from Milwaukee's Legendary Ballpark* (Madison: Wisconsin Historical Society Press, 2017).

2. Paul Dickson, *Bill Veeck: Baseball's Greatest Maverick* (New York: Walker & Company, 2012), chap. 4.

3. Dickson, *Bill Veeck*, chap. 7.

4. Jules Tygiel, *Past Time: Baseball as History* (New York: Oxford University Press, 2000), 172.

5. Gregg Hoffmann, "Milwaukee's County Stadium: A Controversial Construction," in *From the Braves to the Brewers: Great Games and Exciting History at Milwaukee's County Stadium*, ed. Gregory H. Wolf (Phoenix: Society for American Baseball Research, 2016), 5–6.

6. Gregg Hoffmann, *Down in the Valley: The History of Milwaukee County Stadium; the People, the Promise, the Passion* (Milwaukee: Milwaukee Brewers Baseball Club; Milwaukee Journal Sentinel, 2000), 19–22.

7. Bob Buege, *The Milwaukee Braves: A Baseball Eulogy* (Milwaukee: Douglas American Sports Publications, 1988), 12.

8. Hoffmann, *Down in the Valley*, 22–31.

9. The scandal involved the Chicago White Sox's throwing the 1919 World Series. Baseball owners responded by banishing the players involved for life and appointing a commissioner to oversee all of baseball.

10. Ruth did play his last professional season of baseball with the Braves, but he was a mere shadow of the player he had been when he broke in with the Red Sox a generation earlier.

11. Lawrence S. Ritter, *Lost Ballparks: A Celebration of Baseball's Legendary Fields* (New York: Viking Studio Books, 1992), 19–21.

12. This is more than a million fewer than the lowest team recorded in 2016. The Tampa Bay Rays averaged 15,879 per game compared with the Boston Braves, who averaged only 3,653 fans in attendance. http://www.baseball-reference.com/leagues /MLB/2016-misc.shtml.

13. "Atlanta Braves Attendance Data," http://www.baseball-almanac.com /teams/bravatte.shtml. And "Boston Red Sox Attendance Data," http://www.base ball-reference.com/teams/BOS/.

14. Harold Kaese, *The Boston Braves: 1871–1953* (Boston: Northeastern University Press, 2004), 254–55.

15. In 2018 the Milwaukee Brewers still employ Bob Quinn's great-grandson, also named Bob Quinn, in their front office as an executive vice president.

16. Kaese, *Boston Braves*, 282–83.

17. Milwaukee Public Television, *A Braves New World* (Madison: Wisconsin Historical Society Press Studio, 2009), DVD.

18. *The Wisconsin Blue Book, 1950* (Madison: Wisconsin Legislative Reference Library, 1950), 469–92.

19. "Overview of Boston's Population," Boston Redevelopment Authority— Research Division, 2011, http://www.bostonredevelopmentauthority.org/PDF /ResearchPublications/RappaportInstituteAdvBrd.pdf; "Boston Urbanized Area Population & Density from 1920," http://www.demographia.com/db-bosuza1920.htm.

20. "Rumor Milwaukee Will Replace Browns in 1952," *Rome (GA) News-Tribune*, April 1, 1951.

21. "Building a Better City Kept Fred Miller a Busy Man," *Milwaukee Sentinel*, December 18, 1954.

22. Lloyd Larson, "This Is One of Those Super Days in Sports," *Milwaukee Sentinel*, April 1, 1951; Kaese, *Boston Braves*, 284.

23. Bill Veeck with Ed Linn, *Veeck as in Wreck: The Autobiography of Bill Veeck* (Chicago: University of Chicago Press, 2001), 279–80.

24. Charlie Grimm with Ed Prell, *Jolly Cholly's Story: Baseball, I Love You!* (Chicago: Henry Regnery, 1968), 193–95.

25. Robert E. Murphy, *After Many a Summer: The Passing of the Giants and Dodgers and a Golden Age in New York Baseball* (New York: Union Square Press, 2009), 77–79.

26. Veeck, *Veeck as in Wreck*, 281; "Braves Block Bid to Shift Browns," *New York Times*, March 4, 1953.

27. R. G. Lynch, "Exchange of 'Wires' with Perini Tells Why Browns Can't Come Here," *Milwaukee Journal*, March 3, 1953; "Not Unreasonable, Says Veeck of Perini," *Milwaukee Journal*, March 3, 1953.

28. R. G. Lynch, "The World with a Fence around It, That's All," *Milwaukee Journal*, March 4, 1953.

29. R. G. Lynch, "What Is the Truth of the Brave's Statements?" *Milwaukee Journal*, March 5, 1953.

30. "Governor and Senate Add Weight to Milwaukee's Franchise Quest," *New York Times*, March 6, 1953.

31. "Veeck Willing to Shift; Defends Perini's Stand," *Milwaukee Journal*, March 6, 1953.

32. "Shift Does Not Need Approval, Says Frick," *Milwaukee Journal*, March 11, 1953.

33. "Perini Seeks New Rule to Block Browns from Taking This City," *Milwaukee Journal*, March 12, 1953.

34. "Perini Finally Shows His Hand—And How!," *Milwaukee Journal*, March 12, 1953.

35. Lloyd Larson, "Browns Moving to Baltimore for '53; Report Veeck Buying I.L. Franchise," *Milwaukee Sentinel*, March 12.

36. "Milwaukee Acts to Oust Brewers from Stadium to Attract Browns," *New York Times*, March 5, 1953.

37. Arthur Daley, "The Moving of Plymouth Rock," *New York Times*, March 19, 1953.

38. Harold Kaese and R. G. Lynch, *The Milwaukee Braves* (New York: G. P. Putnam's Sons, 1954), 286.

39. "Remembering the Wigwam," http://www.bu.edu/today/2012/braves-field-remembering-the-wigwam-2/.

40. Gary Caruso, *The Braves Encyclopedia* (Philadelphia: Temple University Press, 1995), 324.

41. Phil Eck, *Remembering Fred Miller: From Notre Dame to the High Life* (Springfield, IL: Senators Publications, 2016), 152–53.

42. "Meeting Monday, Says Baseball Paper," *Milwaukee Journal*, March 13, 1953.

43. Sam Levy, "Frick, Giles to Be Present at Conference," *Milwaukee Journal*, March 13, 1953; "Braves Field Price $340,000," *New York Times*, November 1, 1953.

44. "Braves Field Bought by Boston University," *New York Times*, July 31, 1953.

45. "Remembering the Wigwam."

46. "Meeting Called Here," *Milwaukee Journal*, March 13, 1953.

47. Lloyd Larson, "Miller's Death Great Loss to Milwaukee," *Milwaukee Sentinel*, December 19, 1954.

48. The immediate financial success of the Braves in Wisconsin has been referred to as the Miracle of Milwaukee. Fans came out in record numbers for several years in a row and this franchise move became the model for other teams that wanted to cash in on new markets.

49. R. G. Lynch, "'Milwaukee Gets Braves,' Perini Says," *Milwaukee Journal*, March 14, 1953.

50. Joe Knack, "Toledo Not in Yet—But Brewers Close," *Toledo Blade*, March 16, 1953.

51. Kaese, *Boston Braves*, 285.

52. "Perini's Personal Prestige Made Shift of Braves Possible," *Milwaukee Journal*, March 19, 1953.

53. "Boston," *New York Times*, March 22, 1953.

54. "Boston Up in Arms over Braves Shift," *New York Times*, March 17, 1953.

55. "Boston Gets News in Edge of Black," *New York Times*, March 19, 1953.

56. "Boston Fans Resigned but Realize Big Loss," *Milwaukee Journal*, March 19, 1953.

57. Leo H. Peterson, "Owner's Predict More Changes," *Telegraph-Herald* (Dubuque, IA), March 19, 1953.

58. Ron Briley, "Milwaukee and Atlanta, a Tale of Two Cities: Eddie, Hank, and the 'Rover Boys' Head South," *Nine: A Journal of Baseball History and Social Policy Perspectives* 6, no. 1 (1997): 31–32.

59. The eminent domain strategy was attempted by the city of Baltimore in 1984 to seize control of the National Football League's Colts and keep the team in Maryland. Fearing this could actually happen, team owner Robert Irsay arranged for moving trucks to relocate the team to Indianapolis the night before the vote on eminent domain was scheduled to take place. It is not likely that this strategy would have worked in the Boston Braves situation.

60. Arthur Daley, "Sports of the Times," *New York Times*, March 18, 1953.

61. James Quirk, "An Economic Analysis of Team Movements in Professional Sports," *Law and Contemporary Problems* 38, no 1, Athletics (Winter-Spring 1973): 50.

62. Albert Theodore Powers, *Business of Baseball* (Jefferson, NC: McFarland, 2003), 124–25.

63. Paul Dickson, *Bill Veeck: Baseball's Greatest Maverick* (New York: Walker & Company, 2012).

64. Paul Gardner, "Baseball's Notions Counter," *Nation's Business*, April 1950.

65. The caps the Braves used in Milwaukee were initially identical to the ones previously used by the minor league Brewers for several years. The style of the *M* changed slightly over the years, but the cap remained the same until the *M* was changed to an *A*.

66. Louis Effrat, "Braves Move to Milwaukee," *New York Times*, March 19, 1953.

67. "Only 420 Bostonians Bought Season Seats," *Milwaukee Journal*, March 20, 1953.

68. "Club Women Took Her out of Ball Park," *New York Times*, July 19, 1956.

69. "Red Sox Win 4–1 as Fans Boo Braves," *New York Times*, April 12, 1953.

70. Red Thisted, "Braves Top Bosox in Finale," *Milwaukee Sentinel*, April 13, 1953.

71. "Boston's Despair Echoes in Milwaukee Handbags," *New York Times*, March 28, 1953; Robert W. Wells, "Shift Made Our Country Infamous—in Boston," *Milwaukee Journal*, March 20, 1953.

72. "Moving of Braves Upheld by Cushing," *New York Times*, March 23, 1953; "Half of Back Bay Seen Going West Should Braves Capture Pennant," *New York Times*, June 21, 1953.

73. Harold Kaese, "Boston Baseball Fan to a Milwaukee Fan," *Boston Globe*, March 20, 1953.

Chapter 2. Home of the Braves

The chapter-opening epigraph is from R. G. Lynch, "Maybe I'm Wrong: Petitions Circulate to Get Braves on TV," *Milwaukee Journal*, March 25, 1954.

1. Arthur Daley, "Sports of the Times: Brownie Blues," *New York Times*, July 12, 1953.

2. "Veeck Sees His 'Damage' Rectified by Transfer," *New York Times*, March 19, 1953.

3. "Cheers and Beers Will Rise in Milwaukee," *New York Times*, April 8, 1953.

4. "Milwaukee Roars Hello to Braves," *New York Times*, April 9, 1953.

5. "Packer Exhibition Is Cancelled; No Field," *Wisconsin Rapids Daily Tribune*, March 19, 1953.

6. "National League Completes Date Changes Caused by Shift of Braves to Milwaukee," *New York Times*, April 9, 1953.

7. "Braves' Field Chief Likes Stadium Setup," *Milwaukee Sentinel*, March 18, 1953.

8. "Office Gear Follows Braves," *New York Times*, March 22, 1953; Robert Cantwell, "The Music of Baseball," *Sports Illustrated*, October 3, 1960.

9. Robert P. Russell to John L. Doyne, July 16, 1965, box 5, John L. Doyne Collection, Milwaukee County Historical Society.

10. "County Due to OK Braves Lease Today," *Milwaukee Sentinel*, March 17, 1953.

11. "Sidelights on the Financial and Business Developments of the Day," *New York Times*, April 17, 1953.

12. "County Due to OK Braves Lease Today," *Milwaukee Sentinel*, March 17, 1953.

13. "Seek $100,000 for Stadium Traffic Control," *Milwaukee Sentinel*, March 17, 1953.

14. Dickins, "Braves, Faculty to Play on April 32," *Concordia Courier*, April 17, 1953.

15. "Braves Barter Begins," *New York Times*, March 25, 1953.

16. "Ticket Shift Puts Braves in a 'Mess,'" *New York Times*, April 3, 1953.

17. "At 9 A.M. in Milwaukee They Were Seeking Seats for Game 8 Days Away," *New York Times*, April 7, 1953.

18. Harold Kaese and R. G. Lynch, *The Milwaukee Braves* (New York: G. P. Putnam's Sons, 1954), 290.

19. "Happy Milwaukee Flock's for Seats," *New York Times*, March 19, 1953.

20. Kaese and Lynch, *Milwaukee Braves*, 289–90, 296.

21. "Milwaukee Fans Won't See Club Until April 24," *St. Petersburg Times*, April 16, 1953.

22. Robert Creamer, "Milwaukee Is a Real Baseball Town, and This Year the All-star Was a Real Baseball Game. Just Ask the Players," *Sports Illustrated*, July 25, 1955; John Schulian, "National League City," *Sports Illustrated*, June 1, 1998.

23. "Miller Buys Braves Game Radio Rights," *Milwaukee Sentinel*, April 1, 1953.

24. "Braves Broadcasts Continue on WEMP with Earl Gillespie," *Milwaukee Sentinel*, April 1, 1953.

25. "Fans Prod Braves for Series Seats," *New York Times*, June 7, 1953.

26. "Braves Sell Air Rights," *New York Times*, April 1, 1953.

27. Lloyd Larson, "12-Team Majors Silly Idea—Perini," *Milwaukee Sentinel*, November 19, 1953.

28. James R. Walker and Robert V. Bellamy Jr., *Center Field Shot: A History of Baseball on Television* (Lincoln: University of Nebraska Press, 2008), 31.

29. In 2015 Wisconsin was only sixth in the nation, but the per capita consumption was up to 35.8 gallons per year. http://www.marketwatch.com/story/10-states-where-people-drink-the-most-beer-2015-07-07.

30. Kaese and Lynch, *Milwaukee Braves*, 292.

31. Doug Russell, "The Move That Made Milwaukee Cry," http://www.onmilwaukee.com/sports/articles/riseandfallofmkebraves.html.

32. Joseph C. Nichols, "Proud Milwaukee Hails Team Today," *New York Times*, April 14, 1953.

33. Kaese and Lynch, *Milwaukee Braves*, 290.

34. Gilbert Millstein, "More Brooklyn than Brooklyn," *New York Times*, July 5, 1953.

35. Milwaukee Association of Commerce, "Milwaukee Braves Business Attraction Survey," testimony, 406–9, box 1, State of Wisconsin v. Milwaukee Braves, Milwaukee County Circuit Court, MSS-2414, Milwaukee County Historical Society (hereafter cited as Braves Court Case).

36. "Braves to Increase Their Stadium Rent," *New York Times*, June 28, 1953.

37. "Hawks May Shift to Washington," *New York Times*, April 28, 1953.

38. Neil J. Sullivan, *The Dodgers Move West* (New York: Oxford University Press, 1987), 43.

39. Michael Shapiro, *The Last Good Season: Brooklyn, the Dodgers, and Their Final Pennant Race Together* (New York: Broadway Books, 2003), 120.

40. "Milwaukee Pours Favors on Braves," *New York Times*, May 31, 1953.

41. Arthur Daley, "Sports of the Times: Jollier Than Ever," *New York Times*, June 3, 1953.

42. Milwaukee Braves ad, *Milwaukee Sentinel*, August 2, 1953.

43. "Turnstile Story," *Milwaukee Sentinel*, August 2, 1953.

44. Gary Caruso, *The Braves Encyclopedia* (Philadelphia: Temple University Press, 1995), 77–79.

45. "Three-Year Boston Deficit Recouped in Milwaukee," *New York Times*, October 23, 1953.

46. Lou Chapman, "Perini Trio Bats 1,000 at A. of C. Fete," *Milwaukee Sentinel*, October 23, 1953.

47. Jules Tygiel, *Past Time: Baseball as History* (New York: Oxford University Press, 2000), 174.

48. Harry Hill, "A Million Plus Earned by Team, Perini Says," *Milwaukee Journal*, October 23, 1953.

49. Tygiel, *Past Time*, 174.

50. Lynch, "Maybe I'm Wrong."

51. Testimony of William Eberly, March 7, 1966, Braves Court Case.

52. Lou Chapman, "Eberly Braves' 'Most Popular,'" *Milwaukee Sentinel*, December 13, 1953; "Braves' '54 Ticket Sales Up to 7,288," *Milwaukee Sentinel*, December 6, 1953.

53. Larson, "12-Team Majors Silly Idea—Perini."

54. E. V. Durling, "Seattle Could Be Next Milwaukee in Baseball," *Milwaukee Sentinel*, November 6, 1953.

55. "Perini Pledges All-Out Flag Effort for Wisconsin, Milwaukee Fans," *Milwaukee Journal*, March 25, 1954.

56. "Boosters: Milwaukee, State Fans Gather in Florida to See Braves Practice," *Milwaukee Journal*, February 25, 1954.

57. "Braves Not Ready Yet, Grimm Admits," *Milwaukee Sentinel*, March 26, 1954.

58. "Braves Turn Back Red Sox, 3–1, after Welcome Home by 30,000," *New York Times*, April 10, 1954.

59. "Fans Sing 'Jingle Bells' in Snow," *New York Times*, May 5, 1954; "Cardinal Rookie Tames Braves, 2–1," *New York Times*, August 20, 1954; "Baseball's Change of Bases," *New York Times*, August 11, 1954.

60. "45,922 Milwaukee Baseball Fans Raise League's Mark to 1,841,666," *New York Times*, August 30, 1954.

61. "Pennant Talk," *Telegraph-Herald* (Dubuque, IA), August 10, 1954.

62. Lou Chapman, "From Build-up to Let-down—Braves' Story Fabulous," *Milwaukee Sentinel*, September 24, 1954.

63. "15,937,282 Fans Saw Majors Play This Year," *New York Times*, September 27, 1954.

64. John Drebinger, "Baseball," *New York Times*, December 26, 1954.

65. "Braves Raise Their Rent," *New York Times*, September 24, 1954.

66. "Milwaukee to Act on Plan to Add 10,500 Seats to Braves' Stadium," *New York Times*, October 29, 1954.

67. "Foes of Seats for Stadium Score, 14–6," *Milwaukee Sentinel*, November 10, 1954.

68. "Meeting the Traffic Challenge: Dynamic Highway Planning Changes the Face of America," *Milwaukee Sentinel*, March 28, 1954.

69. R. G. Lynch, "Braves' Rooters Whoop It Up for Telecasts of Road Games," *Milwaukee Journal*, March 29, 1954.

70. Lynch, "Maybe I'm Wrong."

71. William Johnson, "TV Made It a New Game," *Sports Illustrated*, December 22, 1969.

72. Johnson, "TV Made It a New Game."

73. Robert D. Warrington, "Departure without Dignity: The Athletics Leave Philadelphia," http://sabr.org/research/departure-without-dignity-athletics-leave-philadelphia.

74. "Athletics' Sale to Be Discussed by League Club Owners Tuesday," *New York Times*, September 24, 1954.

75. "Kansas City Men Return," *New York Times*, September 8, 1954.

76. "Oakland Athletics Attendance Data," http://www.baseball-almanac.com /teams/athlatte.shtml.

77. John Drebinger, "Sports of the Times: Philadelphia's Sad Story," *New York Times*, August 15, 1954.

78. Arthur Daley, "Sports of the Times: The End and the Beginning," *New York Times*, November 10, 1954.

79. "Connie Mack's 1955 Wish: Pennant for Kansas City," *Milwaukee Journal*, December 24, 1954.

80. "Baseball's Change of Bases."

81. John Drebinger, "Dodgers Consider Going to Coast for Spring Exhibitions in 1956," *New York Times*, November 20, 1954.

82. John Drebinger, "California Cities Prime Prospects," *New York Times*, December 7, 1954.

83. John Drebinger, "National League, at Meeting Here, Decides to Defer Plans for Expansion," *New York Times*, January 30, 1955.

84. Bob Buege, *The Milwaukee Braves: A Baseball Eulogy* (Milwaukee: Douglas American Sports Publications, 1988), 98.

85. Ernest Havemann, "Farewell to a Sportsman," *Sports Illustrated*, December 27, 1954.

86. "Building a Better City Kept Fred Miller a Busy Man," *Milwaukee Sentinel*, December 18, 1954.

87. Lloyd Larson, "Miller's Death Great Loss to Milwaukee," *Milwaukee Sentinel*, December 19, 1954.

88. "Brewing Executive Found Beside Flaming Plane with Clothes Afire," *Milwaukee Sentinel*, December 18, 1954; "Brewer and Son Die in Air Crash," *New York Times*, December 18, 1954; "Fred Miller, Son Die in Fiery Plane Crash," *Milwaukee Sentinel*, December 18, 1954.

89. "Civic Leaders Express Sorrow at Miller Death," *Milwaukee Sentinel*, December 19, 1954; Larson, "Miller's Death Great Loss."

90. "Fred C. Miller," *Milwaukee Sentinel*, December 18, 1954.

91. "$200,000 Fund Set Up," *New York Times*, December 8, 1955.

92. "Miller Pays '55 Scoreboard Rent," *Milwaukee Sentinel*, April 7, 1955.

Chapter 3. Bush Leaguers

The chapter-opening epigraph is from Statement, Joseph F. Cairnes Representing the Milwaukee Braves at Meeting of the Parks and Recreation Committee, Milwaukee

County Board of Supervisors, November 26, 1957, Erwin F. Zillman Papers, Milwaukee County Historical Society.

1. "Braves Set New Record for Advance Seat Sale," *New York Times*, November 2, 1954.

2. "11,188 Season Tickets Are Sold, Braves Report," *New York Times*, January 17, 1955.

3. Lou Chapman, "Braves' Ticket Sales Near 1,200,000 Mark," *Milwaukee Sentinel*, April 3, 1955.

4. "Boys in Milwaukee Play Baseball Despite Snow," *New York Times*, January 25, 1955; Arthur Daley, "Innings and Outings of Spring Training," *New York Times*, March 20, 1955; Red Thisted, "46 Braves Hustle Through First Drills," *Milwaukee Sentinel*, March 2, 1955.

5. "County Board Views Changes at Stadium," *Milwaukee Sentinel*, April 7, 1955.

6. Lou Chapman, "Only 400 Fans See Team Arrive," *Milwaukee Sentinel*, April 8, 1955.

7. Henry T. Garvey, "Perfect Braves' Day Except for Score," *Milwaukee Sentinel*, April 10, 1955.

8. Lou Chapman, "Braves Backers Eager for Behind Scenes Tips," *Milwaukee Sentinel*, January 2, 1955.

9. John Drebinger, "Handling of Winning Nationals Gains High Praise for Durocher," *New York Times*, July 14, 1955.

10. "Major League Traffic Job," *Milwaukee Sentinel*, July 13, 1955.

11. "Game Traffic Flows Easily," *Milwaukee Journal*, July 13, 1955.

12. "Shoppers Hug TV Sets during All-Star Game," *Milwaukee Sentinel*, July 13, 1955; R. G. Lynch, "Maybe I'm Wrong: Petitions Circulate to Get Braves on TV," *Milwaukee Journal*, July 13, 1955.

13. "Baseball Attendance Increases Because of Transfer of Athletics," *New York Times*, September 26, 1955.

14. "National League's 1955 Crowds Smaller by 339,107 than in '54," *New York Times*, December 6, 1955.

15. Charlie Grimm with Ed Prell, *Jolly Cholly's Story: Baseball, I Love You!* (Chicago: Henry Regnery, 1968), 218–19.

16. Bob Wolf, "Grimm Quits Manager Job; Haney to Boss the Braves," *Milwaukee Sentinel*, June 17, 1956.

17. Roy Terrell, "Fred Haney Lights a Fire," *Sports Illustrated*, March 18, 1957.

18. "Perini Quits as Braves' President," *Daytona Beach Morning Journal*, January 27, 1957.

19. Terrell, "Fred Haney Lights a Fire."

20. "Milwaukee Braves," *Sports Illustrated*, April 15, 1957.

21. Helen Burrows, "Ladies Boost Game Crowd to 47,176," *Milwaukee Sentinel*, August 9, 1957.

22. "Can't Cheer on an Empty Stomach," *Milwaukee Journal*, August 20, 1957.

23. Ray Grody, "L.A. Fans Couple Attendance Surge with Spending Spree," *Milwaukee Sentinel*, April 29, 1958.

24. "Rival's Souvenirs Ire Perini Salesmen," *Milwaukee Sentinel*, September 26, 1957.

25. This turned out to be true as the Yankees played at Shea Stadium in 1974–75 while Yankee Stadium was undergoing an extensive reconstruction.

26. "Perini, Head of Braves, Predicts Brook Will Leave Ebbets Field," *New York Times,* July 15, 1957.

27. William Barry Furlong, "That 'Big League' Yearning," *New York Times,* June 16, 1957.

28. Furlong, "That 'Big League' Yearning."

29. "This May Be 'Last Free TV Series,'" *Milwaukee Sentinel*, October 3, 1957.

30. "Milwaukee Gets Ready," *New York Times*, September 5, 1957.

31. Robert Creamer, "Yanks vs. Braves," *Sports Illustrated*, September 30, 1957.

32. "Series Empties City Streets as TV Lures Fans," *Milwaukee Sentinel*, October 3, 1957.

33. Jerry Cahill, "Braves Get Red Carpet Treatment at Plane," *Milwaukee Sentinel*, October 4, 1957; Robert Wells, "Braves Welcomed at Airport by Thousands of Well Wishers," *Milwaukee Journal*, October 4, 1957; "Braves' Fans Scalped," *New York Times*, September 27, 1957.

34. Jerry Cahill, "Yanks Rebuff Welcomers," *Milwaukee Sentinel*, October 5, 1957.

35. Lloyd Larson, "Strictly Bush, eh?" *Milwaukee Sentinel*, October 5, 1957.

36. "Everyone Gets into the Act in Bravesville as Baseball Capital Bursts All Its Buttons," *Milwaukee Journal*, October 11, 1957.

37. Ira Kapenstein, "City Hails Champions in a Wild Fete," *Milwaukee Journal*, October 11, 1957.

38. "Aspirin and Sleep Cool Braves Fever; Baseball Capital Resumes Staid Ways," *Milwaukee Journal*, October 12, 1957; "Milwaukee's Night of Revelry Followed by Operation Mop-Up," *New York Times*, October 12, 1957.

39. Lou Chapman, "Braves' Coaching Staff Fired; Sign Wyatt, Fitzpatrick," *Milwaukee Sentinel*, October 27, 1957; "World Champs Fire 3 Coaches," *Palm Beach Post*, October 28, 1957.

40. "County Plans Big Braves Rent Hike," *Milwaukee Sentinel*, June 6, 1957.

41. "Braves Fight Rent Increase," *Milwaukee Sentinel*, November 1, 1957.

42. Joseph M. Sheehan, "Baseball Clubs as Big Business," *New York Times*, June 9, 1957.

43. "No Yielding to the Braves Seen Likely," *Milwaukee Journal*, November 2, 1957.

44. "No Yielding."

45. "Braves Now Having Hassle on Stadium," *Miami News*, November 3, 1957.

46. Herb Hansen, "Records Prove Braves Promised to Hike Rent," *Milwaukee Sentinel*, November 2, 1957.

47. Testimony, William R. Anderson, State of Wisconsin v. Milwaukee Braves, Milwaukee County Circuit Court, MSS-2414, Milwaukee County Historical Society (hereafter cited as Braves Court Case).

48. "Asks County Board Stay Out of Stadium Parleys," *Milwaukee Sentinel*, November 9, 1957.

49. "Milwaukee County Is Right to Ask More Rent for Stadium," *Milwaukee Journal*, November 2, 1957.

50. "Majority Favors Rent Raise for Braves," *Milwaukee Journal*, November 12, 1957.

51. Cairnes statement.

52. Cairnes statement.

53. Cairnes statement.

54. "Braves Reject Terms of Stadium Contract," *Milwaukee Journal*, December 14, 1957.

55. "Braves Reject Terms."

56. Testimony, John L. Doyne, Braves Court Case.

57. Anderson testimony, Braves Court Case.

58. Contract, Milwaukee County and the National League Baseball Club of Milwaukee, Inc., January 24, 1958, box 1, Jerome C. Dretzka Papers, Milwaukee County Historical Society.

59. Contract, Milwaukee County and National League Baseball Club.

60. "Cairnes Is Host to Board, Hopes for Good Relations," *Milwaukee Journal*, May 28, 1958.

Chapter 4. The Beginning of the End

The chapter-opening epigraph is from Arthur Daley, "Sports of the Times," *New York Times*, March 11, 1960.

1. Robert C. Trumpbour, *The New Cathedrals: Politics and Media in the History of Stadium Construction* (Syracuse, NY: Syracuse University Press, 2007), 20.

2. Glen Gendzel, "Competitive Boosterism: How Milwaukee Lost the Braves," *Business History Review* (Winter 1995): 532.

3. John Barrington, "Frick Sees More 'Moves' in Majors," *Milwaukee Sentinel*, October 27, 1957.

4. "Lou Perini Silent," *Tuscaloosa (AL) News*, May 27, 1958.

5. Red Thisted, "Perini Rekindles New York Baseball Embers," *Milwaukee Journal*, May 29, 1958.

6. Arthur Daley, "Sports of the Times," *New York Times*, December 4, 1955.

7. "Milwaukee Owner Urges Expansion," *Victoria (TX) Advocate*, July 27, 1958.

8. "Tebbetts Assigned Key Braves Role," *New York Times*, October 24, 1958.

9. "Tebbetts Named To Braves' Post," *New York Times*, October 12, 1958.

10. Arthur Daley, "Sports of the Times: A Perch for Birdie," *New York Times*, October 16, 1958.

11. Gendzel, "Competitive Boosterism," 548.

12. Lloyd Larson, "Day of Sadness for People behind Scenes at the Stadium," *Milwaukee Sentinel*, January 14, 1959.

13. Lou Chapman, "Braves' Owner 'Surprised' at Quinn's Switch," *Milwaukee Sentinel*, January 14, 1959.

14. "McHale Joins Milwaukee," *Prescott (AZ) Evening Courier*, January 28, 1959.

15. Lloyd Larson, "McHale Makes Favorable Impression in First Meeting," *Milwaukee Sentinel*, January 28, 1959.

16. Red Thisted, "McHale's Debut Impressive," *Milwaukee Sentinel*, January 28, 1959.

17. "Braves Name McHale, Tiger General Manager, to Same Post at Milwaukee," *New York Times*, January 26, 1959.

18. George R. Tebbetts to Milwaukee County Park Commission, June 10, 1959, Jerome C. Dretzka Papers, Milwaukee County Historical Society.

19. Tebbetts to Milwaukee County Park Commission.

20. Tebbetts to Milwaukee County Park Commission.

21. "Braves Getting Ready," *New York Times*, September 13, 1959.

22. Roy Terrell, "Crazy Pennant Race," *Sports Illustrated*, September 28, 1959.

23. Arthur Daley, "Sports of the Times: Westward Ho!," *New York Times*, September 29, 1959.

24. Red Thisted, "Why the Braves Blew It," *Milwaukee Sentinel*, October 4, 1959.

25. Red Thisted, "Haney Quits Braves Post," *Milwaukee Sentinel*, October 5, 1959.

26. "Fred Haney Resigns as Braves Manager," *Eugene (OR) Register-Guard*, October 5, 1959.

27. Clem Hamilton, "Dressen, Always Controversial, Starts Minor Spat with Move," *Milwaukee Journal*, October 24, 1959.

28. Dink Caroll, "Playing the Field," *Montreal Gazette*, July 28, 1959.

29. "Branch Rickey's Continental League May Take Battle for Major League Recognition into Court," *Ocala (FL) Star-Banner*, December 9, 1959.

30. "National League Votes to Expand," *New York Times*, July 19, 1960.

31. Joseph M. Sheehan, "Baseball to Add 4 Cities in Majors," *New York Times*, August 3, 1960.

32. John Drebinger, "Baseball, 1962: 'Play Ball' Echoes in 3 New Stadiums," *New York Times*, April 8, 1962.

33. John Drebinger, "Vote Unanimous on Ten-Club Plan," *New York Times*, December 8, 1960.

34. "New York Yankees Have Ruined the American League," *Lewiston (ME) Evening Journal*, September 2, 1958.

35. "League Squelches Bid by Senators to Move," *Palm Beach Post*, July 7, 1958.

36. Jay Weiner, *Stadium Games: Fifty Years of Big League Greed and Bush League Boondoggles* (Minneapolis: University of Minnesota Press, 2000), 35–44.

37. "Griffith Mum on Transfer," *Daytona Beach Morning-Journal*, October 19, 1959.

38. Weiner, *Stadium Games*, 53.

39. "Griffith, Minnesota May Be in for Success Story," *Ocala (FL) Star-Banner*, March 31, 1961.

40. "Griffith, Frugal Ex-Owner of Twins, Succumbs," *Eugene (OR) Register-Guard*, October 21, 1999.

41. Testimony, William Eberly, March 7, 1966, State of Wisconsin v. Milwaukee

Braves, Milwaukee County Circuit Court, MSS-2414, Milwaukee County Historical Society (hereafter cited as Braves Court Case).

42. Ira Henry Freeman, "Other City Parks Often Lose Money," *New York Times*, April 28, 1960.

43. "Braves Will Mail Forms to Season Ticket Holders," *Milwaukee Journal*, November 27, 1959.

44. "Fan of Braves Only Loyal If Spahn Remains," *Milwaukee Journal*, December 8, 1959.

45. "714,000 Braves' Tickets Sold," *New York Times*, January 17, 1960.

46. Joseph M. Sheehan, "Braves Field Razed," *New York Times*, January 22, 1960.

47. "Stadium Ushers Strike," *Milwaukee Sentinel*, July 5, 1960.

48. "Usher Talks Eyed," *Milwaukee Sentinel*, July 6, 1960.

49. "Ushers Settle Braves Strike," *Milwaukee Journal*, July 9, 1960.

50. "Braves Release Schoendienst and Signal Start of Rebuilding," *New York Times*, October 8, 1960.

51. "Braves' Ticket Prices Rise," *New York Times*, November 27, 1960.

52. "Braves Won't Talk about Passes," *Milwaukee Journal*, June 30, 1960.

53. Eddie Mathews and Bob Buege, *Eddie Mathews and the National Pastime* (Milwaukee: Douglas American Sports Publications, 1994), 155.

54. Jack Mann, "September Song: Strain," *Sports Illustrated*, September 6, 1965.

55. "Analysis of the Braves," *Sports Illustrated*, April 10, 1962.

56. Lou Chapman, "Braves Up Sales to 840,000," *Milwaukee Sentinel*, March 26, 1961.

57. Eberly testimony.

58. "Faults Noted in Beer Ban," *Milwaukee Journal*, June 2, 1953.

59. "Beer Can Ban Tossed Back," *Milwaukee Journal*, June 2, 1955.

60. "Stadium Ban on Beer Eyed," *Milwaukee Journal*, September 4, 1957.

61. "Stadium Beer Toting Ban Again Favored," *Milwaukee Journal*, February 16, 1961.

62. "Milwaukee: Bottles and Cans Are Menace at Stadium; Must Be Banned," *Milwaukee Journal*, April 27, 1961.

63. "Stadium Beer Ban Will Be Enforced, Police Pledge," *Milwaukee Journal*, April 8, 1961.

64. "Stadium Beer Law Repeal Bid Opposed," *Milwaukee Sentinel*, April 19, 1961.

65. "Judge Upholds Beer-Tote Ban at Stadium," *Milwaukee Sentinel*, June 19, 1961.

66. Cleon Walfoort," "Braves Dismissal Baffled Cocky Dressen," *Milwaukee Journal*, August 11, 1966.

67. "Charlie Dressen Fired by Braves Tebbets Named Successor," *Montreal Gazette*, September 4, 1961.

68. Oliver E. Kuechle, "Dressen Fired by Braves; Tebbets Is New Manager," *Milwaukee Journal*, September 3, 1961.

69. Bob Wolf, "Still Perplexed," *Milwaukee Journal*, March 15, 1966.

70. Oliver E. Kuechle, "Braves '61 Blueprint Called for a Pennant," *Milwaukee Journal*, September 3, 1961.

71. Kuechle, "Dressen Fired by Braves; Tebbets Is New Manager."

72. "'Too Far Away' Birdie Made Switch to Get Back to Field," *Milwaukee Journal*, September 3, 1961.

73. Bob Wolf, "McHale Is Appointed President of Braves," *Milwaukee Journal*, September 23, 1961.

74. "Braves Shift Aides," *New York Times*, October 20, 1961.

75. Red Thisted, "Braves Shift Front Office Personnel," *Milwaukee Sentinel*, October 20, 1961.

Chapter 5. Something New

The chapter-opening epigraph is from Lloyd Larson, "11th Season Big 'Marriage' Test," *Milwaukee Sentinel*, April 10, 1963.

1. Bob Wolf, "Braves Lost Money for First Time Despite Player Sales of $425,000," *Milwaukee Journal*, February 2, 1962.

2. "Food Handler Check Urged," *Milwaukee Journal*, March 15, 1962.

3. John McHale to Howard Gregg and the Milwaukee County Park Commission, April 2, 1962, Jerome C. Dretzka Papers, Milwaukee County Historical Society.

4. "Braves' Beer Price Hike Bid Stirs Tempest," *Milwaukee Sentinel*, April 6, 1962.

5. "Braves to Add Tax to Concession Prices," *Milwaukee Journal*, April 16, 1962.

6. "Ban on Canned Beer in Stadium Repealed," *Milwaukee Journal*, June 5, 1962.

7. "Fight Called Year's Worst," *Milwaukee Journal*, July 1, 1962.

8. Walter Bingham, "No More Joy In Beertown," *Sports Illustrated*, July 23, 1962.

9. Bingham, "No More Joy In Beertown."

10. Bingham, "No More Joy In Beertown."

11. Minutes of Special Meeting of Milwaukee County Park Commission, July 20, 1962, box 1, Jerome C. Dretzka Papers, Milwaukee County Historical Society.

12. Minutes, July 20, 1962.

13. Bob Wolf, "Braves Suddenly Have Some Room at the Top," *Milwaukee Journal*, October 6, 1962.

14. Lloyd Larson, "Tebbetts Quits Braves," *Milwaukee Sentinel*, October 6, 1962.

15. "Bobby Bragan Plans to Make His Presence Known," *Nashua (NH) Telegraph*, October 18, 1962.

16. Cleon Walfoort, "Bragan Gets Braves Post as Manager," *Milwaukee Journal*, October 17, 1962.

17. Bob Wolf, "Bragan Is Given an Orange," *Milwaukee Journal*, October 23, 1962.

18. Oliver E. Kuechle, "Time Out for Talk: Choice of Bobby Bragan Well Received," *Milwaukee Sentinel*, October 18, 1962; Lloyd Larson, "Bragan's First Day on the Job Suggests Braves Picked Wisely," *Milwaukee Sentinel*, October 18, 1962; Red Thisted, "Bragan New Manager," *Milwaukee Sentinel*, October 18, 1962.

19. "Rumor Braves on Block for $4,500,000 Price: Milwaukee Writer Says Wife of Perini Wants Him to Quit Baseball, Stay at Home," *Pittsburgh Post-Gazette*, June 16, 1954.

20. "Offer for Braves Refused by Perini," *New York Times*, October 9, 1958.

21. Harry Grayson, "The Scoreboard: Perini Willing to Sell for 7-Million," *Florence (AL) Times*, June 24, 1962.

22. "No Move Contemplated," *Spokesman-Review* (Spokane, WA), June 17, 1962.

23. "No Move Contemplated."

24. Furman Bisher, *Miracle in Atlanta: The Atlanta Braves Story* (Cleveland: World Publishing, 1966), 19–20; Deposition, Oliver E. Kuechle, December 17, 1965, State of Wisconsin v. Milwaukee Braves, Milwaukee County Circuit Court, MSS-2414, Milwaukee County Historical Society (hereafter cited as Braves Court Case).

25. State of Wisconsin v. Milwaukee Braves, Inc., et al., memorandum decision, Sports Collection, box 2, folder 41, Milwaukee County Historical Society.

26. Bob Lassanske, "New Owners Have Own Youth Movement," *Milwaukee Sentinel*, November 16, 1962.

27. State v. Braves, memorandum decision.

28. State v. Braves, memorandum decision.

29. "Atlanta Ignores Man Who First Moved Braves," *Pittsburgh Press*, April 14, 1966.

30. Prospectus for Common Stock Sale in Milwaukee Braves, Inc., March 14, 1963.

31. "Perini Sells 90 Per Cent of Braves: McHale Still Club Prexy," *Palm Beach Post*, November 17, 1962.

32. "Lou Perini Sells Milwaukee Club," *Quebec Chronicle-Telegraph*, November 17, 1962.

33. "Perini Sells 90 Per Cent."

34. "Braves Are Sold," *St. Petersburg Times*, November 17, 1962.

35. Bob Wolf, "Era Finished with Sale of Braves," *Milwaukee Journal*, November 17, 1962.

36. "Wisconsin Men Buy Braves for $5,500,000; Club Will Stay in Milwaukee," *New York Times*, November 16, 1962.

37. Tommy Fitzgerald, "Lou Perini Feels Braves Will Finish in Atlanta," *Miami News*, January 14, 1965.

38. Bobby Bragan as told to Jeff Quinn, *You Can't Hit the Ball with the Bat on Your Shoulder: The Baseball Life and Times of Bobby Bragan* (Fort Worth: Summit Group, 1992), 290.

39. Kuechle deposition.

40. Oliver E. Kuechle, "Time Out for Talk," *Milwaukee Journal*, November 19, 1962.

41. Kuechle, "Time Out for Talk." Lou Chapman, "Phase Two Unfolds," *Milwaukee Sentinel*, April 10, 1963.

42. Robert E. Murphy, *After Many a Summer: The Passing of the Giants and Dodgers and the Golden Age in New York Baseball* (New York: Union Square Press, 2009), 146.

43. David A. Kaplan, "Bud Selig: The Baseball Commissioner's Exit Interview," http://www.reuters.com/article/2015/01/07/us-usa-baseball-selig-idUSKBN0KG12S20150107.

44. "National Sport: Baseball or Football?," *Milwaukee Journal*, December 3, 1961.

45. Whitey Gruhler, "Baseball Man Gives Answer," *Miami News*, December 3, 1961.

46. Grayson, "The Scoreboard: Perini Willing to Sell for 7-Million."

47. Testimony, William R. Anderson, Braves Court Case.

48. "County Agrees to 3-Year Pact with Braves," *Milwaukee Sentinel*, December 12, 1962.

49. Avery Wittenberger, "Supervisors Okay Pact with Braves," *Milwaukee Journal*, December 12, 1962.

50. Anderson testimony.

51. Stadium lease, Milwaukee County and National League Baseball Club of Milwaukee, Inc., 1962, box 1, Dretzka Papers.

52. Robert P. Russell to John L. Doyne, July 16, 1965, box 5, John L. Doyne Collection, Milwaukee County Historical Society.

53. *Securities and Exchange Commission News Digest*, February 11, 1963.

54. Prospectus for Stock Sale, Milwaukee Braves, Inc., March 14, 1963.

55. "Braves See Hope in Atlanta Move," *Tuscaloosa (AL) News*, January 14, 1966.

56. "Braves Fans Balk at Stock Offering," *Chicago Sun-Times*, April 6, 1963.

57. Cleon Walfoort, "State Cites Reason for Poor Stock Sale," *Milwaukee Journal*, January 14, 1966.

58. Lloyd Larson, "11th Season Big 'Marriage' Test," *Milwaukee Sentinel*, April 10, 1964.

59. Bisher, *Miracle in Atlanta*, 25.

60. "Braves Anticipate Pitch, Pay County," *Milwaukee Sentinel*, March 9, 1963.

61. Glen Gendzel, "Competitive Boosterism: How Milwaukee Lost the Braves," *Business History Review* (Winter 1995): 551–54.

62. Jules Tygiel, *Past Time: Baseball as History* (New York: Oxford University Press, 2000), 191.

63. "Atlanta Is Ready for Major League Baseball," exhibit 9, box 8, Braves Court Case.

64. "Atlanta Plans New Stadium for Baseball," *Tuscaloosa (AL) News*, June 9, 1963.

65. Deposition, Ivan Allen Jr., Braves Court Case.

66. Lou Chapman, "It Was Sportswriter vs. Braves in Battle over Move," *Milwaukee Sentinel*, November 21, 1979.

67. Kuechle deposition.

68. Oliver E. Kuechle, "Braves Deny 'Shift' Story," *Milwaukee Journal*, July 21, 1963.

69. "Braves Won't Move Anywhere—Owner," *Ocala (FL) Star-Banner*, July 21, 1963.

70. Kuechle deposition.

71. "Milwaukee Era Thing of Past," *Evening Independent* (St. Petersburg, FL), September 19, 1963.

72. Arthur Daley, "Sports of the Times: Footloose and Fancy Free," *New York Times*, September 19, 1964.

73. "TV 'Gold' May Lure Braves to Atlanta," *Toledo Blade*, September 20, 1963.

74. Oliver Kuechle, "Time Out for Talk: The Braves and TV and Radio Money," *Milwaukee Journal*, September 18, 1963.

75. "Atlanta Bid Admitted by Braves," *Milwaukee Sentinel*, September 11, 1963.

76. "Braves Shift to Atlanta Almost Definite," *Evening Independent* (St. Petersburg, FL), September 21, 1963.

77. "Atlanta Official Denies Braves Moving There," *Milwaukee Journal*, September 21, 1963.

78. Lloyd Larson, "Good Chance That Braves' Long Attendance Skid Will End," *Milwaukee Sentinel*, September 11, 1963.

79. "Braves Will Stay in Milwaukee as Long as They 'Are Welcome,'" *New York Times*, September 24, 1963.

80. "Braves' Head Says Club Will Stay in Milwaukee," *Meriden (CT) Morning Record*, September 24, 1963.

81. Red Thisted, "Braves Will Stay Here," *Milwaukee Sentinel*, September 24, 1963.

82. "Braves Will Stay in Milwaukee," *St. Petersburg Times*, September 24, 1963.

83. "Milwaukee Still Home of Braves," *Toledo Blade*, September 24, 1963.

84. "Doyne Feared Move," *Milwaukee Sentinel*, September 24, 1963.

85. Lou Chapman, "Fans Don't Storm Gates for Braves," *Milwaukee Sentinel*, September 25, 1963.

86. Warren G. Giles, Report to Members of the National League, box 9, folder exhibit 375–80, Braves Court Case.

87. Walter G. Wegner, "Braves Stock $13—No Sellers," *Milwaukee Sentinel*, September 24, 1963.

88. "Groups Push Moves to Up Braves Gate," *Milwaukee Sentinel*, September 25, 1963.

89. "'Go to Bat for Braves,'" *Milwaukee Sentinel*, October 30, 1963.

90. Lou Chapman, "Milwaukee on Trial, Insists Braves' 'Go' Chief," *Milwaukee Sentinel*, November 12, 1963.

91. Chapman, "Milwaukee on Trial."

92. "Braves Lose Money; Orioles Gain Profit," *New York Times*, December 15, 1963.

93. "Finley Plans Possible Suit," *Milwaukee Journal*, January 7, 1964.

94. "Finley Is Ordered to Hold Up Move," *Milwaukee Journal*, January 8, 1964.

95. Bob Wolf, "Finley Finds a Friend in Bragan—or Sort Of," *Milwaukee Journal*, January 8, 1964.

96. "Finley's Meeting with League May Draw Lawmakers," *Milwaukee Journal*, January 14, 1964.

97. "League Votes 9–1 to Keep Finley, A's in Kansas City," *Milwaukee Journal*, January 17, 1964.

Chapter 6. Bringing Down the Curtain

The chapter-opening epigraph is from "Hope in Milwaukee Penetrates Gloom," *New York Times*, October 22, 1964.

1. Bill Veeck, with Ed Linn, *Veeck as in Wreck: The Autobiography of Bill Veeck* (Chicago: University of Chicago Press, 2001), 243–45.

2. Huston Horn, "Bravura Battle for the Braves," *Sports Illustrated*, November 2, 1964.

3. Deposition, Oliver E. Kuechle, State of Wisconsin v. Milwaukee Braves, Milwaukee County Circuit Court, MSS-2414, Milwaukee County Historical Society (hereafter cited as Braves Court Case).

4. State of Wisconsin v. Milwaukee Braves, Inc., et al., memorandum decision, box 2, folder 41, Sports Collection, Milwaukee County Historical Society.

5. Oliver E. Kuechle, "Time Out for Talk: What Happened to the Season Sale?" *Milwaukee Journal*, January 23, 1964. In 1964, the Braves counted more than 910,000 fans through the turnstiles.

6. Lloyd Larson, "Braves' Open House Crowd Lifts Hopes of Revival for Survival," *Milwaukee Sentinel*, April 21, 1964.

7. Bill Mayers, "Sports Talk," *Lawrence (KS) Journal-World*, May 7, 1964.

8. C. C. Johnson Spink, "Braves' Shift Needs Only OK by N.L.," *Sporting News*, July 11, 1964.

9. "Report Say Braves Will Go to Atlanta," *Gettysburg (PA) Times*, July 3, 1964.

10. "Braves' Move to Atlanta Again Talked," *Victoria (TX) Advocate*, July 3, 1964.

11. "Braves Move to Atlanta Seen," *Daytona Beach Morning Journal*, July 4, 1964.

12. Warren Giles to Fred Russell, July 18, 1964, Braves Court Case.

13. Joseph Durso, "Braves Ready to Transfer Franchise from Milwaukee to Atlanta Next Year," *New York Times*, July 3, 1964; Shirley Povich, "For Milwaukee, Too Much, Too Quick," *St. Petersburg Times*, July 10, 1964.

14. Arthur Daley, "Sports of the Times: The Carpetbaggers," *New York Times*, July 12, 1964.

15. Testimony, William R. Anderson, Braves Court Case.

16. Testimony, John L. Doyne, Braves Court Case.

17. "Football Cards Defer Move Plan," *New York Times*, July 19, 1964.

18. Jim Minter, "Battle for the Deep South," *Sports Illustrated*, July 12, 1965.

19. Richard Cecil, interview with author, June 15, 2016.

20. Richard W. Cutler to William C. Bartholomay, September 30, 1964, box 1, folder 22, Eugene Grobschmidt Papers, Milwaukee County Historical Society.

21. William C. Bartholomay to Richard W. Cutler, October 3, 1964, box 1, folder 22, Grobschmidt Papers; Richard W. Cutler to William C. Bartholomay, October 7, 1964, box 1, folder 22, Grobschmidt Papers.

22. "Milwaukee Bargaining on Brave Concessions," *Daytona Beach Morning Journal*, September 25, 1964.

23. William C. Bartholomay to Milwaukee County Board of Supervisors, September 28, 1964, box 1, folder 22, Grobschmidt Papers.

24. "It IS Atlanta's Braves in '65, Says Stockholder," *St. Petersburg Times*, September 24, 1964; Resolution of County Board, 64–915, box 2, Grobschmidt Papers.

25. Eugene Grobschmidt to National League and American League, and Eugene Grobschmidt to 2 U.S. Senators and 10 Congressmen from Wisconsin, September 30, 1964, with attached proposal, box 2, folder 22, Grobschmidt Papers.

26. Press release from Barkin, Herman and Associates, "Schlitz Offers Braves $1,575,000 for Television & Radio Broadcast Rights for the Next Three Seasons," box 9, folder exhibit 461–70, Braves Court Case.

27. Red Thisted, "Solution Attempt Urged," *Milwaukee Sentinel*, October 6, 1964.

28. Red Thisted, "Let Milwaukee Bid on Braves—Frick," *Milwaukee Sentinel*, October 7, 1964.

29. "Cleveland Also Sets Oct. 16 Date," *Milwaukee Sentinel*, October 7, 1964.

30. James G. Wieghart, "Atlanta Waits for Braves to 'Keep Word,'" *Milwaukee Sentinel*, October 8, 1965.

31. "Club Offices Are Shifted to Chicago," *Milwaukee Journal*, October 10, 1964.

32. Laurie Van Dyke, "Braves Shift Top Office to Chicago," *Milwaukee Sentinel*, October 10, 1964.

33. Van Dyke, "Braves Shift Top Office."

34. "Didn't Buy Braves to Move, Boss Says," *Milwaukee Journal*, October 12, 1964.

35. "Braves Considering Offer from Atlanta," *Milwaukee Journal*, October 14, 1964.

36. James G. Wieghart, "Braves Eye Atlanta Bid," *Milwaukee Sentinel*, October 15, 1964.

37. "Owners Said to Agree to Transfer Braves," *New York Times*, October 15, 1964.

38. John L. Doyne to William C. Bartholomay, October 19, 1964, box 1, folder 22, Grobschmidt Papers.

39. "Zablocki Asks FCC to Check on Braves," *Milwaukee Journal*, October 17, 1964.

40. "Falk Warns Braves Would Face Lawsuits," *Milwaukee Sentinel*, October 17, 1964.

41. Richard W. Cutler to Ford C. Frick, October 15, 1964, box 1, folder 22, Grobschmidt Papers.

42. "Milwaukee Businessmen Want Braves," *Palm Beach Post*, October 17, 1964.

43. "Do Not Want Offer, Braves Official Says," *Milwaukee Sentinel*, October 17, 1964.

44. George E. Rice to Ivan Allen, et al., October 17, 1964, box 1, folder 22, Grobschmidt Papers.

45. Arthur Allyn Jr. to Eugene Grobschmidt, October 21, 1964, and Philip K. Wrigley to Eugene Grobschmidt, October 20, 1964, both in box 1, folder 22, Grobschmidt Papers.

46. "Zablocki Asks FCC to Check on Braves," *Milwaukee Journal*, October 17, 1964.

47. "Indians Stay in Cleveland," *Milwaukee Journal*, October 17, 1964.

48. Richard W. Cutler to Thomas A. Reynolds, October 20, 1964, box 1, folder 22, Grobschmidt Papers.

49. State v. Braves, memorandum decision.

50. "Braves Directors Release Brief Statement," *Milwaukee Sentinel*, October 22, 1964.

51. Deposition, William C. Bartholomay, Braves Court Case.

52. "Braves Will Ask League Today for Permission to Shift to Atlanta," *New York Times*, October 22, 1964.

53. "Wisconsin Directors Bristle Over Shift Plan," *Milwaukee Sentinel*, October 22, 1964.

54. "6 Oppose Braves' Move," *New York Times*, October 22, 1964.

55. "Atlanta's Mayor Is a Braves Fan," *New York Times*, October 22, 1964.

56. Lou Chapman, "Braves Made Decision Last April," *Milwaukee Sentinel*, October 22, 1964.

57. "Braves Sign Contract with Atlanta for 1966," *Toledo Blade*, November 10, 1964.

58. Memorandum for Teams, Inc., July 19, 1965, exhibit 166, box 8, Braves Court Case.

59. "Milwaukee," *New York Times*, October 22, 1964.

60. "County Attorneys Take Swift Action," *Milwaukee Sentinel*, October 22, 1964.

61. "Braves Put Off Request to Move to Atlanta Because of a Restraining Order," *New York Times*, October 23, 1964.

62. "League Vote Will Favor Braves' Shift," *Milwaukee Sentinel*, October 22, 1964.

63. Laurie Van Dyke, "Braves Delay Asking League's Ok to Move," *Milwaukee Sentinel*, October 23, 1964.

64. Statement, Eugene Grobschmidt, October 22, 1964, box 1, Grobschmidt Papers.

65. Grobschmidt statement.

66. "Milwaukee vs. Braves in Extra Innings," *Milwaukee Sentinel*, October 23, 1964.

67. Lloyd Larson, "Inner Sanctum Experience: Larson Describes Session with Owners," *Milwaukee Sentinel*, October 24, 1964.

68. "Braves' Owners Fail to Request Permission to Move to Atlanta," *Milwaukee Journal*, October 22, 1964.

69. "Officials Here Deplore Braves' Decision to Seek Transfer," *Milwaukee Journal*, October 22, 1964.

70. Howard D. Martz, "Offer to Buy Club Tops $6 Million," *Milwaukee Sentinel*, October 22, 1964.

71. WTMJ Editorial, No. 3/40, October 22, 1964, box 1, folder 22, Grobschmidt Papers.

72. Anonymous to Eugene Grobschmidt, November 11, 1964, and E. A. Howard to Eugene Grobschmidt, November 14, 1964, both in box 1, folder 22, Grobschmidt Papers.

73. John Roberts to Milwaukee County Board, November 24, 1964, and Joseph R. Konz to Eugene Grobschmidt, December 30, 1964, both in box 1, folder 22, Grobschmidt Papers.

74. Arnold J. Gazinski to Oliver Kuechle, December 21, 1964, box 1, folder 22, Grobschmidt Papers.

75. E. M. Heslin to Board of Milwaukee County Supervisors, October 28, 1964, box 1, folder 22, Grobschmidt Papers.

76. Furman Bisher, *Miracle in Atlanta: The Atlanta Braves Story* (Cleveland: World Publishing, 1966), 104.

77. "Braves Say County Broke Park Lease," *New York Times*, November 3, 1964.

78. "Braves Lose Plea for Federal Court," *New York Times*, November 6, 1964.

79. Laurie Van Dyke, "Braves' Shift Now Said Impossible," *Milwaukee Sentinel*, November 9, 1964.

80. "League Refuses to Allow Braves to Move Till '66," *New York Times*, November 8, 1964.

81. "Milwaukee Has Mixed Emotions," *Sarasota Herald-Tribune*, November 8, 1964.

82. "Atlanta Club Is Purchased by Braves for $285,000," *New York Times*, November 30, 1964.

83. Van Dyke, "Braves' Shift."

84. "Braves Sign Lease, Assure Atlanta Move," *New York Times*, November 11, 1964.

85. "Braves Hopeful of Playing Several Regular-Season Games in Atlanta in '65," *New York Times*, November 13, 1964.

86. "Braves Can't Beat Hitler in Milwaukee," *St. Petersburg Times*, November 14, 1964.

87. It is interesting to note that the Greater Milwaukee Committee was not far off in its prediction. In 1969 Seattle did get an expansion franchise—the Pilots—but they failed in Washington State and were purchased out of bankruptcy court and moved to Milwaukee in 1970. Seattle then received a second expansion franchise—the Mariners—in 1977. Oakland became the eventual home of the Athletics franchise in 1968, and the second incarnation of the Washington Senators, an expansion franchise in 1961, moved to the Dallas–Fort Worth area in 1972.

88. Highlights of Strategy Meeting Concerning Milwaukee Baseball, November 13, 1964, box 9, folder exhibit 441–50, Braves Court Case.

89. Highlights of Strategy Meeting Concerning Milwaukee Baseball.

90. William C. Bartholomay to Ford C. Frick, box 9, folder exhibit 381–90, Braves Court Case.

91. "Milwaukee Gets Assurance on '65," *New York Times*, November 17, 1964.

92. Lou Chapman, "See Exodus of Braves' Brass Soon," *Milwaukee Sentinel*, November 20, 1964.

93. Deposition, Thomas A. Reynolds Jr., Braves Court Case.

94. "Braves' Board Trimmed to 15," *Daytona Beach Morning Journal*, December 11, 1964.

95. Lou Chapman, "Fitzgerald Raps Braves Claim of 'No Firm Offer,'" *Milwaukee Sentinel*, December 12, 1964.

96. Red Thisted, "Be Big, Let Braves Go, Says Quinn," *Milwaukee Sentinel*, December 12, 1964.

97. Lloyd Larson, "Baseball Plot Thickens and It's Still All Confusing," *Milwaukee Sentinel*, December 31, 1964.

98. "Braves Official Denies Offer of $1 Million for '65 Move," *Milwaukee Journal*, December 30, 1964.

99. "$1 Million Offer Denied by Braves," *New York Times*, December 31, 1964.

100. Cleon Walfoort, "3 Conditions Listed Here," *Milwaukee Journal*, December 30, 1964.

101. "Delay Ticket Ban Outside of Stadium," *Milwaukee Sentinel*, December 18, 1964.

102. Arthur Daley, "Sports of the Times: Egg on Their Chins," *New York Times*, November 10, 1964.

103. Arthur Daley, "Sports of the Times: Pie in the Sky," *New York Times*, December 18, 1964.

104. Ray Kenney, "City Promotion Is Obsolete If Braves Move," *Milwaukee Sentinel*, October 23, 1964.

105. Lou Chapman, "Wrigley's Idea: All Major Clubs Play Here in '65," *Milwaukee Sentinel*, December 30, 1964.

106. Lloyd Larson, "Baseball Plot Thickens and It's Still All Confusing," *Milwaukee Sentinel*, December 31, 1964.

Chapter 7. Lame Ducks

The chapter-opening epigraph is from Arthur Daley, "Sports of the Times," *New York Times*, June 10, 1965.

1. Lou Chapman, "See Exodus of Braves' Brass Soon," *Milwaukee Sentinel*, November 20, 1964.

2. Deposition, Thomas A. Reynolds Jr., State of Wisconsin v. Milwaukee Braves, Milwaukee County Circuit Court, MSS-2414, Milwaukee County Historical Society (hereafter cited as Braves Court Case).

3. "Braves Ask Brewery to Renew TV Terms," *Milwaukee Journal*, November 24, 1965.

4. Press Release, Barkin, Herman and Associates, "Decision Made Not to Sponsor Braves Broadcasts," box 9, folder exhibit 461–70, Braves Court Case.

5. "Braves Dropped by Schlitz," *Milwaukee Journal*, December 10, 1964.

6. Deposition, William C. Bartholomay, Braves Court Case.

7. 1965 Braves Yearbook.

8. Reynolds deposition.

9. "Braves Should Remain," *Sarasota Journal*, January 7, 1965.

10. "Bill on Baseball Goes to Congress," *New York Times*, January 5, 1965.

11. E. B. Fitzgerald to John L. Doyne, January 26, 1965, with attached report from Teams, Inc., box 2, John L. Doyne Collection, Milwaukee County Historical Society.

12. Fitzgerald to Doyne.

13. Memorandum, Teams, Inc., July 19, 1965, box 8, exhibit 166, Braves Court Case.

14. Lou Chapman, "Can't Veto Move—Frick," *Milwaukee Sentinel*, January 22, 1965.

15. "Selig Describes Teams' Radio Pact," *Milwaukee Sentinel*, September 30, 1965.

16. "Pabst Signs TV Contract with Tigers," *Milwaukee Journal*, February 25, 1965;

"Atlanta Taking Braves Coverage," *Lewiston (ME) Daily Sun*, February 24, 1965; "Mel Allen Is 'Voice' of Braves in Atlanta," *Milwaukee Journal*, March 9, 1965; Hank Morgan, "A Brief Return to Land of the Braves," *Daytona Beach Morning Journal*, June 30, 1984; "Baseball Slice from Radio-TV Is $25-Million," *St. Petersburg Times*, March 1, 1965; "Pick Allen to Air Tilts in Atlanta," *Milwaukee Sentinel*, March 10, 1965.

17. Lou Chapman, "Million Gate Here in 1965 – Bragan," *Milwaukee Sentinel*, January 25, 1965.

18. Lou Chapman, "Teams, Inc., Recommends: Keep Braves Here for 1965," *Milwaukee Sentinel*, January 25, 1965.

19. "'Good Baseball Town,'" *Milwaukee Journal*, February 6, 1965.

20. 1965 Braves Yearbook, 52–53.

21. Cleon Walfoort, "Braves' Cash Offer Studied," *Milwaukee Journal*, February 12, 1965.

22. Lou Chapman, "Teams, Inc. 'Welcomes' Braves Ticket Proposal," *Milwaukee Sentinel*, February 13, 1965.

23. "Teams, Inc., Starts Its Baseball Push," *Milwaukee Sentinel*, February 18, 1965.

24. Walter Carlson, "Advertising: A City in Search of an Image," *New York Times*, March 8, 1965.

25. WITI Channel 6 Editorial Number 793, Monday, February 22, 1965, box 2, Doyne Collection.

26. "Teams, Inc., Starts Its Baseball Push."

27. "Book Boosts Milwaukee," *Milwaukee Journal*, February 18, 1965.

28. Journal Company, *Milwaukee . . . Major League City* (Milwaukee: Journal Company, 1965), 7–12.

29. Lou Chapman, "Day's Ticket Sale: 2000," *Milwaukee Sentinel*, February 23, 1965.

30. Bobby Bragan as told to Jeff Quinn, *You Can't Hit the Ball with the Bat on Your Shoulder: The Baseball Life and Times of Bobby Bragan* (Fort Worth: Summit Group, 1992), 303; Bob Wolf, "McHale Tells Club to Duck Squabbles," *Milwaukee Journal*, March 2, 1965.

31. Report, Channel 12, March 2, 1965, box 2, Doyne Collection.

32. "Teams, Inc., Sees 'Thawing,'" *Milwaukee Journal*, March 5, 1965.

33. Andrew A. Johnson to John L. Doyne, March 26, 1965, box 2, Doyne Collection.

34. "Packers Predict Sellout Season," *Milwaukee Journal*, March 2, 1965.

35. "60,000 in Atlanta Welcome Braves," *New York Times*, April 10, 1965; Furman Bisher, *Miracle in Atlanta: The Atlanta Braves Story* (Cleveland: World Publishing, 1966), 173.

36. Evans Kirkby, "Bragan Praises Atlanta's Efforts to Integrate; Likes Milwaukee Too," *Milwaukee Journal*, April 15, 1965.

37. John L. Doyne to John J. McHale, April 13, 1965, box 2, Doyne Collection.

38. "Opening Day: Braves Assured of Sellout Crowd," *Wilmington (NC) Morning Star*, March 19, 1965.

39. William N. Wallace, "Braves Expect 20,000 Today as Lame-Duck Season Begins," *New York Times*, April 15, 1965.

40. Laurie Van Dyke, "Cubs Lose 5–1; Fans Score, Too," *Milwaukee Sentinel*, April 16, 1965.

41. William Janz, "They Call It Co-Operation: Owners Miss Braves Opener," *Milwaukee Sentinel*, April 16, 1965.

42. Janz, "They Call It Co-Operation."

43. Lou Chapman, "Pinkerton Guards Keep Writers Out," *Milwaukee Sentinel*, May 1, 1965.

44. "Milwaukee 'Boycott' Effective," *Pittsburgh Press*, May 9, 1965.

45. Mike Christopulos, "City's Love of Baseball Got Team Here," *Milwaukee Sentinel*, November 3, 1982.

46. William N. Wallace, "17,433 Fans See Blasingame Win," *New York Times*, May 21, 1965.

47. "Astrodome Raises Gate in Baseball Over Pace in 1964," *New York Times*, May 14, 1965.

48. Lloyd Larson, "Other Major Cities' Attendance Figures Not Too Impressive," *Milwaukee Sentinel*, April 29, 1965.

49. Jack Mann, "September Song: Strain," *Sports Illustrated*, September 6, 1965.

50. Lloyd Larson, "First Big Test of Attendance for 1965 About to Start," *Milwaukee Sentinel*, June 15, 1965.

51. "Fantastic Support by Negroes for Atlanta Braves—Robinson," *Milwaukee Journal*, June 15, 1965.

52. "Braves Told Where to Go," *Milwaukee Journal*, June 9, 1965.

53. "Owners of Braves Accused of Discouraging Attendance," *Milwaukee Journal*, June 19, 1965.

54. Lou Chapman, "Our Lou Gets 'Red Carpet' Deal as Braves Lift Ban," *Milwaukee Sentinel*, June 21, 1965.

55. James Edward Held to John L. Doyne, June 30, 1965, box 2, Doyne Collection.

56. Held to Doyne.

57. Lou Chapman, "Grobschmidt, Bragan Vie Swap 'Dim-Wit' Blows," *Milwaukee Sentinel*, July 7, 1965.

58. Lou Chapman, "Cleveland's Paul Says: 'AL Club Here? No Chance,'" *Milwaukee Sentinel*, July 23, 1965.

59. Mann, "September Song: Strain."

60. Lou Chapman, "Bartholomay on Series Oops! He Means HERE," *Milwaukee Sentinel*, August 26, 1965.

61. Lou Chapman, "Veeck Sees Antitrust as City's Hope," *Milwaukee Sentinel*, August 3, 1965.

62. "Anti-Trust Before Court," *Sarasota Journal*, July 26, 1965.

63. "New Group Incorporates as Brewers," *Milwaukee Sentinel*, July 30, 1965.

64. Lloyd Larson, "Joy of 1953 Only a Memory as Braves Play Stadium Finale," *Milwaukee Sentinel*, September 22, 1965.

65. Marta Bender, "Spirit Both High and Low at Stadium," *Milwaukee Sentinel*, September 23, 1965.

66. "'Biggest Brave' Sees Finale," *Milwaukee Sentinel*, September 23, 1965.

67. Johnny Logan, "Logan Looks Back," *Milwaukee Journal*, September 22, 1965.

68. "Affidavit in Support of Order to Show Cause, Case No. 332–626," 330–36, box 1, Braves Court Case.

69. Red Thisted, "If Series Is Here—Only 1,300 Tickets," *Milwaukee Sentinel*, September 24, 1965.

70. "No Ticket Freeze," *Milwaukee Journal*, September 24, 1965.

71. "Dodgers Use 6 Hurlers to Blank Braves, 3–0," *Milwaukee Journal*, October 4, 1965.

72. "Braves Throw Party for New Neighbors," *Milwaukee Journal*, October 27, 1965.

73. "Stadium Set for Baseball," *Milwaukee Journal*, April 2, 1966.

74. Reynolds deposition; Bill Veeck with Ed Linn, *The Hustler's Handbook* (Chicago: Ivan R. Dee, 1965), 301.

75. "Antitrust Suit Filed in Milwaukee County," *Spokane Daily Chronicle*, August 3, 1965; "You Are Hearby . . ." *New York Times*, September 4, 1965.

76. "No Talks Yet on Stadium: Grobschmidt," *Milwaukee Journal*, September 27, 1965.

77. "Braves Face Anti-Trust Suit If Club Leaves Milwaukee," *Prescott (AZ) Evening Courier*, November 10, 1965.

78. "Frick Defends Franchise Move If Team Faces Financial Loss," *Miami News*, November 14, 1965.

79. Oliver E. Kuechle, "Frick Invited to a Lie Detector Test," *Milwaukee Journal*, October 28, 1965.

Chapter 8. Milwaukee v. The Braves

The chapter-opening epigraph is from Arthur Daley, "Sports of the Times: Home, Sweet, Home," *New York Times*, March 8, 1966.

1. Deposition, Thomas A. Reynolds Jr., State of Wisconsin v. Milwaukee Braves, Milwaukee County Circuit Court, MSS-2414, Milwaukee County Historical Society (hereafter cited as Braves Court Case); "Park in Atlanta Sold at Auction," *Milwaukee Journal*, October 27, 1965.

2. "West Palm Beach Sign Says 'Milwaukee Braves,'" *Milwaukee Journal*, March 2, 1966.

3. Lou Chapman, "Braves' Fanning Gives VIP Tour," *Milwaukee Sentinel*, March 9, 1966.

4. "Box Office Sales in Majors on Rise," *New York Times*, April 3, 1966.

5. Daley, "Sports of the Times: Home, Sweet, Home."

6. Richard Glaman, "Grobschmidt Gets Pat from Atlanta," *Milwaukee Sentinel*, April 12, 1966.

7. Terry Bledsoe, "Braves in Milwaukee? Ask Allyn," *Milwaukee Journal*, March 17, 1966.

8. Bill Veeck with Ed Linn, *The Hustler's Handbook* (Chicago: Ivan R. Dee, 1965), 300–309.

9. "Baseball Faces Antitrust Trial," *New York Times*, January 26, 1966.

10. Joseph Durso, "Braves Ordered to Prepare to Open Season in Milwaukee," *New York Times*, January 28, 1966.

11. Press release, January 28, 1966, box 9, folder exhibit 351–60, Braves Court Case.

12. Warren Giles, October 18, 1962, Braves Court Case.

13. "Judge Puts Baseball on Alert," *Milwaukee Sentinel*, January 28, 1966.

14. "Wrigley Offers Solution—Split Braves Club," *Milwaukee Sentinel*, January 28, 1966.

15. "Judge Puts Baseball on Alert."

16. "Atlanta Court Issues Order Requiring Braves to Play 1966 Games There," *New York Times*, December 18, 1965.

17. "Federal Judge Acts to Give the Braves a Home in Atlanta," *New York Times*, February 25, 1966.

18. Press release, January 28, 1966, box 9, folder exhibit 351–60, Braves Court Case.

19. Lou Chapman, "Ignore Court Order Here, Braves Told," *Milwaukee Sentinel*, January 29, 1966.

20. "Bartholomay to Defy Order," *Chicago Daily News*, January 27, 1966.

21. Cleon Walfoort, "'White Paper' Will Be Key for Both State and Braves," *Milwaukee Journal*, March 22, 1966.

22. "Ex-Aide Analyzes Braves' Decline," *New York Times*, March 8, 1966.

23. "Braves' Move Called an $18 Million Loss," *Milwaukee Journal*, March 8, 1966.

24. State of Wisconsin v. Milwaukee Braves, et al., memorandum decision, box 2, folder 41, Sports Collection, Milwaukee County Historical Society.

25. "Roller Orders Braves Trial to Continue Today," *Milwaukee Sentinel*, March 18, 1966.

26. Charles L. Buelow, "Baseball Officials Won't Testify Here," *Milwaukee Journal*, March 21, 1966.

27. "Grobschmidt Denies Advocating Harassment of Braves' Owners," *Milwaukee Journal*, March 23, 1966.

28. "Examiner Says Bank's Loan to Braves Was Substandard," *Milwaukee Journal*, March 24, 1966.

29. Deposition, William C. Bartholomay, Braves Court Case.

30. Bartholomay deposition.

31. Bartholomay deposition.

32. Bartholomay deposition.

33. Bartholomay deposition.

34. Cleon Walfoort, "Milwaukee Is No Place for Baseball: Bragan," *Milwaukee Journal,* January 27, 1966.

35. Deposition, John McHale, Braves Court Case.

36. McHale deposition.

37. McHale deposition.

38. McHale deposition.

39. "Witness Says Braves Lost $775,134 in '65," *Milwaukee Journal*, March 25, 1966.

40. "Perini Profit on Sale $5 Million: Accountant," *Milwaukee Journal*, March 26, 1966.

41. "Braves' Profits Here Called Question Mark," *Milwaukee Journal*, March 31, 1966.

42. "Defense Rests in Trial of Braves," *Milwaukee Journal*, April 1, 1966.

43. Cleon Walfoort, "Stadium Set for Baseball," *Milwaukee Journal*, April 2, 1966.

44. Ron Speer, "Atlanta Calm in Face of Braves' Expected Arrival," *Milwaukee Journal*, April 3, 1966.

45. Charles L. Buelow, "State Wants Braves—Or New Club in '67," *Milwaukee Journal*, April 6, 1966.

46. Louis H. Schiff and Robert M. Jarvis, *Baseball and the Law: Cases and Materials* (Durham: Carolina Academic Press, 2016), 304–8.

47. Schiff and Jarvis, *Baseball and the Law*, 304–8.

48. Joe Botsford, "Roller Decision Not Unexpected," *Milwaukee Sentinel*, April 14, 1966.

49. "Legal Moves Planned," *New York Times*, April 14, 1966.

50. Raymond E. McBride, "Bartholomay Says Team Will Appeal," *Milwaukee Journal*, April 14, 1966.

51. Gerald Eskenazi, "Wagner Makes Pitch for the Past at Shea Stadium," *New York Times*, April 16, 1966.

52. "Baseball Would Carry Plea to U.S. High Court," *New York Times*, May 3, 1966.

53. Lou Chapman, "O'Malley Hints Legal Fight to Go On," *Milwaukee Sentinel*, April 14, 1966.

54. Wisconsin v. Milwaukee Braves, 31 Wis.2d 699 (1966).

55. "No Chance of New Team Opening Day," *Milwaukee Sentinel*, July 28, 1966; James G. Wieghart, "Zablocki to Push Baseball Control Law," *Milwaukee Sentinel*, July 28, 1966.

56. "Decision Didn't Kill All Hope Here," *Milwaukee Sentinel*, July 28, 1966.

57. Sue Kaufman, "A Lousy Decision, but Who Cares?," *Milwaukee Sentinel*, July 28, 1966.

58. Joe Pecor, "Crews at Stadium but No Cheers," *Milwaukee Sentinel*, July 28, 1966.

59. William N. Wallace, "Packers Trounce Giants in Last Exhibition, 37–10," *New York Times*, September 4, 1966.

60. "Claims Ruling Won't Hurt Efforts to Get Franchise," *Milwaukee Sentinel*, July 28, 1966; Leonard Koppett, "Next Move Is Up to Milwaukee and Maybe U.S. Supreme

Court," *New York Times*, July 28, 1966; "Spahn Says: Baseball Out in Milwaukee," *Milwaukee Sentinel*, July 28, 1966.

61. Lou Chapman, "No Team Probable for Years," *Milwaukee Sentinel*, July 28, 1966.

62. Edward Kerstein, "Braves Win Supreme Court Decision," *Milwaukee Journal*, July 27, 1966.

63. Oliver E. Kuechle, "Time Out for Talk," *Milwaukee Journal*, August 10, 1966; Lloyd Larson, "Timing Only Possible Element of Surprise in Bragan Firing," *Milwaukee Sentinel*, August 10, 1966.

64. "1965 Attendance Total Surpassed by Braves," *New York Times*, June 19, 1966.

65. "Atlanta Braves Attendance Data," http://www.baseball-almanac.com/teams /bravatte.shtml.

66. Lloyd Larson, "Latest Figures Indicate Majors Still Have Attendance Problems," *Milwaukee Sentinel*, July 9, 1966; Lloyd Larson, "Atlanta Can't Be Very Happy About Attendance Situation," *Milwaukee Sentinel*, September 20, 1967.

67. "Milwaukee Used Wrong Tactics, Perini Thinks," *Chicago Tribune*, March 19, 1968.

68. Oliver E. Kuechle, "Time Out for a Talk: Lou Perini Recalls What Isn't Recalled," *Milwaukee Journal*, March 21, 1968.

69. "Milwaukee Used Wrong Tactics."

Epilogue

The chapter-opening epigraph is from Oliver E. Kuechle, "Time Out for a Talk: Lou Perini Recalls What Isn't Recalled," *Milwaukee Journal*, March 21, 1968.

1. Albert Theodore Powers, *The Business of Baseball* (Jefferson, NC: McFarland, 2003), 131.

2. "MLB Hits 73.159 Million in Attendance, 11th Highest All-Time, Down Slightly from 2015," http://www.forbes.com/sites/maurybrown/2016/10/04/mlb-hits-73-137- million-in-attendance-11th-highest-all-time-down-slightly-from-2015/#1734870c3540.

3. "MLB Attendance Report-2016," http://proxy.espn.com/mlb/attendance ?order=false.

4. "1952 Major League Baseball Attendance & Miscellaneous," http://www.base ball-reference.com/leagues/MLB/1952-misc.shtml.

5. "MLB Attendance Report-2016."

6. Bob Wolf, "Twins Owner Plans Action," *Milwaukee Journal*, August 1, 1967.

7. Lloyd Larson, "Grobschmidt Tells It Like It Is about Brewers' Lease," *Milwaukee Sentinel*, June 15, 1971.

8. Lou Chapman, "25,899 See Brewers Win," *Milwaukee Sentinel*, May 15, 1970.

9. "Old Milwaukee Brews for Their New Braves," *Fort Scott (KS) Tribune*, April 21, 1970.

10. Lou Chapman, "Perini Says Fans Must Be Patient," *Milwaukee Sentinel*, July 20, 1970.

11. Lloyd Larson, "Look at Attendance Figures and You Can't Help Wondering," *Milwaukee Sentinel*, October 2, 1968.

12. Mark Bowman, "Bartholomay Reflects on Move to Atlanta 50 Years Later," MLB.com, April 10, 2015, http://m.mlb.com/news/article/117486044/former-braves-owner-bill-bartholomay-reflects-on-move-to-atlanta-50-years-late.

13. Bob Hertzel, "Will Pirate Drama Follow Script That Sent the Braves to Atlanta?," *Pittsburgh Press*, December 2, 1984.

14. "On the Field, at Turnstiles Success Did Not Follow the Braves," *Milwaukee Journal*, May 27, 1990.

Index

Aaron, Henry, 4, 78, 172, 175, 178, 187, 216

Allen, Ivan, Jr., 119–22, 132–33, 144; criticizes Grobschmidt, 190; happy with decision, 208–10; meets with Bartholomay and Montgomery, 143; wants formal agreement from Braves, 134

Allen, Mel, 165

All-Star Game: 1955, 47, 52; 1963, 121, 199–200

Allyn, Arthur, Jr., 129–30, 145; criticizes Braves ownership, 189–91; no justification for Braves relocation, 164

American Association, 7, 8

American Football League, 137, 159

American League, 23, 44; owners vote against Finley, 130–31, 137; owners vote against Veeck, 23–24, 131, 137

Anderson, William, 51, 65, 69, 107, 115–17, 182, 203, 205

Atlanta Braves, 74, 147, 162, 201, 214, 215, 216, 218; attendance, 210–11, 218; broadcasts, 178; debut in Georgia, 188; season ticket sales, 187–89

Atlanta Braves Booster Club, 171

Atlanta Crackers, 39, 154, 156, 158, 165, 171, 188

Atlanta–Fulton County Stadium Recreation Authority (Stadium Authority), 120–21, 125, 190–95; twenty-five-year lease with Braves, 155

Atlanta, Georgia, 39; integration, 172; officials build stadium, 119–21; officials consider building stadium, 47; urban renewal, 121

Baltimore Orioles, 40, 67, 214

Barkin, Ben, 59, 164–65, 171, 174, 193, 196, 205

Bartholomay, William C. "Bill," 111, 176; Braves future in Milwaukee, 122–23; on buying Braves, 113–14; compensation offered, 175; denies Braves going to Atlanta, 121; deposition in Braves case, 198–200; does not want to sell team, 138, 142; last Opening Day, 173; lease revision, 138–39; meets with Doyne, 137; meets with Frick to move Braves, 133; meets with Montgomery and Allen, 142; Milwaukee no longer major league, 179; on office relocation, 141–42; returns to Milwaukee, 216; on Roller's decision, 205–6; sells Braves, 217–18; testifies on stock sale, 118; White Sox minority owner, 111. *See also* new Braves owners

beer ban, 88–90, 162, 195; repeal, 105–6

Bisher, Furman, 110, 200

Borchert Field, 7, 8, 9, 18

Boston Braves, 8, 9, 21, 34, 36, 44, 53, 72, 150, 192, 214, 215; become Milwaukee Braves, 25; charter member of the National League, 10; fans respond to move, 21–22; World Series, 1948, 11

Boston Red Sox, 10, 11, 18, 20, 26, 31, 36, 38, 39, 40, 210

Bragan, Bobby, 108, 137, 162, 169–70, 172, 199; feud with Grobschmidt, 137, 178; fired as Braves manager, 209; happy with decision, 208–9; hired by Braves, 108–9; make Milwaukee great, 109; target of fan anger, 189

Braves Field ("the Wigwam"), 10, 11, 12, 19, 20, 25, 36, 215

Broeg, Bob, 121

Brooklyn Dodgers, 52–53, 60, 71–72, 79, 149, 190, 201, 214

Buege, Bob, 5

Burdette, Lew, 60–61

253